MW01038413

African Philosophy and Thought Systems:
A Search for a Culture and Philosophy of Belonging

Munyaradzi Mawere
&
Tapuwa R. Mubaya

Langaa Research & Publishing CIG
Mankon, Bamenda

Publisher:
Langaa RPCIG
Langaa Research & Publishing Common Initiative Group
P.O. Box 902 Mankon
Bamenda
North West Region
Cameroon
Langaagrp@gmail.com
www.langaa-rpcig.net

Distributed in and outside N. America by African Books Collective
orders@africanbookscollective.com
www.africanbookcollective.com

ISBN-10: 9956-763-01-2

ISBN-13:978- 9956-763-01-6

© Munyaradzi Mawere & Tapuwa R. Mubaya 2016

All rights reserved.
No part of this book may be reproduced or transmitted in any form or by
any means, mechanical or electronic, including photocopying and recording,
or be stored in any information storage or retrieval system, without written
permission from the publisher

Table of Contents

Preface

As George Orwell tells us: "Writing a book is painful. One would never undertake such a thing if one were not driven on by some demon whom one can neither resist nor understand." *African Philosophy and Thought Systems...* is a book that came out of hardwork and the realisation by the authors of the need to express their unequivocal but fretful minds. This is owing to their past and present experiences and those of fellow Africans in and outside the continent that are both excruciating and resplendent in some way. It is a critical philosophical text that examines, with some profound dexterity, a gamut of topical themes in African philosophy and philosophy in general.

While a number of African philosophy texts have been produced around the African continent since the beginning of the decolonisation projects from the 40s to the present, there has been little contribution from the Southern African region especially Zimbabwe, in terms of African philosophy texts. Hitherto, there has been an intellectual gap and dearth of literature by philosophers in Zimbabwean institutions of higher learning with coherently systematic themes that hinge on the making and unmaking of African cultures and thought systems. In light of this, to the best of my knowledge, this book is the very first by philosophers in Zimbabwean institutions to attempt to synthesise African philosophy into a single thematic volume.

The production gap in African philosophy texts has always had far reaching consequences to the expansion and vibrancy of philosophy as a discipline in Zimbabwean universities. The gap has seen philosophy wholly as a discipline offered in only two universities out of the fifteen universities in the country. This means that philosophy, though one of the most critical disciplines that in fact should be compulsory in academia, has assumed a backseat position in the curricula of many universities in the country. It is from this realisation that Great Zimbabwe University, as a university that was accorded the special mandate by the Zimbabwe government to promote African arts, culture and heritage, took a bold step by introducing African philosophy and thought course as a university-wide module – a module taught to all first year university students regardless of their areas of specialisation. On this note, the publication of this impeccable text is not only timely but a positive gesture towards the fostering of Great Zimbabwe University's prime niche and African heritage on the global stage. This book is unique, groundbreaking and original. It is the first book, at least in the region, in which indigenous African philosophical ideas and values are examined in detail alongside contemporary trends in philosophy.

Furthermore, the book is, to the best of my knowledge – also the very first volume where the emergence, development and implications of ideals, ideas and values in African political systems of governance and logical reflective thought are studied in relation to indigenous African contexts.

Be that as it may, this text has the potential to generate more insights and debate while influencing national, continental, and global trends not only in the field of African philosophy but African studies altogether. That said, as the Vice-Chancellor of Great Zimbabwe University, I would like to express my profound gratitude and unhidden exhilaration to the two scholars – Professor Munyaradzi Mawere and Mr Tapuwa R. Mubaya – for coming up with a genial project that has resulted in this cherished and well researched foundational text for the African Philosophy and Thought module offered across our university by the School of Arts, Culture and Heritage Studies.

ProfessorR. J. Zvobgo (Ph. D)
Vice-Chancellor, Great Zimbabwe University

Chapter 1

What Philosophy Is and Is Not

Philosophy is the birthbed of all knowledge. It is the mother of all sciences. It is the beginning of all searching and theorisation. This is premised on the idea that philosophy pursues questions in every dimension of human life and its techniques apply to problems in any field of study or endeavour. Basing on this understanding, it is generally accepted that no single definition expresses in fullness the richness and diversity of philosophy. This implies that philosophy may be described in many ways (APA 1981). That being the case, there are as many answers to the question "what is philosophy?" as there are philosophers. This is largely because the question asks more than one could answer. As that may, each philosopher seeks to define this disarmingly daunting question in his or her own unique conceptualisation and interpretation, hence the multiplicity of definitions. In view of this, different scholars from diverse ideological backgrounds and different historical epochs have attempted to proffer their own respective definitions of philosophy which, however, have all never been adequate and exhaustive enough to address the various nuances that fall within the confines of philosophy. Consequently, defining philosophy has proven to be an extremely an elusive task (even to the philosophers themselves) and indeed a challenging endeavour tantamount to chasing the wind.

The term "philosophy" has somehow become complicated to pin down or define with precision especially under one rubric. On this note, we concur with Schneider (2011) who in light of the challenges and controversies regarding the definition of philosophy argues that the word "philosophy" covers a wide continent, with unclear borders and regions. As alluded to above, it is evident that there is no one single sense of the word

1

philosophy. Precisely, there is no universally accepted definition of the word, thus, philosophy can be understood in a myriad of ways and can also be defined from a number of perspectives. In sync with this obtaining reality, Martin Heidegger (1956: 2) in his reflections on the nature of philosophy remarked that "we seem to live in such a time where contemporary philosophers share no unified conception of what philosophy has been or should become. In conformity with Heidger, Peter van Inwagen (2004: 332) noted that disagreement in philosophy is pervasive and irresoluble. For this reason, Inwagen made the conclusion that there is almost no thesis in philosophy about which philosophers agree. Taking into account the complexities surrounding the definition of the term philosophy, many writers and scholars abandon the attempt to define philosophy and instead, turn to the kinds of things philosophers do and don't do (see also Bryson 2009). The present chapter, thus, is a response to the dual question 'what philosophy is and is not?'

Definition(s) of philosophy: An unfinished business

The word philosophy is derived from two Greek words: *philein* which means love and *sophia* which means wisdom (Deluze and Guattari 1994; Barnett 2008). These two words when joined together create the word philosophy which can be loosely translated to mean "the love of wisdom." It is fundamental to set the record straight right from the onset that the definition of philosophy can be offered from a number of perspectives some wider and others narrower. As Sodipo (1973: 3) tells us, philosophy is reflective and critical thinking about the concepts and principles people use to organise their experiences in religion, moral, social and political life, law, psychology, history and the natural sciences. As an academic discipline, philosophy exercises the principles of reason and logic in an attempt to understand reality and answer fundamental questions underpinning human lives in all realmsof existence. This conceptualisation of philosophy is corroborated by Deluze and Guattari (1994) who define philosophy as an activity that people undertake when they seek to understand fundamental truths about themselves and the world in which they live. Taking it from Deluze and Guattari, all disciplines generally qualify as philosophy as long as they seek to understand fundamental truths about some people and the world around. For Maziarz (1987), philosophy implies both the process of questioning and the results of this interrogation as embodied in a personal or public enterprise of value to mankind. A similar understanding is offered by Gyekye (1987) who understands philosophy as a conceptual response to basic issues and human problems. For scholars such as Honderichn (1995: 666) and Quinton (1995), philosophy is a body of knowledge concerned with the general nature of the world (metaphysics or theory of existence), the justification of belief (epistemology or theory of knowledge), and the conduct of life (ethics or theory of value). Honderichn and Quinton drew their definitions from the basic branches of philosophy such as metaphysics, logic, epistemology, and ethics (moral philosophy).

According to Warburton (1999), the main concern of philosophy is to question and understand very common ideas that people take for granted and use every day without thinking seriously about them. He gives examples of experts in different areas of study in terms of how they differ from a philosophy expert in view of their object of study, type of questions they ask, and their questioning style. He, thus, argues that a historian may ask what happened at some time in the past, but a philosopher will ask, "What is time?" A mathematician may investigate the relations among numbers, but a philosopher will ask, "What is a number?" A physicist will ask: what atoms are made up of or what explains gravity, but a philosopher will ask how we can know there is anything outside of our own minds. A psychologist may investigate how children learn a language, but a philosopher will ask, "What makes a word mean anything?" Anyone can ask whether it's wrong to sneak into a movie without paying, but a philosopher will ask, "What makes an action right or wrong?" (Warburton 1999: 27). This understanding of philosophy is shared by Brandom (n.d) who argues that philosophy unpacks and evaluates notions that other disciplines take for granted. He infact, argues that "when we engage in philosophical questioning, we throw ourselves into uncertainty about fundamental beliefs and concepts" (even if, as human beings, we remain deeply comitted to those beliefs and concepts). Insofar as it involves refusing to take things for granted, philosophy is an exercise in rational autonomy. For a scholar such as Morris (1999), philosophy is more of an activity that utilises unique skills and methods of thinking in order to provide practical advice for living. Thus, Teichmann and Katherine (1999) define philosophy as: "a study of problems which are ultimate, abstract and very general" (p. 1). For them, these problems are concerned with the nature of existence, knowledge, morality, reason and human purpose.

Some scholars see philosophy as a double-edged discipline. Nussbaum (2000), for example, defines philosophy as an irritating gadfly that keeps asking questions about the core concepts-both its own (irritatingly, but valuably) as well as those of other disciplines and people. Regardless of their ultimate goals, philosophers probe foundational concepts to increase clarity; they have, in Nussbaum's words, "a commitment to the critical scrutiny of arguments that makes them good at refining distinctions, detecting fallacies," and understanding both sides in a dispute.For Priest (2006), "philosophy is precisely that intellectual inquiry in which anything is open to critical challenge and scrutiny" (p. 202). The critique-centred nature of philosophy serves to produce three features, on Priest's account, that is: 1) subversive, 2) unsettling, and 3) of universal import (Priest 2006: 202-203). Presumably, because philosophers are prepared to challenge everyday common beliefs, philosophy is subversive. It is the making of challenges that shows philosophy's universal import. There is no assumption a philosopher cannot question and no position a philosopher cannot challenge, hence its unsettling nature. Add to that, Nyarwath (2010) postulates that philosophy is the discipline that seeks to address the most basic/fundamental principles/issues in the world concerning reality. Nyarwath went further asserting that philosophy asks questions that appear very obvious and are normally taken for granted. It is concerned about the existence of things, for instance, the existence of God, ideas, and other such entities. It also grapples with basic concepts such as justice, ultimate reality, truth, and others, thus, it seeks to understand and establish certain fundamental principles (Nyarwath 2010) and truths.

Though there is no consensus on the finer details concerning the precise meaning of the term philosophy as highlighted above, some working and seemingly convincing definitions have been conjured up. Below are some of the five generally accepted definitions of philosophy:

a). Philosophy is a way of simplifying complex ideas and statements about our experiences in life in order to make us understand them or make sense out of them.

b). Philosophy is a rational attempt in finding solutions to fundamental problems of mankind.

c). Philosophy is a constant and endless quest by human beings in trying to find out many riddles of the universeso that they can find out a meaningful framework for the expression of all thoughts, actions, and observable phenomena.

d). Philosophy is what an individual accepts as his guiding principles, which prompt him/her to act, indifferent ways at different times, places and circumstances.

e). Philosophy is a rational investigation which examines the nature and reasons behind events happening in the world. This understanding of philosophy is largely informed by what philosophers are known to do.

Basing on this discussion, the reader is bound to agree with us that it is not easy to pin down or define philosophy with in a precisely expected manner as it is an extremely broad term covering a very wide range of intellectual activities.

Again, the scope of the word 'philosophy' has itself varied considerably throughout history, not to mention the fact that there has probably never been a time at which it meant the same thing to everyone (Craig 2002). Recently, something rather strange has happened to it. On the one hand, it has become so broad as to be close to meaningless, as when almost every commercial organisation speaks of itself as having a philosophy – usually meaning a policy. Similarly, philosophy has been spoken of as a way of life for both individuals and groups such it has become difficult to determine who is a philosopher and who is not. In fact, basing on the understanding that philosophy is a way of life, it follows that everyone has a philosophy as long as s/he has a way of life. On the other hand, the definition of philosophy has become very narrow (Craig 2002). Makumba (2007) argues that if one were to look closely at the generally acceptable definitions of philosophy, even the purely etymological one as *love of wisdom,* it is very clear that philosophy is an all-inclusive enterprise, hence it is not cultural or time bound. Philosophy rather targets and points to the human person as a rational entity with faculties of reason. As a universal experience, it is not limited to a particular race or group of people. What may be called into question is the level of systematised thoughts, which certainly cannot be the same everywhere.

The two senses of philosophy

Common/Popular Sense

In an attempt to clarify and simplify what philosophy is Akinpelu (1981) identified two senses in which the term can be used namely, the common and technical senses. Commonly, philosophy is taken to refer to one's attitude to life, which is as a result of one's assumptions, beliefs, attitudes and prejudices to things. In this sense, everyone has his/her own likes, dislikes, prejudices as a result of one's own experiences, upbringing, and background. In line with this understanding, it can be noted that everyone has his/her own philosophy of life, which guides and directs how s/he conducts himself/herself (see Jaeas 1960). Such an understanding could lead to questions like: "what is the philosophy of your school? or what could be the philosophy of his actions?"

Professional/Technical Sense

In its technical sense, Akinpelu (1981) sees philosophy as an academic discipline in which scholars devote their time and energy. As such, for him philosophy is characterised by logical, consistent, and systematic thinking, so as to reach conclusions that are sound, coherent and consistent in all their parts. According to Akinpelu, to philosophiseis to engage in a strenuous activity of thought and to pursue it with no other aim than to satisfy the questioning of human mind (ibid). Under this technical sense, philosophy is conceived as *action*; as *content* and as *attitude*. As activity, it involves analysing, speculating, synthesising, prescribing or even criticising issues and assumptions. As content, it involves those issues that make up a course of study, and as attitude it refers to the distinctive attributes or dispositions, which are often required in doing philosophy (Ibid). These attitudes include logical consistency, critical thinking, tentativeness and comprehensiveness.

It is of paramount importance to note that philosophy in the technical sense, critically examines issues and problems from impartial point of view, thereby exposing biases or prejudices, whether political, economic, social or cultural (Ibid). In this sense, personal philosophy falls short of the idea of philosophy because it only embodies some rudimentary aspects of it. In other words, personal view of philosophy does not provide a thorough, rigorous, and hard look at issues, with a view to analysing them and offering a deep reflection to produce an alternative system, as does philosophy in the technical sense.

Why studying philosophy?

By and large, there are quite a number of benefits associated with the study of philosophy. To begin with, philosophy students or generally philosophers tend to have exceptional aptitude for analytical thinking, critical thinking, careful reasoning, problem solving, and communication skills valued in the legal and medical business among a host of other professions. Specifically, training in philosophy may increase one's ability to use logic, make nuanced distinctions and reasoning, recognise subtle similarities and differences, detect unstated assumptions, and decrease the likelihood of being prone to superficiality and dogmatism (Barnett 2008).This is one reason, among others, why professional disciplines such as law and jurisprudence study some philosophy courses. In fact, they borrow extensively from such branches of philosophy as logic, ethics, and epistemology. In the same vein, Priest (2006) notes that philosophy is a highly constructive enterprise arguing that philosophy is responsible for creating many new ideas and systems of thought. From this, it can be inferred that philosophy is instrumental in the creation of new ideas.

Adding to that, the study of philosophy enhances, in a way no other activity does, one's problem-solving capacities. Most importantly, philosophy helps one to critically analyse concepts, definitions, arguments and problems (APA 1981). Moreover, philosophy contributes to one's capacity to organise ideas and issues, to deal with questions of value, and to extract what is essential from masses of information. In simple terms, philosophy helps one to distinguish fine differences and similarities between given views and to discover common ground between opposing positions. In short, philosophy helps one to synthesise a variety of views or perspectives into a unified whole (ibid).

Apart from that, philosophy also contributes uniquely to the development of expressive and communicative powers. In fact, through its branches like philosophy of language, logic, philosophy of history, and philosophy of law, philosophy provides some of the basic tools of self-expression, for instance, skills in presenting ideas through well-constructed, systematic argument that other fields either do not use, or use less extensively. This way, philosophy helps one to express what is distinctive of one's view; enhances one's ability to explain difficult material; and helps one to eliminate ambiguities and vagueness from one's writing and speech (ibid).

Last but not least, philosophy provides training in the construction of clear formulations, good arguments, and apt examples. It thereby helps one develop the ability to be convincing. Through studying philosophy, one learns to build and defend one's own views, to appreciate competing positions, and to indicate forcefully why one considers one's own views preferable to alternatives (ibid).

Fields of philosophy

Normally, philosophy is usually divided into a number of fields. Ultimately, these are all interwoven, and it is difficult to pursue a question in any one field without soon finding yourself in the others, too (Solomon and Higgins 2010). Thus, philosophy as a discipline is more of an activity rather than a body of passive knowledge. In other words, people learn philosophy by doing it, that is, by philosophising, hence philosophy is considered as an activity. Three types of philosophy can be identified namely; speculative, prescriptive and the analytic (Akinpelu 1981).

Speculative philosophy

To begin with, speculative philosophy as the word rightly suggests contemplates, ponders, reflects critically or speculates about and upon all things. This type of speculation islimitless as it deals with the real as well as the abstract. Notably, speculative philosophy is interested in the search for order, wholeness and linkages in the realm of experience (Akinpelu 1981). For instance, the Millesian philosophers wanted to discover the laws that governed the universe.They also searched for explanations of life and creation. What method did they use? They made use of pure reasoning with which they speculated or reflected critically as they searched for explanations. This was a typical example of speculation. They wanted to understand the mystery of creation through speculation. This type of philosophy can be sub-divided into Metaphysics and Epistemology (Bamisaiye 1989; Akinpelu 1981). The meaning of metaphysics and epistemologies will be expounded in the ensuing sections.

Prescriptive philosophy

According to Kneller (1964), prescriptive philosophy seeks to set standards, grounds or criteria for the judgment of values, conduct and art. It seeks to establish the objectivity or subjectivity of concepts such as good and bad, right, and wrong, beautiful and ugly, among many others. In other words, do these qualities adhere in things or are they mere projections of the individual mind? Prescriptive philosophy also seeks toestablish some fundamental laws for judging which actions are worthwhile and which are not (Bamisaiye 1989; Akipelu 1981). What this entails is that prescriptive philosophy is judgemental.

Analytic philosophy

Analytic philosophy is concerned with the conceptual meaning of words. It analyses the meaning of words such as education, teaching, learning, intelligence, indoctrination, freedom, authority, curriculum, among many others. It endeavours to show where appropriate and how inconsistencies may come into logical presentation through the use of certain words (Hans-Johann Glock 2008; Dagfinn 1996; Danto 1980). Branches of philosophy such as philosophy of language fall within the armpit of analytical philosophy as they seek to understand the use of language in terms of the meaning of words used.

Continental philosophy

According to Critchley (1998), continental philosophy is a set of 19th and 20th century philosophical traditions from the mainland Europe. The term 'continetal philosophy' originated from the English-speaking philosophers of the time who used it to mean a range of philosophical traditions outside the realm of analytic movement. Such traditions included phenomenology, Germany idealism, existentialism, hermeneutics, structuralism, post-structuralism, French Feminism, Psychoanalytic theory, critical theory and Western Marxism. Michael Rosen (1998) has identified common themes that characterise continental philosophy namely: i). As opposed to analytic philosophers, continental philosophers generally reject the view that the natural sciences are the only or most accurate way of understanding natural phenomena. ii). For continental philosophy, meaning is determined at least partly by factors such as context, space and time, language, culture, or history. iii). Continental philosophy typically holds that human agency can change conditions of possible experience. iv). Continental philosophy sought to redifine the method and nature of philosophy.

Traditional branches of philosophy

Historically, philosophical concerns have been treated under the following broad categories: Metaphysics, logic, epistemology, and axiology. These could be represented diagrammatically as below:

Metaphysics	Logic
Epistemology	Axiology

In addition to the broad categories mentioned above, philosophy also deals with the systematic body of principles and assumptions underlying a particular field of experience. For example, there are philosophies of science, education, art, music, history, law, mathematics, and religion. Any subject pursued far enough reveals within itself philosophical problems (the task of philosophers) it grapples with. It is important to note that the main branches of philosophy are divided according to the nature of the questions asked in each area. It is therefore imperative to note that the integrity of these divisions cannot be rigidly maintained, for one area overlaps into the others. However, the major branches of philosophy are discussed in detail below.

a) Metaphysics

From an etymological point of view, that is, the root of the word, metaphysics, means "after the things of nature". It came from two Greek words: '*meta*' meaning "after" or "beyond", and *physika* meaning "nature" (Nyarwath 2010). Metaphysics is, thus, the study of theory beyond nature which Aristotle called "first philosophy". This is why metaphysics is referred to as an enquiry into the world and the world beyond (ibid). This makes metaphysics a foundation of philosophy and the pivot of philosophical enquiries. From a technical perspective, metaphysics is that branch of philosophy, which studies the nature of reality. That is, metaphysics investigates reality as distinct from that which is illusionary. As such, it is vital to highlight that philosophers do not agree on the nature of reality (Barnett 2008).

Basic issues in metaphysics

Metaphysical problems are perennial problems, which keep on recurring. Pre-Socratic philosophers like Parmenides of Elea have discussed them; they have been studied by scholastics and even modern philosophers. Even the un-philosophical mind keeps on wondering about his/her own creation, the creation of the physical world, the world beyond and a host of issues that keep on fascinating people (Omoregbe 1999). As underlined earlier, people resort to philosophy when things are not working well for them or for humanity in general. That is why philosophy is sometimes referred to as a child of failure. It is interesting to note that the greatbooks written in philosophy were authored by those who were worried, disappointed, or fascinated by the happenings of their times. For instance, Plato's *Republic* disillusioned was written out of Plato's disillusionment of the politics of his time culminating into the death of his master, Socrates. Leibniz's works were as a result of his perplexity and fascination as a result of scientific discoveries of his days (Ibid).

Consequently, Plato's *Republic* was in search of an ideal society by teaching what constitutes justice. Omoregbe identified the basic issues in metaphysics as follows: the problem of being, the problem of substance, the problem of essence and existence, the problems of universals, the problem of appearance and reality, the problem of unity and diversity, the problem of change and permanence, the problem of causality, the problem of body – mind interaction and the problem of freedom and determinism (ibid). Let us take the issues one after the other to see the issues and controversies at stake.

The problem of being

For Parmenides whatever exists is being. According to his understanding, being is one, eternal and unchanging. For Aristotle, this being is God whom he considered the pure being. St. Thomas Aquinas arguing from a Christian perspective of metaphysics maintains that God is the being par excellence. The Scholastic philosophers however made a distinction between necessary being and contingent being. A necessary being owes his existence to noother being outside himself whilst acontingent being is not responsible for its ownexistence, and does not contain within itself the sufficient reason for its existence. Let us hasten to highlight that philosophers are divided over this metaphysical issue of reality. Some see being as whatever exists, while others take a mystical approach and see it as a hidden, mysterious reality which is both immanent and transcendent, and which is the source of all things.

The problem of substance

This metaphysical problem has continued to attract the attention of philosophers. Aristotle distinguished between substance and accident. Substance is whatever exists on its own, while accident is whatever cannot exist on its own but only inherent in other things. According to John Locke, when we look at things what wesee are actual qualities such ascolour, height, size, and so on. But we know qualities cannot exist independently as they must exist in something which supports them.

The problem of essence and existence

Sartre's main contention is that existence precedes essence, as opposed to traditional Western philosophy, which gives primacy to essence over existence. Philosophers are divided over which comes first? Is it existence or essence? This isa standing controversy that remains topical even today.

The problem of universals

Philosophers in succession hold that things such as beauty, justice, goodness, whiteness, humanity etcetera are universals. They are universal concepts and not just ideas in the mind. We recognise them in things that exhibit them, and this means that theyare real, though they are not physical. Socrates was the first philosopher in the West to articulate the issues of universals. He insisted on the distinction between the universals and the things that exhibit them.

The problem of appearance and reality

It is true that appearance deceives and that our senses often deceive us. We cannot, therefore, always take things as they appear to us, nor can we always relyon our senses, since they sometimes deceive us. Parmenides, Plato and Rene Descartes mistrust senses as a means of acquiring knowledge. For instance, Bertrand Russell says, we assume as certain many things which on closer scrutiny are found tobe so full of apparent contradictions that only a great amount of thought enables us to know what is it that we can really believe without reasonable doubt. The controversy here is whether appearance is the same thing as reality or appearance is one thing and reality is another.

Problem of unity and diversity

It is true that unity and diversity are observable in the universe. How is it that there isa basic unity in the midst of amazing diversity of things in the universe? The Ionians, the earliest philosophers in the West, were struck by the unity as well as diversity of things in the universe. These philosophers adopted a monistic explanation and held that all these are basically one though in various forms. In Western Philosophy, three approaches have been adopted, namely; the monistic, the dualistic and the pluralistic approaches so as to explain the problem of unity and diversity in metaphysics.

The problem of change and permanence

One of the earliest problems in Western philosophy is the problem of change andpermanence. Which of the two elements, that is, change or permanence is primary? Heraclitus and Parmenides held extreme positions which subsequent philosophers tried to reconcile. While Heraclitus held that change was the basic feature of theuniverse, Parmendies held that permanence was the primary feature.

The problem of causality

Cause is that which is responsible for bringing something into existence. The statement, "everything has a cause" is taken to be of universal application. Sincethere is no event that has no cause, nothing ever happens without cause. Scientists tell us that the universe is an orderly cosmos, not chaotic universe where anything can happen. In other words, it is a universe governed by laws and things happen only according to these laws. This is the basic presupposition of modern science, and all that scientists do, is to understand these laws so as to know the kind of causes that can produce certain kinds of desirable effects.

Problem of mind-body interaction

The question of the nature of the human mind and its relation with the body has longbeen a controversial issue. Different philosophers have conceived mind differently. Plato, Augustine, Aquinas and Descartes conceive the mind as a separate substance that exists on its own without the body. Others like David Hume and Bertrand Russell have denied that the mind is a separate substance that can exist independently of the body. This problem, like other philosophical problems, still remains unsolved to the satisfaction of all philosophers.

The problem of freedom and determinism

It is commonly believed that man is free; that he makes use of his freedom the way he likes and is, therefore, held morally

16

responsible for whatever he does. The theory of determinism, however, denies that man is really free. The future is irrevocably fixed and man can do very little to change it. Logical determinists claimt hat every future event is caused and so it must either occur or not occur and so what we call history is the manifestation of divine will. Albert Einstein, the greatest scientist of the last millennium, argued along these lines. In presenting the position of freewill, Enoh (2001) argued that it does present a direct opposition to determinism. According to him, the position recognises that man lives in a world that is orderly and stable and, therefore, having laws, which control the flow of things. Man cannot therefore be an exception and this subjects him to these forces. To this aspect, his actions are to some degree determined. He then concludes that what gives man dignity as a human being is his capacity to transcend the bonds of such determinism and choose certain cause of action.

From the foregoing discussions on metaphysics, it can be seen that man is a metaphysical being. In other words, metaphysics is part and parcel of man. Man is always fascinated byhis creation on earth, the universe, the existence of God and all he sees around. Although some philosophers see metaphysics as meaningless, it appears real in human life. Metaphysically people have seen that man's imaginative and explorative activities in search of knowledge and wisdom go beyond sense perception.

(b) Epistemology

The word epistemology is a derivation from two Greek words, *episteme*, meaning knowledge, and *logos*, meaning study (Nyarwath 2010). Literally, therefore, it means the study of knowledge. More commonly, however, it is known as the theory of knowledge by which we mean the branch of philosophy which is concerned with posing, reflecting and examining questions related to knowledge or knowing. In general, epistemology is the branch of philosophy concerned primarily with the nature, sources, limits and criteria knowledge (Barnett 2008). Some of the questions addressed are as follows; what is the human mind capable of knowing? From what sources do we gain our knowledge? Do we have any genuine knowledge on which we can depend, or must we be satisfied with opinions and guesses? Are we limited to knowing the bare facts of sense experience, or are we able to go beyond what the senses reveal?

There are three central questions in the field of epistemology:

• What are the *sources* of knowledge? Where does genuine knowledge come from or how do we know what we claim to know? This is the question of origins.

• What is the *nature* of knowledge? Is there a real world outside the mind, and if so can we know it? This is the question of appearance versus reality.

• Is our knowledge *valid?* How dowe distinguish truth from error or falsehood? This is the question of the tests of truth, of verification.

Traditionally, most of those who have offered answers to these questions can be placed in one of two schools of thought—rationalism or empiricism. The rationalists hold that human reason alone can discover the basic principles of the universe. The empiricists claim that all knowledge is ultimately derived from *sense experience* and, thus, that our knowledge is limited to what can be experienced. It should be clear that there is a necessary relationship between metaphysics and epistemology. Our conception of reality depends on our understanding of what can be known. Conversely, our theory of knowledge depends on our understanding of ourselves in relation to the whole of reality.

Sources of epistemic knowledge
Types of knowledge vary with their sources, their methods of acquisition and validation.

Empirical knowledge

This is the type of knowledge people obtain through experimentation and observation of the things around them, through their senses and personal experiences from actions in which people are involved. It is the characteristic of knowledge in the science, both natural and social (Ayer 1995). Knowledge acquired through seeing objects, hearing sounds, tasting flavour, feeling something or smelling odour is empirical knowledge (ibid). In short, our endowed senses ofseeing, hearing, smelling, tasting and feeling are the gateways to scientific knowledge. This is a very important type of knowledge and it is very much valued in today's world of science and technology. But do senses alone furnish us with knowledge, as scientists would hold? It must be noted that the senses alone without the co-operation of reason cannot furnish us with all the knowledge we can rely on. Until reason interprets them and gives them meaning, they are simply raw data without meaning. For example, the direct object of the sense of sight is simply colour, when we look, we can only see colour. That is, all the sense of sight can furnish us with. It is reason, which tells us that what we are seeing is a tree, a table, a blackboard, an animal, a human being and so on (ibid).

Furthermore, the direct object of the sense of hearing is sound. The ears do not tell us where the sound comes from. We hear the sound of an aeroplane passing, the sound of gunshot, or that of a thunder. It is our reason that tells us, for example, that the sound we are hearing is that of thunder notthat of aeroplane or gunshot. Our ears only register the sound without telling us the meaning of the sound. The same applies to all other senses. When we perceive an odour, for example, it is our reason that interprets the odour we are perceiving and tells us that it is the odour of a decaying animal or cosmetics (ibid). When a blind man touches something, the sense of touch does not tell him what he is touching. It is reason that interprets his experience and tells him what he is touching. All these imply that the senses alone without reason cannot furnish us with knowledge (ibid).

Rational knowledge

This is the knowledge derived from reasoning that is not by observation, but by inferring new knowledge from what we already know. Mathematicsis a good example of rational knowledge, so also are subjects such as philosophy and logic. Given some hypothesis or premise, we can go ahead to deduce a number of conclusions that must necessarily follow (Ayer 1995). For example, given the premise that a man is a bachelor, it follows as of necessity that he is not married. Or the fact that there is a teacher implies that there must be a learner. From the presence of the teacher, we logically infer or deduce that there must be a learner or some learners whom he teaches (ibid). The hallmark of this type of knowledge is that the conclusions being inferred must logically and necessarily follow from what went before. It is a law of reasoning and argumentation, which applies to most school subjects. Hence, in mathematics, for example, the teacher should not just mark the answer to a mathematical question correct or wrong, rather s/he should award credit to the logical steps by which the student reaches the answer (ibid). This is also the practice in philosophy; it is not so much in the final conclusion that matters as the reasoning process in arriving at the conclusion.

Revealed knowledge

This is knowledge gained through revelations. It is the characteristic of religions, especially the revealed ones. The religions which most of us are familiar with are Christianity and Islam, through the Bible and Quran. This type of knowledge was revealed to the prophets of these religions who faithfully recorded the knowledge for mankind and imparted the contents to their followers (Ayer 19950). The method of the original acquisition was by vision or trance, possible only to those who are holy enough or those to whom God or Allah had chosen to reveal Himself (ibid). This type of knowledge is not open to observation or empirical tests. Neither can it be proven by logic and human reasoning. It just has to be accepted by faith. This type of knowledge is considered as the final word of God Almighty, which cannot be subjected to empirical tests or rational analyses (ibid).

Intuitive or Insight knowledge

This is knowledge that comes to us in flashes without going through the process of reasoning. It is knowledge that is acquired directly by an immediate contact of the mind with the object without going through the process of reasoning. It comes as a flash into the mind. It can come in form of inventive intuition when in a flash; a certain bright idea comes to our mind as a kind of vision. Archimedes was reported to have had a vision of the law of floatation in a flash while taking his bath. He was so overwhelmed by the vision that he rushed naked to record such a very important insightful knowledge before it escaped his memory. Musicians and artists do enjoy such intuition occasionally, and the result is beautiful pieces of artwork or music.

Conditions of knowledge

In an attempt to answer these questions with regards to what constitute knowledge, A. J. Ayer (1955) gave three conditions of knowledge as follows:

- What one said to know should be true (thruth condition);
- That one should be sure of it (ability to justify), and
- That one should have the right to be sure (certainty).

The words that stand distinct in Ayer's conditions of knowledge are: certainty, and justification for knowledge. Knowing is being in the appropriate position to certify or give one's authority or warrant to the truth of what is said to be known. The man who has a true opinion is the man who has the right to be sure. "I know", therefore, is related to "I" guarantee (ibid).

Similarly, Austin (1961) argues: If you say you know something, the most immediate challenges take the form of asking: Are you in a position to know? That is, you must undertake to show not merely that you are sure of it, but that it is within your cognisance. What is the implication of this? The implication of this is that a person who knows has cause to be sure, certain, and to guarantee what is known. To know is stronger than to believe or hold an opinion. This is because knowledge enlarges and enriches one's ideas, choices, alternatives and initiatives to make an action deliberately. Roderich Chisholm (1963) on the other hand argues that a person can be said to know something if he believes it, if he is justified in believing it, in the sense that his believing it is reasonable or acceptable. No wonder why philosophers like Plato define knowledge as a true justified belief, that is, a belief that is true and justifiable.

From the foregoing, it is clear that belief is not the same as knowledge because knowledge must be based on conclusive evidence and it must be certain. Belief, in contrast, is not based on conclusive evidence. For instance, if one hears over the radio that someone is dead, one cannot say that s/he knows that the person has died. S/he can only say that s/he wants to believe that the person is dead, since he himself heard that over the radio. His only evidence is the news broadcast from the radio. This is not conclusive evidence. Knowledge, however, entails belief in the sense that a person cannot say that s/he knows something but that s/he does not believe it. S/he knows it but s/he doesn't believe it, is an incongruous statement for anybody to make. It makes sense, however, to say "I do not know it but I believe it".

It is vital to note that belief can pass into knowledge. What was formerly an object of belief can become an object of knowledge (Ayer 1995). This happens when what was formerly believed becomes justified. There were many beliefs, which became either justified true knowledge or refuted as false through ample evidence. For instance, before Copernicus, the earth, it was believed, was the centre of the solar system and all other heavenly bodies revolved around it. Copernicus' work refuted the belief with the discovery of the sun as the centre of the solar system and which all other planets revolved around. Today, it is a justified true knowledge (ibid).

Criteria for knowledge

Bamisaiye (1989) in her contribution to what constitutes knowledge enumerated five criteria for knowledge: viz: existence, certainty, validity, veracity and utility. What does each of these terms convey in relation to knowledge? Firstly, existence means that knowledge should have existential reference. In other words, what should constitute knowledge should be that which exists. The geography teacher, for instance, teaching the relief features of Africa should make reference to such features that exist. If he makes reference to Kilimanjaro Mountain, it is with the understanding that Mount Kilimanjaro exists somewhere in Africa. What does not exist should not constitute knowledge (ibid). Secondly, certainty means that knowledge should be validly proved. Thirdly, validity means that knowledge should not be self-contradictory. In fact, veracity means that knowledge expresses truth. As a result, falsehood does not constitute knowledge. It is the truth inherent in knowledge that makes it reliable and certain. Last but not least, utility means that knowledge is either useful in its direct benefit to the knower or in its potential for creating further knowledge (ibid).

(c) Axiology

Axiology is the study of values. It is the branch of philosophy that is concerned with various criteria, which underline the choices we make (and do not make), or with the factors, which affect our desires, interest, needs, likes and performances (Enoh 2001). Axiology is divided into two parts; ethics and aesthetic. Ethics is a branch of philosophy that is concerned with human actions and behaviour in the society. Ethics can be understood etymologically as derived from the Greek word *ethos* meaning character/ personal character (Nyarwath 2010). It is, therefore, an investigation into the nature of a virtuous life or the right way to live. Ethics is concerned with understanding/evaluating the character of individuals. It studies moral values and standards by which we ought to live (Ibid). Wojtyla and Aguas (2013) note that ethics study the norms or standards or codes that would define or determine the morality of human act or conduct. It is, therefore, apparent that ethics is all about human relationships. In broad terms, ethics concerns itself with the question of morality. Morality is derived from the Latin word *moralis* which means customs or manners. Commonly, people speak of people being ethical or moral to mean good or right and immoral to mean wrong or bad (Bloom 2010). This shows that morality is something that enables people to distinguish right from wrong and it also serves as a guide to people's actions. Philosophers are divided on whether morality is a function of reason or a function of passions. While some hold that morality is a function of reason, others maintain that morality is a function of passions. Omoregbe (1993), for instance, contends that morality is the integrated function of both reason and the passions. He argues that both rationality and passions are essential ingredients of morality. Man is the only being that combines rationality and passions; hence, morality is uniquely human. Man is, therefore, a harmonious blend of passions and reason.

On the other hand, aesthetic deals with the norm of beauty. In other words, this branch of axiology is concerned with appreciating beauty in nature and art. It attempts to evaluate the various criteria of beauty that is a justification we make for preferring a certain work of art to another (Enoh 2001). It is in the very nature of man to appreciate beauty in the work of art, in man, music etc. It is in the light of satisfying man's quest for beauty that the display of works of art are organised at local, national and even at international levels to satisfy and appreciate beauty (Ibid).

d) Logic

The term 'logic' comes from the Greek word '*logikě*' which meant "thought" or "reason." It is the systematic study of arguments. It tests the validity and soundness of arguments. By validity we mean relation of coherent support between the assumption of an arguments and its conclusion. An argument is said to be sound when it is both valid and its premises are true.

Logic can be further categorised into four groups namely; informal logic, formal logic, sysmbolic logic and mathematical logic. On one hand, informal logic studies natural language arguments, for example, fallacies. On the other hand, formal logic studies inference with purely formal content. *Inference* is not to be confused with *implication*. An implication is a sentence of the form 'If p then q', and can be true or false. An inference, on the other hand, consists of two separately asserted propositions of the form 'p therefore q'. An inference is not true or false, but valid or invalid. Aristotle's works contan the earliest known formal study of formal logic. Modern formal logic, thus, follows and builds on Aristotle's formal logic.

As name suggests, symbolic logic studies symbolic abstractions that capture the formal features of logical inference (Whitehead and Betrand, 1967; Hamilton 1980). Symbolic logic is often divided into two branches naley propositional logic and predicative logic. The last category of logic, mathematical logic, is simply an extension of symbolic logic into other areas such as proof theory, model theory, recursion theory and set theory. Though what logic studies seem to be clear, the definition of logic remains elusive.

What philosophy is not

Unfortunately, in addition to saying what philosophy is, it is also necessary to say what it is not or opposite of what philosophy is.Philosophy is neither cultural criticism nor political activism. We neither deny that culture as politics or any other realm of life prompts philosophical questions nor that philosopher(s) may, or even should, play an active public role. But to the extent that different realm of life should, they just satisfy a broader obligation, applying to publicly funded intellectuals more generally. Philosophy is not cognitive science either. The study of the brain, like the one of language by linguistics, is an important area of scientific research to which philosophy can contribute. But this should not motivate us to cannibalise ourselves by allocating resources that are in short supply elsewhere to research which is not primarily philosophical. While both interaction with the sciences and with the more general culture are important and can provide useful inputs for philosophy itself, philosophers should concentrate on the core of their discipline, i.e. the most central, general, and therefore, difficult questions of metaphysics, epistemology, logic, aesthetics, and ethics. In particular, they should focus on their problems, rather than on themselves (Keller 2006). Philosophy is not a contribution to human knowledge, but to human understanding. It seeks to advance understanding and not to produce new knowledge. Nevertheless, it is this understanding that provokes people to produce new knowledge.

More so, philosophy is neither an empirical science nor an a priori one, since it is no science qua science. What philosophy does, however, is to question the empirical science and *a priori* ones.

Conclusion

The chapter has shown that 'philosophy' finds its place of origin in the language of ancient Greece. The word philosophy is thus translated to mean 'love of wisdom.' There has not been large collective convergence to the question what philosophy is? The term is hard to pin down precisely. What philosophy is has always been – and hopefully always will be – a much debated question. Some expect from philosophy profound answers to life's deepest questions, while others simply ignore it as meaningless drivel. We can reverently approach it as the most important of human endeavours, or dismisses it as idle speculation about the most problematic of concerns. Many consider it to be a subject that, since it concerns everyone, must be a simple matter and thus comprehensible to all, whereas others consider philosophy so difficult that it is pointless even to attempt to understand it. And indeed, what has often been presented in the past as philosophy provides ample evidence to warrant such contradictory ideas about its nature.

Chapter 2

Africa and its Philosophical Thought: Nature, Scope and Pragmatics

"No brutality, mistreatment, or torture has ever forced me to ask for grace, for I prefer to die with my head high, my faith steadfast, and my confidence profound in the destiny of my country, rather than to live in submission and scorn of sacred principles [...] Do not weep for me my dear companion. I know that my country which suffers so much, will know how to defend its independence and its liberty. Long live the Congo! Long live Africa!" (Patrice Lumumba 1961).

A critical look at disciplines across the fields of knowledge attests to the fact that philosophy has become one of the most regionalised of all disciplines. It is one discipline where, though without rendering jejune the discipline as a whole, we can talk in spacio-blocks and hunks, for example, talking of philosophy in the West (Western philosophy), Africa (African philosophy), East (Eastern philosophy), and America (American philosophy). The prefixing of philosophy with reference to Africa has fiveif not more major implications: Firstly, that there is African philosophy traceable to a particular geographical space. It affirms the existence of a philosophy in Africa. Secondly, that the prefixing confirms the denialist position of African philosophy, that is, it acknowledges the existence of a camp that rebuts and outrightly denies rationality and the existence of an African philosophy independent of Western philosophy. This is because where there is no denial of such a philosophy as we see in science in general, there is no need to affirm and distinguish this philosophy from that philosophy. Thirdly, the prefixing confirms that philosophy is not universal as we see in science. Instead, African philosophy, though might be overlapping with other philosophies, is distinctive in terms of both essence and methodology. Fourthly, the prefix "Africa" implies that philosophy is attached to race. Fifthly, the prefixing of philosophy implies the possibility of us having a pluriversal rather than universal philosophy in much the same way we have pluriversal epistemologies and ontologies.

The five implications pointed out above suggest that while the existence of philosophy in Africa could be widely acknowledged, the nature, scope, and interpretation of that philosophy is never homogenous such that no single scholarly work can sufficiently exhaust the subject and methodology of African philosophy. No wonder scholars like Makinde (2000: 103) admits that philosophy in Africa "means more than African Philosophy… [it refers to] the activities of doing, writing and teaching philosophy in Africa." This means that the question: "what makes a philosophy African?" is enduring and will continue to boggle our minds for many more years to come. It is not a question that can be addressed in humpty-dumpty and hastily manner, lest it escapes our reason like a butterfly in its erratic flight. Neither is it a question that can be adequately addressed in a single scholarly piece of work. Yet, fundamental as is, the question cannot be ignored in any serious text about African philosophy. As such, it is part of the objective of this book to address the inexorable question; to try to respond to the question within the boundsand matrix of cultural and geographical frames. While we appreciate the universality of philosophy as a discipline anchored on rationality and critical inquiry, we examine the question in cultural and geographical frames in order to try to bring out to the surface that which distinguishes African philosophy from other philosophies such as Western philosophy or Chinese philosophy. We do this on the pretext that as one looks at philosophy in different societies, the context they examine may differ though the methods of investigation of the content may overlap.Emphasising the same point, Oduor's (n.d: 3) observation is apt and worth quoting as such:

> I have often marvelled that no one asks about African physics, African chemistry, African biology, African mathematics, and so on. People seem to understand that each of these disciplines have their own subject matter, methodology and specialist language that transcend cultural contexts. I look forward to the day when this will be true of philosophy. I look forward to the day when people will understand that what makes a philosophy African, Asian, American or European is the cultural context in which it is produced, rather than its methodology and language.

This implies that the onerous question on the existence of African philosophy has come of age. It is a question worth surrendering into abyss of oblivion not to resurface again. Yet, while the question on the existence of African philosophy has come of age, it remains an ineffaceable mark; a question that no serious African philosopher can afford to ignore. Enduring as always, the question continues boggling and lingering in the minds of many non-Africans and Africans, non-academic and academics alike even today some decades after it was first raised especially by African-American thinkers, due to its gory effects that are strapping and hard-wearing. In fact, given the colossal ineffaceable energised chicanery waves of neo-colonialism and globalisation with their current sweeping effects on Africa, the question, though has been long debated still warrant further interrogation and reflection in order to respond to the demands of the aforesaid 'dramatic' forces. In this view, the relentless questions that would merit careful attention and treatment are: Does Africa exists? Does African philosophy really exists? If it does exist, what is it? How does it differ from Western philosophy? Does it have the same import as Western philosophy? Why is it important to demonstrate the existence of African philosophy? And above all, should Africa continue

31

trusting *snakes* in the grass in managing its own affairs? While some of these questions such as the second one has been long-debated by scholars (Tempels 1945; Hountondji 1983; Odera Oruka 1978, 1991; Olela 1981; Asante 1990, 2000; Wamba-dia-Wamba 1991) and others addressed in chapter 3 of this book, in this chapter we shade more light on the debates on African philosophy and the conceptualisation of Africa paying particular attention to the key responses that were proffered through time. The first question about whether Africa exists or not is given primary attention for the major reason that the same responses provided to it could also be used to respond to the other questions we raised above such as those to do with the existence of African philosophy. This is done with a view to show where the debate on Africa and African philosophy stands at the moment and the direction it is possibly assuming as Africa responds to the different forces from within and outside the continent as well as the past penumbra of lies conjured by Euro-centric thinkers against the African people.

Does Africa really exist?

While the discourse on Africa studies has its own peculiar themes, it borrows from other discourses in philosophy especially African philosophy. Moreover, given the parallels in philosophical status between African Philosophy and African studies, there is sufficient validation for philosophy to shed light on the discourse on the conceptualisation or rather theorisation of Africa. The need to do so becomes even more evident and urgent now than ever when one realises that the arguments that have been put forward by Eurocentric scholars against the existence of African Philosophy have also been politically deployed to desecrate the existence of Africa (see for instance, Radu 2001; Kant trans. 1950; Hegel trans. 1956). These Eurocentric perceptions and propaganda –Eurocentrism–, often cast in a mythical style, were produced and perpetuated by

32

the Eurocentric scholars based on the false impression that the West is more superior, in all respects, to all other racial groups on earth. As superbly captured by Mohanty Chandra (1984), Eurocentrism is produced when "third world legal, economic, religious and familial structures are treated as phenomena to be judged by Western standards [...] when these structures are defined as 'underdeveloped' or 'developing'" (p. 71). Thus, tracing the history of the feral racism, ethnocentrism, and Eurocentrism of the global north, one is surprised to note that the history goes back to the West's most revered culture heroes such as David Hume, Georg Hegel, John Locke, and Levy-Bruhl, among others, who theorised and wrote as if they were oblivious of rational consciousness of people of other continents. These scholars are infamous as proponents of "philosophical racism" (Immerwahr 1992) which yielded the balderdash chagrin of colonialism. The Eurocentric scholar, Hegel, for example, had a racist biased perception of the Negro and the African in general. He provocatively and unashamedly wrote:

> In Negro life the characteristic point is the fact that consciousness had not yet attained to the realisation of any substantial existence [...]. Thus, distinction between himself as an individual and the universality of his essential being, the African in the uniform, undeveloped oneness of his existence has not yet attained (Hegel 1956: 93).

Hegel, together with many other Eurocentric scholars such as John Locke and Stuart Mill denied sovereignty to Africa arguing that Africans had no idea of a government or state. For them, Africa was stateless with people who are ignorant of diaphanous relations or anything closer to good governance. Others like Levy-Bruhl and Linnaeus even denied Africa of knowledge of God, worse still, having a philosophy. Yet, "philosophy is not a science in the ivory tower, but has to contribute to the betterment of the life of the people – it has to be practical. Philosophers have to deploy the results of their thinking to the well-being of their communities" (Graness 2012: 2). That said, the philosophical rejoinders offered in the field of African philosophy generally can be of great benefit to scholars preoccupied with the theorisation of Africa both as a concept and as a geographical space.

The term "Africa" comes from the Greek *aphrike* meaning not cold; from the Latin *Aprica* meaning sunny or *Afriga* meaning land of the *Afrigs*, the Roman term for the peoples living in the southern part of the Roman Empire (see Wamba-dia-Wamba 1991). The Encyclopaedia Britannica (2011) also alludes to the same understanding with regards to the etymology of the word "Africa":

> In antiquity the Greeks are said to have called the continent Libya and the Romans to have called it Africa, perhaps from the Latin *aprica* ("sunny") or the Greek *aphrike* ("without cold"). The name Africa, however, was chiefly applied to the northern coast of the continent, which was, in effect, regarded as a southern extension of Europe. The Romans, who for a time ruled the North African coast, are also said to have called the area south of their settlements *Afriga*, or the Land of the *Afrigs*—the name of a Berber community south of Carthage (n.p).

As further asserted by Wamba-dia-Wamba, etymologically, the term "Africa" is a reflection of a European attempt at grasping un-European difference given that European philosophy has, for a long time, been theorising this difference, not as apositive other, but as a target, a colonisable target. No wonder scholars like V. Y. Mudimbe conceptualise Africa as a construction of Europe in the sense that the later [Europe] needed its other [Africa] on which to project its fears and aspirations. This means that for Mudimbe as with Wamba-dia-

Wamba, Africa was never an equal other; the reason why some Westerners even doubt the existence of Africa.

It is clear from Hegel's statement above and the analysis here elaborated that an African is a person whose roots – origin – can *directly* be traced to the continent of Africa. The word "directly" is emphasised here to show that while Africa is considered as the cradle of mankind, not everyone is considered an African except those whose ancestry could be unswervingly traced to the continent of Africa. Otherwise, even the Europeans who are believed to have originated from Africa could count as Africans too. We will not pursue this question here except to underscore that the question on whether Africa and Africans exist or not is a question that does not warrant any further debate especially given that it is generally agreed that Africa is the cradle of mankind: it is a continent where all humanity originated. Archaeological evidences to support this claim are abounding. Besides, prior to the advent of the trans-Atlantic slave trade and the most nefarious, horrendous and atrocious scheme of colonialism, Africa was generally described positively as a land full of gold. Some Europeans even believed that Africa was the earthly paradise where milk and honey flow, and where the Biblical Garden of Eden with all sorts of animals and fruits could be found. Even the colour ascribed to the people of this geographical space – Africa – was aesthetically described, hence the adage "black is beauty."

With the ushering in of trans-Atlantic slave trade and the partitioning of the African continent in 1884, the tables were turned upside down against Africa. Colonialism and racial segregation were super-imposed on Africa. Both trans-Atlantic slave trade and colonialism in Africa were "supported by a broad range of popular and scholarly literature which highlighted fundamental differences between Europeans and Africans, and which reinforced ideas of European superiority" (Ciaffa 2008: 124) with the major objective of reinforcing the need for colonising Africa and subjugating the African people while appropriating their valuable envisaged resources. With this new phenomenon – colonialism – the question that used to acquiesce positive answers yielded typically different responses altogether. Even the existence of Africa and anything typically African was subjected to question if not doubted with some people especially in the Western world thinking it to be imaginary. Africa's ability to contribute anything positive towards world civilisation was, in fact, doubted; hence the denial of the label "African." This was in spite of the fact that the term 'African' has been used to define those things, material or otherwise, that are indigenous to Africa. As Rodney (1981) and Ngugi wa Thiongo (1998) remind us, terms such as traditional African valuesand return to aspects of Africa's indigenous civilisation have the direct implication that there are such things as traditional values and indigenous civilisations that are unique to Africa, hence the legitimacy of the term "African."

With the increasing magnitude of globalisation, this taken for granted question – who is African? – has become more complex than ever. More often than not, people now face difficulties in distinguishing Africans from non-Africans. This difficulty in itself entails that even the question on whether there is something called Africa could be a tantalising difficulty to answer though normally taken for granted to mean a geographical space in the southern hemisphere, hence it merits unpacking.

We start off this section with a vignette from an unidentified blogger at: http://wssbd.com/wx/201503/a_Does_Africa_really_exist_.html, who on 17 March 2015 posted the following comment about Africa: 'I have never been to Africa […] I don't believe it is actually there. The only proof is photoshopped pictures. It's like Narnia, we pretend it's there but not really. Stop an African in the street and ask […] no it's made up [...] like Narnia.'

From what we hear from the blogger, the question "does Africa really exist?" would seem to be asking an unrealistic question, on one hand. On the other hand, the question would seem to be begging a decidedly negative answer. The blogger's thinking could be influenced by the very idea of "Africa" or let us say the word "Africa" having originated from outside Africa, starting with Herodotus who coined it and also the knowledge that the most influential African pan-Africanist, Kwame Nkrumah, was inspired by "black" American and Caribbean thinkers such as W. E. B. Du Bois and Marcus Garvey. But could this be enough evidence to doubt the existence of Africa?

It is surprising that even scholars like Michael Radu (2001: 2), though was once lecturer at Witwatersrand University but now leaving in the global north, also doubts the existence of Africa. This is confirmed in his comment on the 1963 Organisation of African Unity's (OAU) changing of name in July 2001 in Lusaka, Zambia to African Union (UN), possibly on the imitation of European Union (EU):

After all, who could be against African unity? But there is no such thing as "Africa" in any meaningful political and cultural sense, and there is no reason to think that the newly minted AU will be any more effective than the OAU was. What the continent needs is not another fictional show of unity or layer of bureaucracy […] Africa, like Asia and unlike Europe or Latin America, is not a cultural, political, or economic entity. It is a geographic collection of fifty-three states, virtually all postcolonial and recent inventions. Some countries have French as the official language, some Portuguese, Arabic, or English. Some have a mostly Black population, some Arab or mixed. Some are mostly Christian, some Islamic, some a mix. A handful has functional democratic systems, most are autocracies, many are kleptocracies, and all but a few (South Africa, Libya) are among the poorest in the world. Simply put, beyond accidents of geography, there is no such thing as "Africa" – except vis-a-vis the rest of the world.

Radu (2001: 2) even goes on to say: "But there is no such thing as 'Africa' in any meaningful political and cultural sense, and there is no reason to think that the newly minted AU will be any more effective than the OAU was." In his sense, Radu is of the view that Africa is a failed continent and hence, it does not exist at least in the political, economic and cultural sense. Radu (Ibid), thus, believes that "simply put, beyond accidents of geography, there is no such thing as 'Africa' except vis-à-vis the rest of the world."

The thinking of Radu and that of the blogger mentioned above is not new especially from the Western world's historic theoretical perspective. There are many Eurocentric scholars who, in spite of hordes of accretion that Europe and America are historically known to have acquired from Africa, have preposterously reasoned that Africa exists perhaps only as a mental figment and not in reality. These scholars have looked at Africa with negative lens. David Hume, Georg Wilhelm Friedrich Hegel, Immanuel Kant, John Locke, Stuart Mill, and more recently Levy-Bruhl's filthy racist opinions are worth elaborating. David Hume (repub.1978), in his: *The Treatise of Human Nature* and particularly his essay 'Of national characters' first published in 1748, for example, notes:

> I am apt to suspect the Negroes, and in general all the other species of men (for there are four or five different kinds) to be naturally inferior to the whites. There never was a civilised nation of any other complexion than white, nor even any individual eminent either in action or speculation. I am apt to suspect the Negroes to be naturally inferior to the whites. There scarcely ever was a civilised nation of that complexion, or even any individual eminent either in action or speculation.

The German scholar, Kant (repub.1950: 21), who never travelled more than a day's ride away from his home town, Prussia, and wrote in an age before televisions and mass communications were envisaged to be part of human civilisation, for example, claims something very obnoxious and abhorrent about Africa:

> The Negroes of Africa have by nature no feeling that rises above the trifling. Mr. Hume challenges anyone to cite a single example in which a Negro has shown talents, and asserts that among the hundreds of thousands of blacks who are transported elsewhere from their countries, although many of them have even been set free, still not a single one was even found who presented anything great in art or science or any other praiseworthy quality, even though among the whites some continually rise aloft from the lowest rabble, and through superior gifts earn respect in the world. So fundamental is the difference between these two races of man, and it appears to be as great in regard to mental capacities as in colour. The religion of fetishes so widespread among them is perhaps a sort of idolatry that sinks as deeply into the trifling as appears to be possible to human nature. A bird's feather, a cow's horn, a conch shell, or any other common object, as soon as it becomes consecrated by a few words, is an object of veneration and of invocation in swearing oaths. The blacks are very vain but in the Negro's way, and so talkative that they must be driven apart from each other with thrashings.

On the same note, another German scholar, Georg F. W. Hegel denied some Africans, particularly those of the northern part of the continent, their identity. He defined Africa and Africans in terms of geographical boundaries. He called North Africa either "European Africa" or "Asiatic Africa" basing on the colour of the people of the northern part of Africa which he said is lighter than that of the people of the southern part of the continent. The philosophy of divide and rule that Europeans used at the 1884 Berlin Conference and later in their colonies, thus, was crafted way back by such scholars as Hegel. As if this was not enough, Hegel went on to deny Africa the ideas of rationality, morality and that of God. He thought of Africans as a backward people living in a *dark continent*. One big question that strikes the back of critical minds is: In what sense is Africa a dark continent? After all is there a bright continent? Calling Africa a dark continent as if it was covered in a thick blanket of miasma had dramatic effects on the African people. It meant that Africa was a continent that required nothing less than European civilisation and enlightenment to kindle its flame of progress. Hegel, thus, sees nothing praiseworthy and admirable in the African people as he saw all of them equals to inane beings. In his *Lectures*, Hegel (repub.1956: 93) blatantly writes:

> The peculiarly African character is difficult to comprehend, for the very reason that in reference to it, we must quite give up the principle which naturally accompanies all *our* ideas-the category of Universality does not apply. In Negro life the characteristic point is the fact that consciousness has not yet attained to the realisation of any substantial objective existence-as for example, God, or Law-in which the interest of man's volition is involved and in which he realises his own being. This distinction between himself as an individual and the universality of his essential being, the African in the uniform, undeveloped oneness of his existence has not yet attained; so that the Knowledge of an absolute Being, an Other and a Higher than his individual self, is entirely wanting. The Negro, as already observed, exhibits the natural man in his completely wild and untamed state. We must lay aside all thought of reverence and morality-all that we call feeling-if we would rightly comprehend him; there is nothing harmonious with humanity to be found in this type of character. The copious and circumstantial accounts of Missionaries completely confirm this, and Mahommedanism appears to be the only thing which in any way brings the Negroes within the range of culture.

Worth noting is the fact that Hegel does not only deny rationality, knowledge and a sense of morality to Africa and the

African people. He even denies the existence of Africa itself, at least in a historical and economic sense. In fact, Hegel conceived Africans as a people that lack history, political progress, and worse still economic enterprising. In his *Lectures of 1830-1831*, Hegel (repub.1956: 99) goes on to unleash an uninvited barrage of attacks on Africa:

> At this point we leave Africa, not to mention it again. For it is no historical part of the World; it has no movement or development to exhibit. Historical movements in it – that is in its northern part – belong to the Asiatic or European World. Carthage displayed there an important transitory phase of civilisation; but, *asisNahoenician* colony, it belongs to Asia. Egypt will be considered in reference to the passage of the human mind from its Eastern to its Western phase, but it does not belong to the African Spirit. What we properly understand by Africa, is the Unhistorical, Undeveloped Spirit, still involved in the conditions of mere nature, and which had to be presented here only as on the threshold of the World's History.

As late as the 1920s, some Western scholars were still hanging on the racialist descriptions of Africa and the African people. The French scholar, Lucien Levy-Bruhl (1910, 1922), for example, presented what he calls savage states of mind. While Levy-Bruhl does not deny the existence of Africa and the African people, he argues that, the minds of the latter are so primitive and radically different from the Western logical ones. Basing on his ethnographic findings, for he was a philosopher-cum-anthropologist, Levy-Bruhl describes the mentality of Africans as pre-logical and mystical meaning that they are dominated by feelings. This description, given that it was based on what is generally considered as first-hand data – ethnographic field data – had far reaching consequences for Africa and the African people. No wonder, Ndaba (1999: 174-75) argues that 'Levy-Bruhl embodies the worst expression of racism against

African people since Joseph Conrad's main but monstrous character of Kurtz as depicted in his *Heart of Darkness*. Levy-Bruhl was even described as being too subtle, for he means by 'pre-logical' little more than unscientific or uncritical, that primitive man is rational but unscientific or uncritical (see Evans-Pritchard 1965: 18). In fact, for him, to be an African means to be ahistorical and mythical.

It is clear that even today, many Euro-centric scholars and organisations in the global north still support the idea that "Africa" is stuck as a tag such that it remains nothing less than an idea. Harold Macmillan's "wind of change" in 1960, Bob Geldof's "Do they know it's Christmas?" in 1984, and *The Economist's* "Hopeless Continent" in 2000, all widely rebut the idea of "Africa" as a reality and a continent capable of doing what other continents like America and Europe could do. The global ruling class increasingly derives its conversation from *The Economist* such that as recent as December 2011, the Magazine's cover proclaimed: "Africa Rising". On reading the magazine's cover, one wonders whether Africa was asleep or is being raised from the dead.

In 2013, Simon Kuper also wrote an article '*Africa? Why there is no such place?*' Kuper, in fact, doubts the existence of Africa. For him, Africa is just a figment, fantasy in the mind of an emotional *imaginator*. In the aforementioned article, Kuper argues that Africa does not exist. He, thus, argues:

> True, the word "Africa" still expresses an emotional reality. Since the 1940s, many Africans have come to feel African. It's one of the identities they have, beside a local and national and perhaps global identity. "African" can be a positive identity. Often, though, it is simply used to mean a victim, a member of the lowest economic category. If that's the identity, then nobody wants to be African [...]. Some geo-political phrases obscure reality rather than reveal it. Like "the Islamic world" or "the international community", "Africa" doesn't exist.

42

As could be seen from different descriptions, imaginations and conceptualisations of Africa, the central question is reason and therefore the questioning of the *philosophiness* of African philosophy. By *philosophiness* of the African philosophy we mean the quintessence of and the degree to which African philosophy could qualify as philosophy. Even if African philosophy is equated to simple lore, one should understand that any lore that deepens and widens people's horizons and presents food for thought is the beginning of philosophy, hence its philosophiness.The question of reason comes to the fore for the major reason that some cultures such as those of Africa were considered as "cultures devoid of reason" which in fact is a necessary and indispensable tool for philosophical reasoning and logical reflection. One of the prominent African scholars, Dismus A. Masolo (1994: 1) put this aptly when he notes:

> The birth of the debate on African philosophy is historically associated with two happenings: Western discourse on Africa and the African response to it […]. At the centre of this debate is the concept of reason, a value which is believed to stand as the great divide between the civilised and the uncivilised, the logical and the mystical […]. To a large extent, the debate about African philosophy can be summarised as a significant contribution to the discussion and definition of reason.

The conceptualisations and imaginations of Africa such as those elaborated above had extensive and repugnant consequences to Africa and the African people. They were promulgating a Eurocentric perspective as universal and the sole adjudicator. Arguing from a Latin American perspective, Quijano (in Vallega, 2011) contends that:

> The Eurocentric perspective of knowledge operates as a mirror that distorts what is reflected, as we can see in the Latin American historical experience. That is to say, what we Latin

Americans find in that mirror is not completely chimerical, since we possess so many and such important historically European traits in many material and inter-subjective aspects. But at the same time we are profoundly different. Consequently, when we look in our Eurocentric mirror, the image that we see is not composite but also necessarily partial and distorted. The tragedy is that we have all been led, knowingly or not, wanting it or not, to see and accept that image as our own and as belonging to us alone. In this way, we continue being what we are not (p. 207).

Besides, the conceptualisations and imaginations elaborated were sowing the seeds of destruction, at least socio-economic and political demise, on the African soil and plunging the whole continent under a thick blanket of miasma. The nauseating fruits of these imaginations and appellations ranged from self-hate to chasm, lack of self-confidence to self-denial, and from mental slavery to intellectual poverty. As one of the authors of this book aptly puts it:

This imagination *[as expressed above]* no doubt retards and frustrates the African people's intellectual emancipation and passion for reunion and hope. It is the same realisation that provoked Kuper to write his book: *The invention of primitive society* in which he argues that such a construction of Africa *[as a primitive society]* demanded a projection and imposition of the Westerners' own hegemonic societal values on other societies such as Africa in the false name of civilisation (Mawere 2014: ix).

These pejorative labellings and stereotypes are further accentuated by some Africans who remain trapped in the colonialistic and Eurocentric stereotypes panoramas. This reasoning is further supported by Umar Johnson (2011) in his: *Hidden Colours,* who bemoans that the problem with Africans is that their lives is prescribed by a Eurocentric template which unfortunately makes Africans move away from what they are,

Africa and Africans with African structures and systems of being and doing, to what they can be, Europeans, and Europeans with European structures and systems of being and doing. If such is the template that underwrites the leadership and its governance in the independence period, then it might not be difficult to observe the negatives especially to the marginal spaces and classes.

It is in the context of the above elaborated sad histories and situations that contemporary critical philosophers as African politicians of the time find themselves, deeply entangled in a cobweb of mangled situations and histories that make them finding it difficult or even impossible to react with *kid blows* or at least to be neutral when treating issues to do with African philosophy especially vis-a-vis Western philosophy. Ochieng-Odhiambo and Iteyo's (2012) comment on the situation of contemporary African philosopher is apt:

> History, therefore, makes it difficult for the African philosopher to remain neutral, because whatever the philosopher is working in or on about Africa does have political consequences. Given that this history has made the African philosopher labour under all sorts of burdens, given that it has interfered with her/his being, identity, culture and society, she or he would find it difficult to be neutral; for this would be tantamount to one abandoning one's responsibility to oneself and one's society (p. 177).

It is in view of sniping labelling and unabashed caricaturing such as those discussed above, especially the iniquitous denial of reason to African cultures that many African scholars mainly those from the discipline of philosophy such as Kwasi Wiredu, Kwame Gyekye, D. A. Masolo, Henry Odera Oruka, and revolutionary luminaries across the continent, felt obliged to respond at least in defence of Africa and African philosophy. In line with this imperative, a revolutionist-cum philosopher,

Patrice Lumumba, pronounced before his execution in 1961 that:

> No brutality, mistreatment, or torture has ever forced me to ask for grace, for I prefer to die with my head high, my faith steadfast, and my confidence profound in the destiny of my country, rather than to live in submission and scorn of sacred principles [...]. Do not weep for me my dear companion. I know that my country which suffers so much, will know how to defend its independence and its liberty. Long live the Congo! Long live Africa!

In the same manner, Okot p'Bitek (1979), appeals for a cultural revolution by African scholars, a revolution that would initiate reverse of the unpardonable gains of barbarism-cum-brutalism of the global north imperialists:

> A proper understanding of Africa can offer a new vision for its future: The African scholar has two clear tasks before him. First, to explore and destroy all false ideas about African peoples and culture that have been propagated and perpetuated by Western scholarship. Vague terms as *Tribe, Folk, Non-literate* or even innocent looking ones such as *Developing*, etc., must be subjected to critical analysis and thrown out or redefined to suit African interests. Second, the African scholar must endeavour to present the institutions of African peoples as they really are (p. 7).

Similarly, Senghor (1975) associates Africa and the African people with beauty and life. In his poem: *Black Woman,* Senghor (Ibid: 96) romanticises the beauty of the "black race" – what we prefer calling indigenous African people – as comparable to no other human race on earthwhen he says:

Naked woman, black woman!

Clothed with your colour which is life, with your form which is beauty!

In your shadow I have grown up; the gentleness of your hands was laid over my eyes.

And now, high in the sun-baked pass, at the hearts of summer, at the heart of noon,

I come upon you, my promised land, and your beauty strikes me to the heart like the flash of an angel.

In Senghor's poem, "black", becomes beauty and life. He uses the concept of *Negritude* to symbolise what the black man or an African in general stands for. His association of life with Africa resonates with the popular view that Africa is the cradle – motherland and fatherland – of mankind basing on the widely accepted scientific view that the oldest ever known human fossils (of Homo sapiens) in the world were discovered in the 'remote' region of Herto in Ethiopia. As the archaeologist Berhane Asfaw (2003) tells us, these fossils are five times older than those found in Europe and are the oldest ever direct predecessors of humans. This caused Asfaw to declare that "Ethiopia is the Garden of Eden: the whole history of human evolution is here." Prior to this archaeological discovery, the famous remains found in Ethiopia was Lucy – a three and a half million-year-old complete skeleton that was unearthed at Hadar in 1974. In Tanzania at Olduvai/Odupai Gorge, *Homo habilis* fossils dating approximately 1.9 million years by Mary and Louis Leakey in 1929. Recently, even older human lineage fossils dating 2.8million-year-old were found in Afar region of Ethiopia (Sample 2015). It is even surprising to realise how Eurocentric scholars who deny others – Africans – philosophy contradict themselves to the extent that they believe in the non-existence of Africa and the view that Africa is the cradle of mankind at the same time. One would wonder how one continent could be the cradle of mankind and non-existent at the same time.

Nature and scope of African philosophy

In many African countries, the discipline of African philosophy is relatively young and often studied as a sub-set of African Studies. It is different from philosophy in Africa which entails the participation of Africa in the universal enterprise of philosophy. In fact, while African philosophy presupposes pluriversality in so far as it implies the existence of a distinct philosophy in Africa with a distinct approach – a philosophy with a distinct way of doing philosophy – philosophy in Africa implies that there is participation of the continent as a whole in the enterprise of philosophy.

While through professional African philosophy, African philosophy as a discipline is fast gaining prominence in academia either replacing or taught alongside Western philosophy in African universities where the latter was normally taught since the introduction of formal education on the continent. Nevertheless, this is not sufficient to describe African philosophy in terms of its nature and scope. Mesembe (2013) acknowledging the same notes that: "African philosophy as a component of academic global philosophy has become very respectable in its contributions to shaping the history and experiences of the African people and that work on African Philosophy must be persistent and sustained."

An attempt to understand the nature and scope of African philosophy begs an understanding of two things: what it means to do philosophy and; the prefixing "African" of African philosophy we highlighted above. Doing philosophy entails a process. It is a process of rational and critical reflection or a reflective examination of things in the realm of existence. Ezeani (2005) puts this aptly when he notes:

> To philosophise is to think, and to think is to question. To philosophise is to ask questions and question the answer to the question and continue the process until one arrives at the ultimate

48

answer – the truth […] through the process of critical questioning and reflection the philosopher attempts to confront his or her existence, assumptions and also contribute to the development of thoughts (p. 11 & 7).

From the above, one notes that all humans have the capacity and right to think rationally: they have the capacity and right to philosophise or to do philosophy. In fact any tradition or lore that raises people's nadir of curiosity widens people's knowledge base, and presents food for thought to the present and future generations marks the beginning of philosophy. The enterprise of critical reflection in Africa, therefore, qualifies as philosophy. It is what it means to do philosophy in Africa. It is also what we mean when we talk of Western philosophy or when we talk of American philosophy – how they do philosophy in the West and in the Americas. It is from this understanding that it becomes absurd to ask whether there is philosophy in Africa, in Europe, or in Asia. For as long as there are people who can engage in critical investigation of things, there is philosophy. Yet, when this or that thing is tagged "African," it means the thing is related to Africa in some special way. This may be in terms of origin, place of existence, or some other forms of attachment; hence we can talk of African philosophy as a philosophy that belongs to Africa. The same understanding alludes to the question on the content/nature of philosophy in Africa, by which we mean the study, writing, teaching, and practice of philosophy in Africa. It is on the basis of such understanding that scholars like Anyanwu (2010), has come to understand African philosophy as that which concerns itself with the way in which African people of the past and present make sense of their destiny and the world they live. For Janz (2009), African philosophy is philosophy produced by African people. Asukwo (2009: 30) understands African philosophy as "a subjective world-view packaged and anchored with the mind-frame in order to ask and answer questions that can solve the immediate problem at hand within a given socio-economic and political environment." Bodunrin summarises African philosophy as "the philosophy done by African philosophers whether it be in the area of logic, ethics or history of philosophy" (Sogolo 1993: 2). We should, however, note that to discuss philosophy in Africa is necessarily to discuss African philosophy. By African philosophy we mean the contextualised critical thinking, articulation of ideas, and attempts to seek solutions to problematic situations by Africans. This is because tagging a philosophy "African" or "American" or "European" is contextualising it. It is showing that the philosophising exercise is being executed in the specific context in question. In the case of African philosophy, it means that philosophy tools and techniques are being utilised to explore reality of things from the view point of Africa. We, thus, concur with Ezeani (2005: 7) who understands African philosophy as "contextualised critical thinking of or a philosophical product by an African [...] it is (or part of it is) an articulation by an African philosopher of his or her ideas or thoughts in a coded format meant to provide an answer to a mindboggling question or a solution to a contextualised social or political problem" (p. 9). On this basis, African philosophers should not be criticised for being linked to the kind of philosophy they study, teach, or practice simply because it is reflects on the existential experiences of the African people or is different from Western philosophy. Makinde (2000), thus, is right when he warns and encourages African philosophers "to do [philosophy] in the way they think it should be done including of course, the writing and teaching of it" (p.125). So is Sodipo, in his assertion that "when you say African philosophy you are drawing attention to that aspect of philosophy which arises from a special problem and the unique experience of African people" (Uduigwomen 2009: 6). In fact, African philosophers must hold onto their position as long as they maintain the main function of philosophy, that of searching for truth in its entirety (Nze 1990). This way African philosophy can maintain its uniqueness as an equal philosophy and grow its influence beyond Africa as Western philosophy has done over the years. Otherwise, African philosophy, as has been done to the African people during trans-Atlantic slave trade and colonialism, will be devalued and subjected to lower order hierarchically, when it is actually an equal philosophy – in the sense that we speak of Western philosophy – with only a different approach to the investigation of the truth. On this note, Ozumba and Chimakonam (2014) are right when they argue that Western thought and African philosophy differ in approach: whereas Western thought is exclusive and dichotomised innature, African thought is complementary, integrative and inclusive. Chimakonam's (2011) cry for a pronounced African Logic is worth considering as it is this logic that acts as the identity mark of African philosophy. Chimakonam's critical question: "Why can't there be an African Logic?" and his further explanation on the uniqueness of African philosophy is apt:

> Among the characteristics of African logic is the uniqueness of its approach. Western logician, for instance, takes the middle position between A and B and only asserts one when he has fully drawn out his proof. The African logician, however, asserts one A and B before drawing out his proof to justify this position. This is principally why, by the standard of Western logic, any such reasoning pattern is said to be guilty of bias and prejudice and is accused of lacking in objectivity. It is by this standard that African thought pattern is said to be illogical (p. 143).

We add that, why can't there be African epistemology? Why can't there be African metaphysics? Why can't there be African ethics? The existence of areas such as these would, in doubt, show the uniqueness of African philosophy as well as the context in which the philosophy in question – African philosophy – is studied.

African philosophy and pragmatics

The utility of African philosophy is yet to be fully explored if not realised. In the past years, scholars have been concentrating more on debates surrounding the existence of African philosophy. Insignificant attention has been paid to the value and significance of African philosophy to Africa and the African people and even those beyond.

Due to the inexorably unpardonable forces of westernisation and its attendant process of globalisation compounded with political strife, civil wars, and sprouts of xenophobic attacks across the African continent in the recent years, African philosophy seems to be fast losing its value. Nevertheless, the value of African philosophy to Africa and the people of Africa and beyond cannot be underestimated.

In view of misconceptions and misrepresentations about Africa by Eurocentric scholars such as Hegel, Kant, Hume, Levy-Bruhl, and others, there is need to pulverise Western misrepresentations and re-write Africa from within and set the record straight for the world to know the truth about Africa and the African people. As such, there is no doubt that African philosophy being Africa-oriented is one discipline with the potential to debunk and correct all Eurocentric misconceptions and misrepresentations about Africa and its people.

By correcting Eurocentric misconceptions and misrepresentations about Africa and the African people, Africans are afforded the opportunity to reclaim their cultural identity as well as self-identity. This resonates with what scholars like Walter Rodney and George James longed when they wrote their historic and legendary books: *How Europe underdeveloped Africa* and *Stolen legacy* respectively. In his *Stolen legacy*, for example, James explained how Europe and how much Europe stole from Africa to enrich itself without even acknowledging and recognising the role of the later [Africa] in the civilisation of Europe and the world as a whole. On the basis of this realisation,

Rodney and James argue for the need for Africa to reclaim its cultural identity, dignity, and position in both global politics and politics of world development and civilisation. Mawere (2015a) even argues that the need for the reclamation of what is duly African is more urgent now than ever. He thus, avers:

> There is need for African scholars [and *people*] to drink deep, soberly, solicitously and wholly in the past and present, for little learning is always dangerous and unsustaining [...]. The people of Africa should not afford to remain undecided and uncertain of their position in this fast changing world; they must reawaken their intellectual proclivity and dig deep into their existential experiences and cause of existence the *Sankofa* way (p. 3).

This is what Aime Cesaire (1939; 1969) meant when he urged the people of Africa to go back to their rootsup to the remotest point and re-establish or recuperate her distorted identity as a people. As Cesaire points out the distortion which was inflicted by the colonists' aggression and socio-cultural imperialism, could only be dislodged through resistance of the colonial values and resilience as well as determination of the African people to counter the legacy of colonial self-hatred and convalesce their own values to re-establish their identity as a people.

It goes without mention that through its emphasis on moral values such as Ubuntu/Unhu and MAA'T, among others, African philosophy promotes a culture of sharing, love, unity/oneness and respect amongst the people and of the surrounding environment, including that of other beings[1].

---

[1]Munyaradzi Mawere (2015b) prefers to use the term "other beings" to Bruno Latour (1987; 1993; 2005) and others' (i.e Callon 1986) "nonhumans," reasoning that there are some "creatures"/entities that are difficult to classify as either humans or nonhumans, as they are part human and part nonhuman. Mawere gives examples of vampires and werewolves (see Kosek 2010, 672), which he says, are part human and part nonhuman beings that result from

Ubuntu/Unhu philosophy, for example, is one African philosophical tradition that emphasises humaneness, respect, and sharing among human beings (within the community and even those outside the community such as strangers) and other beings. This philosophy, thus, is both an inter- and intra-relational epoxy resin adhesive that binds together all creation on earth to allow it to live together as per the order of the creation.

The MAA'T and Ubuntu/Unhu philosophical traditions also establish grounds for good governance and justice system in a way that promotes good governance and preservation of life in society. The 42 Admonitions of the MAA'T, for example, act as cardinal law that guide human behaviour, conduct, and help preserving life in society as a whole. The principles of respect and love embedded in Ubuntu/Unhu philosophy also emphasise the same thing. Where there is respect and unconditional love, there is likely to be good governance – governance that satisfies all community members.

Also, considering Africa's colonial history with the colonists' emphasis on mimicry and cultivation of a culture of inferiority among the colonised, it is widely agreed that there is need for the African people [the formerly colonised] and the Europeans [the former colonists] to decolonise their minds. This is what Ngugi wa Thiongo urged in his literary-cum-philosophical masterpiece: *Decolonising the mind: The politics of language in African literature.* In fact, wa Thiongo as with many other critical African writers such as Julius Nyerere, advocates linguistic

---

the contagion of the battlefields. Basing on his ethnographic studies in the Norumedzo Area of southeastern Zimbabwe, Mawere also gives other examples such as *vadzimu* [ancestors], *mhondoro* [lion spirits] and *njuzu* [mermaids/half-fish, half-human creatures] that, according to his interlocutors in the Norumedzo, are not purely human. Neither are they purely nonhumans, but are simply referred to as *zvisikwa zvaMwari* [other beings created by God]. On this note, we follow Mawere's use of the terms "humans" and "other beings," to refer to all those entities that cannot be classified as humans, both in part or in totality.

decolonisation and anti-imperialist perspective in virtually all spheres of life in post-colonial Africa.

Conclusion

The present chapter has problematised the conceptualisation of Africa and African philosophy with a view to unpack the nature, scope, and value of African philosophy to contemporary societies in Africa and beyond. It has underscored the fact that while the question of the existence of African philosophy is long dead and buried, it remains fundamentally important even today if African philosophy as a discipline is to be well grasped and its direction determined. The chapter has also acknowledged that while discussions on and around African philosophy have taken place in many circles inside and outside Africa, little attention has been given to the question of the value and significance of African philosophy: more attention has been devoted on arguments seeking to prove the existence of African philosophy as well as those distinguishing African philosophies from other philosophies such as Eastern philosophy, Western philosophy, and American philosophy. We have argued that it is the value of African philosophy to both the contemporary and future generations that will make the study of African philosophy viable and tenable around the world; hence the need to study the discipline wholesomely. In our next chapter, we focus on Henry Odera Oruka's trends of African philosophy, which we consider as an attempt not only to prove the existence of African philosophy but to show that African philosophy just like its philosophers is no different from other philosophies around the world besides being attached existentially and methodically to the context of Africa.

Chapter 3

African Philosophy, Debates, and Henry Odera Oruka's Four Trends

"Africa is a hopeless continent"– *The Economist Magazine 13 May 2000.*

African philosophy is a story of wonderful, courageous, resilient and high spirited people told falsely by bigotry and prejudice of thecolonial monsters, neo-colonialist bustards, and the Euro-centric minds riddled with discrimination, intolerance and malarkey. It is a story that needs to be told sanguinely, rightly, naturally, accurately, beautifully, truthfully and in good faith. It is a story that needs not only deconstruction but reconstruction: a story that needs new minds and think-tanks to be told genuinely and objectively. This is the story we cheerfully capture in this chapter and indeed in this whole book; a great story that need to be retold in entirety without swindling for the new generation to hear and sap the truth from the real source, and most importantly to be schooled rightly, honestly and productively. The fruits of this adventure, will no doubt, enable Africans to think outside the box, move away from the trap of desperation, break away from the vicious circle of misery and insolence, and allow Africa to re-assume its important role and position in international affairs. But how can this be possible if Africa and African philosophy itself continue to be doubted even several decades after the evil towering ghost of colonialism has vamoosed the African soil? (Mawere 2015). How can this be possible if the former imperialists continue to be lionised and wax-lyricalisedby scholars and their own governments alike regardless of the fact that the damage that the Western imperialists inflicted on other cultures was more than venial to be forgiven?

Given that much of the highlighted issues have been discussed in our previous chapter, and a number of African scholars have contributed significantly and positively on debates about reclaiming African dignity and its lost glory and philosophy, the larger part of this chapter focuses more on Odera Oruka's novel contribution to African philosophy through his trends of contemporary African philosophy.

Henry Odera Oruka's trends of African Philosophy

In response to the acrimonious debate on the existence of African philosophy, racist pronouncements and claims against Africans' ability to reason, worse still to philosophise, the Kenyan philosopher, Henry Odera Oruka, enunciated what has come to be widely known invariably as *trends* in African philosophy (Oruka 1997), *schools* of African Thought /Philosophy (Oruka 1987), or *currents* in African philosophy (Outlaw 1987).

Henry Odera Oruka was a dexterous, productive, audacious, well-read and prolific scholar who wrote a number of books, journal articles and presented many papers in conferences around the world. He contributed significantly to almost all fields of philosophy which included but not limited to logic, philosophy of religion, philosophy of culture, epistemology, metaphysics, ethics and African philosophy. However, it is in the latter field that Odera Oruka is best remembered and credited. He identified and branded six approaches – trends – in his response to the question on what African philosophy really is or could be. These are ethno-philosophy, philosophic sagacity, professional philosophy, nationalistic-ideological philosophy, hermeneutic philosophy, and artistic or literary philosophy (Odera Oruka1998: 101) although he outlined and elaborated only the first four of these trends. The two other trends– literary philosophy and hermeneutical philosophy – Odera Oruka claims to be trends in contemporary philosophy also worth considering. But given that these two trends easily fall within the purview of the four trends of contemporary philosophy especially ethno-philosophy and professional philosophy, we will not discuss them in this book. For now, let us look at Odera Oruka's aforementioned four trends of contemporary philosophy in some detail.

Ethno-philosophy

The term 'ethno-philosophy' is not unique to Henry Odera Oruka. Prior to its usage by Odera Oruka, it hadbeen used in the context of the discourse on the nature of African philosophy by Kwame Nkrumah (1970) and PaulinHountondji in his 1983 publication, *African philosophy: Myth and reality*. Hountondji, for example, used the term ethno-philosophy to refer to the philosophy that Placide Tempels and many others across the African continent such as Alexis Kagame, Fouda, Mgr Makarakiza, Marcien Towa, Lufuluabo, Bahoken and Mulago (Hountondji, Ibid) were 'discovering' or rather unearthing. We should note that though it is often assumed that the word ethno-philosophy was coined by Hountondji, it was in fact Kwame Nkrumah who coined it. Nkrumah had actually registered for a PhD dissertation at the University of Pennsylvania in 1943 and had proposed to work on what he termed 'ethno-philosophy.' This means that even though the term is now largely associated with Odera Oruka, ethno-philosophy as an approach to African philosophy is directly linked to Nkrumah and later Tempels, particularly his book *LaPhilosophie Bantoue,* first published in 1945 and later (in 1959) translated under the title *'Bantu Philosophy.'*

The book by Tempels marked the birth of modern African philosophy– particularly ethno-philosophy – given that it was, in many ways, contrary to what many scholars in the West were writing about Africa. For this reason, Tempels' book generated a lot of debate among scholars in both Europe and those that were beginning to emerge in Africa. But what ethno-philosophy is all about?

For scholars like Bodunrin (1984: 1) ethno-philosophy refers to the seminal works of anthropologists, sociologists and ethnographers who interpret the "collective world views of African peoples, their myths and folk wisdom" as that part of the treasure of the African people that can be considered as African philosophy. Serequeberhan (1991) shares the same view as that of Bodunrin. He explains ethno-philosophy as characterised by the conviction that the starting point of African philosophy is the "mythical religious conception, world views and ritual practices" (p. 17).

As could be seen from the above discussion, the idea behind ethno-philosophy is that unlike Western philosophy which is more of an individual exercise, African philosophy is alived communal philosophy. This means African philosophy is exercised as a collective wisdom of thepeople and not as a preserve, exercise or adventure of any one person. African philosophy, thus, belongs to every member of the society, young or old, born or yet to be born, from which it is rooted. It is rooted from the shared lived experiences of the African people as a whole. On this note, African philosophy includes proverbs, idioms, folktales, maxims, and aphorisms, among other shared experiences and wisdoms of the African people.

Ethno-philosophy is very much closer to cultural philosophy and philosophic sagacity although Odera Oruka tells us that the former [cultural philosophy] is a first order activity while the latter [philosophic sagacity] is a second order activity. Philosophic sagacity is a second order activity in that it involves critical reflection of the first order conformity [cultural philosophy]. In other words, philosophic sagacity is generally reflective and rationalistic as compared to cultural philosophy and ethno-philosophy which are in fact deeply embedded in culture and tradition. However, an ordinary sage though is also known as a culture philosopher, there is a thin line of difference between cultural philosophy and ethnophilosophy. As Odera Oruka, tells us:

> Cultural philosophy consists of the beliefs, practices and myths, taboos andgeneral values of a people which govern their everyday life and are usuallyexpressed and stored in oral vocabulary of the people. Ethno-philosophy, on theother hand, is a written work of some scholars claiming to offer an objectivedescription of the culture philosophy of a people. As a trend of thought, ethno-philosophy is much recent than culture philosophy which dates back to the daysof the first ancient. In historical order, philosophic sagacity antedates ethno-philosophy but is second-order to culture philosophy (Odera Oruka 1991: 6-7).

While ethno-philosophy is undoubtedly believed to be rich in philosophy, it has met with serious criticisms from many scholars over the years. In fact, there is a significant amount of literature that is critical of ethno-philosophy as a trend of contemporary African philosophy. One of the novel criticisms levelled against ethno-philosophy is offered by Paulin Hountondji who argues that ethnophilosophy is a misrepresentation of the African people. In one of his numerous critiques of ethno-philosophy, Hountondji (2002: 107) writes:

> The return of the real thus shatters into smithereens the founding myths of ethno-philosophy: the myth of primitive unanimity – the idea that in 'primitive' societies, everyone is in agreement with everyone else – from which it is concluded that there could not possibly exist individual philosophies in such societies, but only belief-systems. In reality, an unbiased reading of the existing intellectual production reveals something else. The African field is plural, like all fields, a virgin forest open to all possibilities, to all potentialities, a host to all contradictions and intellectual adventures like all other sites of scientific production.

Similarly, scholars like Barry Hallen (2010) view ethno-philosophy as debased philosophy unworthy of the name philosophy given that it emphasises the myth of unanimity through its embracing of communality. Hallen (Ibid), thus, notes:

1). Ethno-philosophy presents itself as a philosophy of *peoples* rather than of *individuals*. It is communal and not individualistic. In Africa one is, therefore, given the impression that there can be no equivalents to a Socrates or a Kant. Ethno-philosophy speaks only of Bantu philosophy, Dogon philosophy, Akan philosophy; as such its scope is collective (or 'tribal'), of the world-view variety; 2). Its *sources* are in the past, in what is described as authentic, *traditional* African culture of the *pre*-colonial variety, of the African prior to 'modernity'. These can be found in cultural by-products that were primarily oral: parables, proverbs, poetry, songs, and myths – oral literature generally. Obviously, since such sources do not present their 'philosophies' in any conventionally discursive or technical format, it is the academic scholars, rather than African peoples, who interpret or analyse them, and thus come up with what they present as the systematised 'philosophy' of an entire African culture; 3). From a *methodological* point of view, ethno-philosophy therefore tends to present the beliefs that constitute this 'philosophy' as things that do not change, that are somehow timeless. African *traditional* systems of thought are, therefore, portrayed as placing minimal emphasis upon rigorous argumentation and criticism in a search for truth that provides for discarding the old and creating the new. Tradition somehow becomes antithetical to innovation. Disputes between academic ethnophilosophers, thus, arise primarily over how to arrive at a correct *interpretation* of a static body of oral literature and oral traditions (p. 75-76).

The historian of philosophy, Wamba-dia-Wamba (1991) in his: *Philosophy and African Intellectuals: Mimesis of Western Classicism,*

Ethno-philosophical Romanticism or African Self-Mastery? also argues against communal philosophy as embraced by ethno-philosophy. For him, in Africa as elsewhere in the world, the question of philosophy should and indeed is necessarily connected to the formation and development of intellectuals as a social class. And, intellectuals, as a social class, emerged as a result of the need to distinguish manual labour from intellectual labour in a given society. The separation between intellectual labour and manual labour is necessary and was prompted by the desireto increase production in society through the means of production. The need to increase production, in turn, necessitated the need to clearly distinguish between manual labour and intellectual labour. Making reference to the historical evolution of humankind, Wamba-dia-Wamba goes on to argue that now that the human society has evolved in relation to its social division of labour, this separation resulted in a social class of intellectual producers who kept growing not only in numbers but diversity and even complexity. Examples of such intellectual producers are philosophers. This means that for Wamba-dia-Wamba, bunching African philosophy as communally owned hinder philosophical progress in African societies such that we cannot talk of philosophy where ideas are collectively owned. Wamba-dia-Wamba (1991: 8), thus, says:

> Philosophy-doing, as a relatively autonomous social activity, emerged as ahistorical outcome of that separation. In pre-class divided communities, whereintellectual work was not fundamentally separated from manual labour, philosophy as a social activity did not exist. This does not mean, however, thatpeople were not thinking. But most likely they were not thinking systematically about thinking.

As could be seen in the paragraph above, Wamba-dia-Wamba denies the existence of philosophy in societies where ideas are communally owned. He, in fact, argues that the emergence of African philosophyas a specific way of philosophising cannot be traced to pre-class divided African societies but must be traced to the colonial as well as neo-colonial forms ofseparation between intellectual labour and manual labour. Wamba-dia-Wamba, therefore, sees African philosophy as a product of colonialism in Africa that was used as watch-dog to safeguard the colonial ideology. For him, the watch-dogs (what he calls intellectual workers) were found in the name of missionaries and ethno-philosophers. The works of these intellectual labourers was not only critical to the colonial regime that founded them but even to the militant propagandists of dominant ideas towards the masses, Wamba-dia-Wamba would argue. Basing on this reasoning, Wamba-dia-Wamba (1991: 10) asserts: 'ethno-philosophy is a philosophy of and for the dominated Africa. It does not matter whether or not actual ways of thinking of some real Africans fit inthis way of viewing things. The fact is that this specificity is discovered, theorised in the face of humanity that dominates it and requires it to be sodominated.'

In short, Wamba-dia-Wamba views ethno-philosophy as philosophy of the dominating group or of the dominated if at all it could be considered as philosophy. It is in this view that ethno-philosophy is viewed by Wamba-dia-Wamba as a suspicious contribution to African philosophy and, in fact, as a philosophy of domination that falls short as an authentic philosophy: ethno-philosophy as an approach to African philosophy, thus, is guilty of misrepresenting Africa and its values.

Yet besides all the challenges that ethno-philosophy encounters, Bodunrin (1984), is still confident that it has potentials worth waiting, and thus, warns that:

> The African Philosopher cannot deliberately ignore the study of the traditional belief system of his people. Philosophical problems arise outof real life situations. In Africa, more than in many other parts of the modern world, traditional culture and

beliefs still exercise a great influence on the thinking and actions of men. At a time when many people in the West believe that philosophy has become impoverished and needs redirection, a philosophical study of traditional society may be the answer (p. 13).

Professional philosophy

Professional philosophy as an approach to African philosophy was a direct response or rather an antithesis of ethno-philosophy or what Peter Bodunrin (1984) referred to as 'cultural philosophy'. Those scholars who considered themselves as professional philosophers like Bodunrin argue for a 'universal philosophy' as posited against the idea of 'cultural philosophy.' For Bodunrin, philosophy, whether African, Asian, American, or European, is culturally neutral in so far as philosophy is a professional and theoretical discipline which like physics and mathematics has a universal application, character, and methodology. Thus for Bodunrin, ethno-philosophy as an approach to African philosophy was too simplistic and uncritical. Instead, philosophy (and in fact any approach to African philosophy) was supposed to be "critical, discursive and independent, contrary to the insinuations of ethno-philosophy" (Ochieng-Odhiambo and Iteyo 2012: 174). Scholars in the professional philosophy, thus, rallied together and accused ethno-philosophy and its proponents of doing a de-service to African philosophy by their embracing of myths and denial of reason to ethno-philosophy. For this group of scholars, Tempels' hands (and those of all his disciples) were not all that clean for he was the one who championed ethno-philosophy arguing that it is a philosophy embedded in myths, extra-rational traditionalism and magic (Tempels 1945/1959). Tempels (1959: 24) expresses this view when he avers:

> We do not claim that Bantus are capable of presenting us with a philosophical treatise complete with an adequate vocabulary. It

is our own intellectual training that enables us to effect its systematic development. It is up to us to provide them with an accurate account of their conception of entities.

From the assertion above, it is clear that while Temples agrees that there is philosophy in Africa and among Africans, he admits that the 'owners' of that philosophy are unable to express it in clear terms unless they are trained by the Westerners. It is for this reason that scholars like Wamba-dia-Wamba argues that ethno-philosophy is a tool for the colonialists who use it to safeguard their interests. For him and others in the camp of professional philosophy, ethno-philosophy and its proponents though they seem to have an Afro-centric tone, are "settling for aninferior and idiosyncratic conception of philosophy which lacks the intellectual rigour of Western philosophy and thereby virtually guarantees its own marginalisation in the world market" (Van Hook 1993: 36).

While professional philosophy has accused ethno-philosophy of doing a de-service to African philosophy, it "too can and indeed has been accused of the same" (Ochieng-Odhiambo and Iteyo 2012: 175). Professional philosophy and its proponents have been accused of working within a framework that is distinctively Western and not African. This framework continues privileging the West: the West remains more of a compass with the mandate to dictate the rules of the philosophical game. As Ochieng-Odhiambo (2010: 108-109) rightfully puts it, "in professional philosophy, there is an apparent over-glorifying of how philosophy is practiced in the West inthe name of universalism. They, thus, play the game as the West would have it played, and bythat very token, guarantee its irrelevance to issues, problems and struggles of Africa." In fact for Ochieng-Odhiambo, professional philosophy only does copy-paste of Western philosophy. It lacks originality as a trend of contemporary African philosophy.

Besides the above critique, some scholars argue that professional philosophy just like Western philosophy from where it emanates is essentialistic in nature. In fact, what professional philosophy (and Western philosophy at large) claims to be universal is indeed not universal in so far as it is drawn from the historical and ideological context of the Western world. Hallen (2009), for example, takes a particularistic stance. He argues that universalist philosophers "such as Wiredu, haveembraced a paradigm of cross-cultural rationality that is too extreme and too Western in orientation and, therefore, unfairly discriminates against the rationality of certain African modes of thought and beliefs" (p. 57). Outlaw (1987) alsocriticises the critique offered by professional philosophers that African philosophy should be rational and disengage itself from its cultural roots. For Outlaw, rationality is in fact a cultural product (particularly Western culture) in much the same way ethno-philosophy is a cultural product (of the African culture) (see p. 35). Onyewuenyi (1982) and other particularists like Outlaw, Hallen and Sogolo (2003) voice their concern against the emphasis on universalising this or that aspect of human cultures. Their reason for rejecting universalism is that each culture is different or unique to itself such that to universalise a particular aspect will not do enough justice to other cultures. For them universalise a particular feature will result in some cultures losing their essential features that are unique to themselves.

Philosophic sagacity

The phrase 'philosophic sagacity'was used by Odera Oruka to describe a reflective evaluation of thought of a particular distinguished individual African elder/sage (and not a group of people) who is a repository of knowledge, wisdom, and painstaking critical thinking and logical reasoning: it is not a communal but purely an individual enterprise. Philosophic sagacity, thus, is more of a conversational or dialectical approach to philosophy given that it involves interviews, discussions, and dialogue/conversations with specific individuals who are known, believed to be sages or are well versed with the wisdom and tradition of their people. In this sense, philosophic sagacity describes the kind of philosophic activity which the Nigerian philosopher, Campbell Momoh, calls "Ancient African philosophy" (Momoh 1985: 77-78, 1988, 1989) and the Ghanaian philosopher, Kwasi Wiredu, referred to as 'Traditional African thought or philosophy' (Wiredu 1980). By the latter, Wiredu meant a critical evaluation of thought by an individual African sage who is a repository of knowledge, wisdom, and rigorous thinking. Philosophic sagacity is one of Odera Oruka's most cherished contributions to African philosophy. Emphasising Odera Oruka's contribution to African philosophy, Ochieng-Odhiambo and Iteyo (2012: 170) comment:

> Odera Oruka is best remembered, especially with respect to philosophic sagacity which he is credited to have introduced within academic circles. In philosophic sagacity, emphasis is laid on reason in matters pertaining to African cultures and belief systems [...]. Odera Oruka's major contribution to philosophy in general, and to African philosophy in particular, is his philosophic sagacity.

But how philosophic sagacity has been understood by other philosophers? How does it differ from professional philosophy and ethno-philosophy?

Philosophic sagacity or what Hountondji (1983: 81) terms a *literature de pensée* was criticised by Hountondji, who himself is normally criticised[2] for being too theoretical, elitistic and

---

[2] For more on criticism against Paulin Hountondji, read Oyekan Owomoyela (1987: 92), 'Africa and the imperative of philosophy: A sceptical consideration,' African Studies Review, Vol. 30 (1) who argues that Hountondji's suggestion that African Studies is suspect because it was invented by Europeans and is, therefore, part of the European tradition, is as

insufficiently political for an African philosopher. Yet, following Odera Oruka's understanding of philosophic sagacity, Ochieng-Odhiambo and Iteyo (2012) describeit [philosophic sagacity] as a philosophy deeply connected to culture and worth pursuing. Making reference to the Kenyan culture, Ochieng-Odhiambo and Iteyo (2012: 181) describe philosophic sagacity as:

> The map in intellectual terms (based on reason) of the disposition of forces which will enable Kenyan society to digest the inconsistent ethnic elements in Kenya, and develop them in such a way that they fit into the Kenyan personality. The Kenyan personality is the cluster of humanist and coherent principles which underlie the traditional Kenyan society.

Unlike ethno-philosophy, philosophic sagacity is considered by scholars like Wamba-dia-Wamba as a de-colonising philosophy, an emancipatory endeavour meant to liberate human mind of the African people.

Besides, philosophic sagacity was a philosophical trend meant to address the problems associated with both ethno-philosophy and professional philosophy. Elaborating on the objective of philosophic sagacity, Odera Oruka (1978: 17) wrote that its purpose was to "invalidate the claim that traditional African peoples were innocent of logical and critical thinking." Odera Oruka made it clear that African philosophy in its uncontaminated traditional form does not begin and end in folk thought and collectivity as professional philosophers thought. For him, African people even before their contact with the

---

strange as his denigration of ethno-philosophy. Olabiyi Yai is also another critic of Hountondji. In his (1997) publication "The theory and practice in African philosophy: The poverty of speculative philosophy," Yai charges Hountondji of "eliticism, philosophism, and scientism" (p. 16) and of being a speculative philosopher who ignores the issues of praxis in his theorising. It is also widely agreed that in his attempt to rubbish ethno-philosophy, Hountondji ignored the vitality and possibilities inherent in indigenous African traditions, norms and values.

outside world have always been logical, critical and engaged in debates and dialogue such that to say their philosophy begin and end in folk is a misnomer that should not go unchallenged. In his seminal work: "sagacity in African philosophy" (1983), Odera Oruka, thus, maintained that among the traditional folk of Africa, uninfluenced by modern education, there are genuine philosophers – individuals capable of fundamental reflection on man and the world, and able to subject the folk philosophy of their own communities to criticism and modification. He referred to such individuals as 'philosophic sages'. Put differently, Odera Oruka argued that philosophy can be found in African traditional cultures because there are indigenous thinkers – philosophic sages/opinion leaders – who although they lack modern education think logically and critically without even resorting to ethno-philosophy or to professional philosophy, the latter of which is yoked in Western framework. This important feature of philosophic sagacity is confirmed by Ochieng-Odhiambo and Iteyo (2012: 181) who remind us that:

> Philosophic sagacity is a product and a reflective evaluation of the culture philosophy. The philosophic sage makes a critical assessment of the culture and its underlying beliefs. He produces a system within a system, an order within an order. He operates at a second-order level, which is generally open-minded and rationalistic.

No wonder scholars like Azenabor (2009: 74) is careful to remind us that 'philosophic sagacity is a reflection of a person who is both a sage and a critical thinker, because a person can be a sage and not a critical thinker (this would be an *ordinary sage),* while the one who is both a sage and a critical thinker is a *philosophic sage'.* It is on the basis of this understanding that Oruka then makes an elucidatory distinction between an ordinary sage, whom he calls a 'culture philosopher', and a philosophic sage. Being a sage, "does not necessarily make one a philosopher as some of the sages are simply moralists and the disciplined, die-hard faithful to a tradition. Others are merely historians and good interpreters of the history and customs of their people" (Oruka 1983: 177). Yet, a 'philosophic sage' is not only wise, but also capable of being rational and critical in understanding or solving the inconsistencies of his or her culture, and coping with foreign encroachments on it.

Given that philosophic sagacity is rich in logic and critical analysis, Odera Oruka is of the view that philosophic sagacity should put as its major objective to "trace African Philosophy by wearing the uniforms of anthropological fieldwork and using dialogical techniques to pass through anthropological fogs to the philosophical ground" (Odera Oruka 1991: 3). By this, Odera Oruka meant that the major task of philosophic sagacity was to prune both ethno-philosophy and professional philosophy of undesirable features while maintaining those that are desirable for purposes of progress in African philosophy. Odera Oruka, thus, was one progressive African philosopher who had the dream of merging the African quintessence in ethno-philosophy with the professional perspicacity in professional philosophy so as to come up with a genuine objective African philosophy, a philosophy that is devoid of both myth and hegemonic character as is the case of ethno-philosophy and professional philosophy respectively. Odera Oruka, thus, writes in one of his works that philosophic sagacity "is the only trend that can give an all-acceptable decisive blow tothe position of ethno-philosophy. Neither of the other two trends – nationalist/ideological philosophy and professional philosophy – can objectively play this role" (Odera Oruka 1983: 384-385). However, we should be quick to comment that for him philosophic sagacity was not meant to exterminate ethno-philosophy. Neither was it meant to throw professional philosophy into the dustbin of oblivion. Instead, Odera Oruka's philosophic sagacity was meant to build bridges between ethno-philosophy and professional philosophy to produce one African philosophy that is more objective and unadulterated.

Nationalistic-ideological philosophy

Nationalistic-ideological philosophy (also known as African partisan philosophy) is more concerned with the prescriptions of African statesmen (or politicians) and intellectuals strategically involved in the emancipatory project and complete independence of Africa and the African people from the ghost and shackles of colonialism and imperialism. It is concerned with the preservation, upholding of African ideological ideas. The philosophy is, to a larger extent, partisan to a particular ideology, and in this case African political ideology. Okot p'Bitek (1979: 7) captures well the imperative task of an African scholar and in particular African nationalistic-ideological philosopher, for example, when he asserts:

> The African scholar has two clear tasks before him. First, to explore and destroy all false ideas about African peoples and culture that has been perpetuated by Western scholarship. Vague terms as *"Tribe"*, *"Folk"*, *"Non-literate"* or even innocent looking ones such as *"Developing"*, etc., must be subjected to critical analysis and thrown out or redefined to suit African interests. Second, the African scholar must endeavour to present the institutions of African peoples as they really are.

What p'Bitek means is that the genuine responsibility of a real African philosopher is to serve the African interest in the global community, deconstruct and reconstruct what was destroyed by imperialists in a way that promotes the identity and consciousness of the oncevanquished and marginalised African cultures. For Ochieng-Odhiambo and Iteyo (2012: 176) 'this is the role ethno-philosophy and professional philosophy never took up seriously.' Thus, Ochieng-Odhiambo and Iteyo (Ibid) concur with Imbo (2002: 160) who observes that:

> Sometimes explicitly, sometimes implicitly, a very tensed, gendered northern European rationality came to claim universality […]. One legacy of this claim has been the definition of rationality as the true discovery by the human mind of the pure essence of reality with the result that non-European influences have been consigned to the realm outside positive knowledge and in some cases accused of irrationality.

Spelling out the role and responsibility of an African scholar and in particular an African philosopher especially one who identifies himself/herself as an African nationalistic/ideological philosopher, Ochieng-Odhiambo and Iteyo (2012: 176) follow p'Bitek's understanding elaborated above as they say:

> The genuine African philosopher, besides being concerned with discussing the subject matter and finer points of philosophy as a discipline, has the special responsibility of deconstructing mainstream philosophy with a view to liberating the identity, consciousness and culture of the marginalised African "other". This is the role ethno-philosophy and professional philosophy never took up.

What Ochieng-Odhiambo and Iteyo say is what African nationalist figures have emulated and gallantly and chivalrously displayed in their participation in the struggle for the liberation of Africa and the African people. Most of these figures – Kwame Nkrumah, Julius Nyerere, Muammar Gaddafi, Samora Machel, Robert Mugabe, Nelson Mandela, Keneth Kaunda and Seko Toure, among many others – have managed to demonstrate, throughout history, their unwaveringbottomless support of African identity, culture and consciousness.

Conclusion

In this chapter, we have highlighted the philosophical foundations of Africa and the African people, how Africa and by extension African philosophy has been conceptualised by different scholars especially those from the global north. We have then extensively discussed how some African philosophers have laboured not only to prove the existence of Africa but to show that African philosophy is an equal philosophy to other philosophies in the world. On this note, we have thoughtfully discussed Henry Odera Oruka's trends of African philosophy. The foundations, imaginations, conceptualisations, and trends of African philosophy have been discussedwith a view to turn things round, demonstrate that Africa is not a punch-bag or patio for others to plunder as they deem necessary, to reclaim Africa's lost glory, and set the records on Africa straight for the next generation to take the relay-stick forward.This demystification, will no doubt, clean Africa of all the bunkum and twaddle that have soiled its people for centuries. It will indeed capacitate Africans to think outside the box, break away from the vicious circle of misery and insolence, free Africans of the myth of a society without history, and most importantly help Africa to move away from the trap of desperation and allow it to re-assume its important role and position in international affairs.

Chapter 4

Philosophical Genres and Movements in Africa

Introduction

Philosophy on the continent of Africa as elsewhere is as old as humankind. This is true given that philosophy is a gift endowed to all races on earth by virtue of their ability to think abstractly and reason. However, while rich in many respects, philosophy on the continent has a varied history, both interesting and sad with rib-racking sensations, which dates at least as far as pre-dynastic African culture and thought. Interestingly, while philosophy in Africa seems to be largely entwined with culture it is not homogenous. Neither is it individualistic, at least from a traditional point of view. Each geographical space on the continent is, therefore, identified with a distinct philosophical genres (or philosophical tradition). Though distinction can be made between philosophical genre and philosophical tradition, in this book we use the two interchangeably for the major reason that we understand both as unique styles, arts, expressions, or work that distinguish themselves from many others such that they can be categorised as distinct. In fact as we can see, genres are so distinct in as much as philosophical traditions are.

While there are many philosophical genres[3] that could be identified across Africa, for purposes of this book, we focus on

---

[3]While we use the term "African philosophical genres," other African scholars such as Maurice Makumba (2007) use the term "African indigenous philosophies" to refer to the different philosophical traditions found across the continent of Africa. We refer to these philosophical traditions as genres (though using the two interchangeably) simply because we understand a philosophical tradition just like a genre as a unique style, art, expression, or work that distinguishes itself from many others such that it could be categorised as distinct.

what we think are the most prominent ones namely; Bantu philosophy, Yoruba philosophy, MAA'T philosophy, and Ethiopian philosophy.

Surprisingly, these philosophical genres, unlike philosophical movements on the continent, are hardly discussed in philosophy texts in the area of African philosophy. This is in spite of the extraordinary philosophical nature and resilience of the genres given that they have existed since pre-colonial era and survived all the colonial onslaughts from both the European imperialists and Euro-centric scholars. It is this observation that partly prompted us to commit ourselves to write this chapter and indeed the whole book. The sections that follow, thus, discuss in some detail the selected philosophical genres that existed in pre-colonial Africa through colonial period and the present time before looking at the different philosophical movements that could be identified on the continent.

Ethiopian philosophy

As already alluded to, ethno-philosophy is one of the distinct genres of philosophy in Africa. But before discussing this philosophical genre, we need to understand the geographical areas that the philosophy covered in the past, and continue to cover in contemporary times.

In pre-colonial Africa, the names Abyssinia, Ethiopia, Kush, and Nubia – which are found south of Egypt – were all used to refer to the same land, Ethiopia (Snowden 1976; see also Makumba 2007: 81). As Makumba tells us "Ethiopia in Greek means 'burnt-faced men'. It came to have a geographical meaning, referring to the land, the colour of whose inhabitants ranges between brown and dark. Thus, it could refer to the Negroes, Nubians, Nilotes, Hamites or Kushites."

The philosophy which is pervasive in the horn of Africa and the whole area covering the larger part of southern Egypt (what we call here ancient Ethiopia) assumes the name of a country,

Ethiopia, which is closely associated with it. In philosophy terms, this whole area is famous for its philosophy, best known as Ethiopian philosophy. But one would want to understand what this philosophy was (and is) all about? How is it unique from other philosophical genres on the continent?

Ethiopian philosophy occupies an important position within the larger realm of African philosophy. Traditionally, Ethiopian philosophy upholds prowess, good relations, humanism, nobility, probity, piety and, love of others. This is becauses Ethiopians always knew that when people have little or nothing, they need each other most. It is out of this realisation that they see the need to form tightly-knit communities. We add that it is when people have little or nothing that they value sharing; that they excel in their creativity; that they pride oneness, value social ties, mutual relationships, and friendships. Such, was the philosophy that traditionally, the people of Ethiopia lived by. Makumba (Ibid) captures this aptly when he notes that "among the ancients, in the Greco-Roman world, Ethiopians were famed for their creativity, military prowess, diplomatic relations, and piety. This explains the presence of some 'red Ethiopian' in Egypt. The Greeks, for one, spoke favourably of the Ethiopians and did not hide their admiration of them, referring variously as the 'uttermost men,' 'tallest and handsomest men,' and 'noble Ethiopians" (see also Snowden 1976: 20). Their military prowess, for example, enabled them, at one time, to conquer Egypt, allowing some of the Ethiopians migrating into Egypt and other parts of the Greco-Roman world. Today, Ethiopian philosophy refers to the philosophical corpus of the present-day countries of Ethiopia and Eritrea. The philosophy, which has evolved through time together with its associated culture and trading partners such as the Arabs and Greeks, was preserved in both oral and written form through Ge'ez (Ethiopic) manuscripts. Ancient Ethiopian philosophy in its written form includes translated works such as: *The life and maxims of Skendes* (written in 11th AD); *The treatise of Zaar a' Ya o'qob* (1667); *The fisalgwos* – *The Physiologue* (written in the 15th century); and *The book of the wise philosophers* (written in the 1510/22) (see also Makumba 2007).

Due to Ethiopia's early contacts with the Arabs and Greek societies, its traditional philosophy has assumed creative assimilation in such a way that it turned some of the philosophies borrowed from outside into traditional modes of thought while also offering some modes of thought to the outside world. As underlined above, many works were translated from Arabic and Greek from as early as the 11th century. Yet, Ethiopian written philosophy was not only limited to translated works as there were also original works by the local Ethiopians. As Doresse (1967) notes in his book: *Ethiopia*, while the 14th and 15th centuries were prosperous literary periods in Ethiopia as many works were translated to Ethiopic language, local Ethiopians were also busy writing their voluminous biographies relating to pious founders such as Gabra-Manfas-Qeduss or Abba Libanos. Thus, by the 14th and 15th centuries, Ethiopia had already established herself in written literature in both philosophy and other fields of knowledge. Scholars like Sumner even go a step further to demonstrate that the exchange of ideas between Ethiopia and Greece during the time was reciprocal and mutual. In one of his works with the title: *Ethiopia: Land of diverse expression of philosophy, birthplace of modern thought*, Sumner shows the Greek origin of some Ethiopian philosophical works just to demonstrate the existence of African philosophy in pre-colonial ancient Africa. He extensively compares Zera Yacob and Rene Descartes, his contemporary, to show that Africa had the same talent or perhaps greater than that of the West. In his comparison, for example, Sumner tells us that in terms of method, both Descartes and Yacob used critical investigation: both emphasised on the need for an inquiry in their quest for the truth. However, unlike in the case of Western philosophy which emphasises abstract thinking and argumentation, the consequence of the synthesis of the Ethiopian traditional modes of thought and the outside philosophies was largely an Ethiopian-Christian synthesis that embraces moral reflection, use of narratives, maxims, parables, and imagery.

Though an old philosophical tradition, Ethiopian philosophy has in the few past decades, particularly in the 17th century, been popularised by one of the prominent philosophers in the region, the continent, and beyond by the name Zera Yacob[4] (1599-1692). He wrote: *The treatise of Zera Yacob* (1667) which became Ethiopia's first autobiography as well as her first [original] philosophical text. In the 17th century, Ethiopian religious and philosophical ideas were challenged by King Suseynos' adoption of Catholicism and the subsequent presence of Jesuit missionaries, who attempted to forcefully impose Catholicism upon Ethiopians. In the forefront of this exercise was the philosopher Zera Yacob, who though a philosopher, had a culture that was entirely theological. He had intellectual capacities of repute and extensive knowledge of Jewish and Islamic religions. He liked David's Book of Psalms most, which both inspired and comforted him (see Sumner 1976).

Having seen the contradictions between the Christian and Ethiopian traditions, Yacob relegated the latter and all other traditions that fall outside the purview of Christianity. His reason for refusing tradition was that tradition is infested by lies, because men, in their arrogance believe that they know everything and thus refuse to examine things with their own mind, blindly accepting what has been transmitted to them by their forebears. Yacob, thus, accepts as unique authority his 'reason' and accepts from the Scriptures and dogmas, only what resists a rational inquiry. As he clearly spelt in his *Hatata* (piece-meal examination), Yacob believed that the human mind can find the truth if it searches it [the truth] and does not get

---

[4] This seventeenth century renowned writer and philosopher, Zera Yacob should be distinguished from the fifteenth century Emperor, Zera Yacob. This is in spite of the fact that the names of the two, the Emperor and the writer-cum-philosopher, carry the same meaning – Seed of Jacob.

discouraged by difficulties and adversity (see Sumner 1976; 1985). He, for example, through *Hatata*, arrives at an argument for the existence of God who he considered as an essence uncreated and eternal, basing on the impossibility of an infinite chain of causes. Using the same logic, Yacob argued that the Creation of God is good because God Himself is good. Yacob, thus, identified the will of God with what is rational to reject as blasphemy some of the Ethiopian traditions, Jewish and Islamic moral precepts such as sexual interdictions, fasting, and polygamy.

Yet, through Yacob's disciple, Walda Heywat, whose work is normally considered as "more Ethiopian" than Yacob's, Ethiopian philosophy synthesises tradition and Christianity to form "traditional-Christian inspired wisdom" (see also Sumner 2004; Kiros 2014). Besides, through Heywat's work, it is clear that Ethiopian philosophy is not speculative, but addresses social, practical, and moral problems of the time. This is clearly noted in Heywat's *The treatise of Walda Heywat*.

Bantu philosophy

The other widely recognised genre of philosophy found in Africa is Bantu philosophy. Generally speaking, Bantu philosophy is philosophy of the people who are referred to as the Bantu – all the indigenous people found in sub-Saharan Region. Besides sharing a philosophy, these people share a culture that is similar in many great ways with their different languages sharing almost similar click sounds when spoken.

Bantu philosophy is famous for its philosophical traditional known as Ubuntu philosophy (or *Unhu* philosophy in Shona language), which is generally a philosophy of humanness that underscores and embraces the spirit of sharing, love, oneness, and caring. In this book we, therefore, use the terms *Unhu* and Ubuntu interchangeably. While the philosophy of *Unhu* has always been pervasive in the Shona and many other cultures of

Zimbabwe, it was introduced into education through the work of Samkange and Samkange: *Hunhuism or Ubuntuism: A Zimbabwean indigenous political philosophy* that was published at the eve of national independence in 1980. Samkange and Samkange (1980) made this significant contribution to the Zimbabwean education by coming up with a philosophy that intended to promote the perceptions and worldviews of the indigenous people. For Samkange and Samkange, *unhu*/ubuntu inspires, permeates, and radiates high mental and moral attributes such that it promotes brotherliness, togetherness, sharing, caring for one another, kindness, courtesy and good relations. Samkange and Samkange's conceptualisation ubuntu/*unhu* resonates with that of Nziramasanga (1999) who notes that hunhu/ubuntu is humanness in the fullest and noblest sense. We add that hunhu/ubuntu is a philosophy of humanness that emphasises love, camaraderie and hospitality to all. This means that the philosophy of *unhu*/ubuntu stresses the values of respect, collectivism, social cohesion, consideration for others and the respect for life and nature: it is a collectivistic approach to life as opposed to Euro-centric approaches that are largely individualistic. Above all, it shows us one's level of 'educatedness' such that we consider one to be educated if s/he embraces and demonstrates all aspects of Ubuntu philosophy. We thus consider one 'uneducated' if s/he is ignorant of what is good or bad, of what is to be said and not said in public and if one doesn't respect own culture and other people's cultures and personas including their ideas. No matter how many diplomas or degrees that person has, in the Shona and many other cultures of Zimbabwe, s/he is uneducated. The person is only learned and not educated for that individual is not socialised to properly fit in as a member of a society and can hardly contribute positively to the well-being of the society.

As such, it could be argued that Ubuntu sums up Bantu philosophy given that it touches the whole terrain of Bantu philosophy. For this reason, we use the terms Bantu philosophy and Ubuntu philosophy interchangeably in this book. Along the same lines, Ramose (1999: 49) captures this aptly when he argues:

> *Ubuntu* is the root of African philosophy. The being of an African in the universe is inseparably anchored upon *ubuntu*. Similarly, the African tree of knowledge stems from *ubuntu* with which it is connected indivisibly. *Ubuntu* then is the wellspring flowing with African ontology and epistemology. If these latter are the basis of philosophy then African philosophy has long been established in and through *ubuntu*. Our point of departure is that *ubuntu* may be seen as the basis of African philosophy.

In this section, we do not discuss Ubuntu in detail as this is done in chapter 5, besides emphasising that *unhu* as a philosophy of humanness emphasises on the importance of social ties, mutual relationships, respect, oneness, sharing, and love.

MA'AT philosophy

MA'AT philosophy is one of the philosophical genres found on the African continent. It is a philosophy that flourished (and continue to flourish) in North Africa, particularly in Egypt and Sudan. Given that Egypt is widely embraced as a country that is central to the development of ancient philosophy, MAA'T philosophy is sometimes known as Kemet (Egyptian) philosophy. But what is MAA'T philosophy? In other words, what MA'AT philosophy is all about?

According to Lesole (2002), MA'AT (Maat) is an ancient Egyptian deity with the mandate to explain key elements and principles of human perfection. MA'AT philosophy generally understood is, therefore, a philosophy of truth and justice as the word 'MAA'T' literally translated means truth, justice or that which is considered as right. It had forty-two Admonitions which acted as guidelines for good and correct human moral behaviour namely;

1. I have not done iniquity [injustice or sin].
2. I have not robbed with violence.
3. I have not stolen.
4. I have not murdered or bid anyone to slay on my behalf.
5. I have not spoken lies.
6. I have not plundered the Netchar.
7. I have not diminished obligations.
8. I have not defrauded offerings.
9. I have not snatched away food.
10. I have not transgressed.
11. I have not dealt deceitfully.
12. I have not caused shedding of tears.
13. I have not committed fornication.
14. I have not caused pain.
15. I have not acted guilefully.
16. I have not wasted food.
17. I have not been angry and wrathful except for a just cause.
18. I have not set my lips in motion against any person.
19. I have not been an eavesdropper.
20. I have not defiled the wife of any man.
21. I have not polluted myself or my purity.
22. I have not caused terror.
23. I have not stooped my ears against the words of Right and Truth.
24. I have not evilly slaughtered the animals.
25. I have not filched the food of the infant.
26. I have not sinned against the Netchar of my native town.
27. I have not plundered the offerings to the blessed dead.
28. I have not defrauded offerings of the Netchar/ God.
29. I have never cursed the Netchar/God.
30. I have not spoken scornfully or behaved with ignorance.
31. I have never fouled the water.

32. I have never cursed the king.
33. I have done neither harm nor ill.
34. I have not multiplied words exceedingly.
35. I have not acted with insolence.
36. I have not worked grief.
37. I have not stirred strife.
38. I have not judged hastily.
39. I have not polluted the earth.
40. I have not done which is abominable.
41. I have not cursed.
42. I have not laid waste to the land
(Cited in Mawere 2014: 28; see also Bandele 1992).

As noted by Lesole (2002), Koka (1996), and Broodryk (2002) and as could be seen from the forty-two admonitions given above, "MA'ATphilosophy whose principles cohere with those of Unhu/Ubuntu [...] had its admonitions written approximately 1, 500 years before the discovery of the Christian Ten Commandments *by Moses at Mt Sinai*" (Mawere 2014: 26). Mawere (Ibid), explains that "the MA'AT Admonitions were virtues enshrined in the philosophy of the life of the indigenous African people ... The principles of the MA'AT like those of Ubuntu/Unhu are applicable to all facets of life including business, morality, education, medicine, natural environment, and governance."

Given the age and similarities between the Biblical Commandments and the Admonitions enumerated above, some scholars like Koka and Lesole have come to believe that MA'AT philosophy has over the years influenced both the Christian and Islamic traditions.

Yoruba philosophy

Another rich and resilient genre of philosophy that has existed since pre-colonial through colonial and contemporary times is the Yoruba philosophy. The Yoruba are people found in West Africa especially in present Nigeria and Ghana as well as some parts bordering Cameroon.

In West Africa, the most distinctive and prominent pre-colonial (or what others call pre-modern) philosophical traditions has been identified as the Yoruba philosophical tradition. This philosophical tradition has emerged as a result of thousands of years of its development through the interaction of the Akan, Dogon, Dahomey, and Yoruba people. It is a philosophy tradition that is very rich in ethnophilosophy especially proverbial lore. Some of the famous proverbs of the Yoruba Philosophical Traditions (though also common in other African philosophical traditions) include:

- What an old man sees seated, a youth does not see standing (trans: wisdom goes by age). The proverb reflects that in African societies (and in particular the Yoruba society) wisdom is viewed as something associated with age – the older one is the wiser s/he is expected to be due to his/her accumulated experiences.
- Problem shared is half a problem (trans: sharing one's problem reduces its impact on his/her life). The proverb entails African socialism as it emphasises the need for one another in society.
- Truth never rots (trans: whatever is done in secret will always be known). This proverb projects truth as a virtue that cannot be hidden forever. The proverb discourage people from lying, being unfaithful or cunning.
- Even a four-legged horse stumbles and fall (trans: No one is perfect). This proverb reminds human beings of their imperfection and mortality regardless of their status in society.
- A storyteller does not tell of a different season (trans: The past is not seen as fundamentally different from the present but all history is contemporary in a way). This proverb shows the close connection between the past, the present and the future. This is one reason why in Yoruba society of Nigeria (as that of

Ghana traditional societies of the Akan people) strongly believe in the *Sankofa* (reach back and get it). *Sankofa* is an Akan (of Ghana) word derived from the Akan *San-* (to return) and *ko –* (to go) and *–fa* (fetch/seek/take) (see also Seeman 2010). It is an expression that urges the people of Africa – people who undoubtedly had lost confidence in themselves and their culture during their contact with the colonists – to go back to their traditional norms and values for that they have forgotten in order to reclaim their past and move forward. Kwame Gyekye calls this "cultural revivalism" (Gyekye 1997: 233) with which he assumes a basically reverential attitude towards the African cultural heritage in its totality, a heritage that was disturbed and destabilised by colonialism. As excellently captured by Frantz Fanon (1967) in his *The Wretched of the earth*:

> Colonial domination, because it is total and tends to simplify, very soon manages to disrupt in spectacular fashion the cultural life of a conquered people. This cultural obliteration is possible by the negation of national reality, by new legal relations introduced by the occupying power, by the banishment of the natives and their customs to outlying districts by the colonial society, by exploration, and by the systematic enslaving of men and women (p. 190).

Contrary to the principles of colonial domination outlined above by Fanon, *Sankofa* thus, is an emphasis to learn from the past.

• Even a bird with a long neck cannot see the future (trans: The future will always remain a mystery to the living). The proverb reminds us that the future remains beyond our knowledge as our knowledge of it is limited.

• One ignorant of his history is nonhuman (trans: History is the integral part of all humanity). The proverb reminds us that history is fundamentally important as it enables us to learn from the past, improve our present situations, and project into the future.

• A large eye does not mean keen vision (trans: Do not judge things or people by mere appearances). The proverb reminds us to be always critical and cautious when making judgments about others.

All the proverbs cited above, which are indeed pervasive in other African societies) show the richness and philosophical sophistication – epistemological, ethical, logical, metaphysical, and psychological thought – of the Yoruba society.

Historically, the West African (as with the North African) philosophical traditions have had a significant impact on Islamic philosophy as a whole as much of the Islamic philosophical tradition was subject to the influence of scholars born or working in the African continent in centres of learning such as Cairo in Egypt and Timbuktu in Mali.

African philosophy and movements

African philosophical traditions together with the African political experiences inspired some Africans to engage in intellectual political movements. Among the most important political thinkers influenced by philosophy to come up with (or involve themselves in) intellectual political movements are Kwame Nkrumah, Nelson Mandela, Kenneth Kaunda and Julius Nyerere. Out of the many intellectual political movements in Africa in the 20th and 21st centuries with philosophical interest have been *négritude* and pan-Africanism (see also Appiah 1998). In the next sections we discuss the aforementioned philosophically and politically inspired movements.

Négritude

Negritude is a cultural and political ideological philosophy developed by Francophone African political and philosophical thinkers. The word negritude takes its root from the Latin Niger, which was used exclusively in a racist context within France, to refer to Black people as art nigre. In its present sense, the term was first used by Martinican (from Martinique) poet Aime Cesaire in his poem: *Notebook of a return to my native land* published in French in 1939. Cesaire studied in Paris, France, where he re-discovered Africa through his Negritude Movement.

As a movement, negritude was initiated in the 1930s by a group of young Black students and scholars, primarily from France's colonies and territories, such as Cesaire, Leopold Sedar Senghor (the first president of Senegal in 1960), and Leon Damas (a French Guyanese). These three are normally considered as "the Three Fathers of Negritude" because their encounter with each other in 1931 in Paris marks the beginning of a collective exploration of their (and Africans) complex cultural identities as black, African, and French. In 1934, the trio launched the pioneering journal *L'Etudiant noir* (*The Black Student*), which aimed at breaking nationalistic barriers among Black students in France. All of them were dissatisfied, disgusted and indeed at conflict with Black French assimilation, French racism, and colonial injustices that affected the African peoples. They argued for the need for the African people to rally together for a common goal, hence their movement is arguably rooted from African socialism.

Besides, the three revolutionists used a realist literary style that embraced Marxist ideas in their writing invented negritude to resist and oppose French colonialism. Cesaire, for example, saw Negritude as – the self-affirmation of the Black people – the fact of being black, acceptance of this fact, and appreciation of the history and culture of the Black people. For Cesaire, the emphasis on the fact of 'blackness' was the only way through which Western imperialism could be reversed and decolonisation of the African mind collectively made possible. On a similar note, Senghor tried to actualise and promote the African desire – that of being recognised an equal race – through preaching the need for the restoration of African culture, communalism, identity, and pride. Senghor, like his other colleagues, realised the power and potency of unity as is embedded in African communalism. Franken (1969) captures this power and potency of African communalism when he notes:

> The people of Africa had a philosophy of life. People lived in small communities. They needed one another. The women could not go individually to fetch wood and water in the forest, or grass for the roofs. Nor could the hunter go by himself to provide food for his family. They had to join forces and live together. From this natural need grew a certain philosophy of life. Everybody accepted the duty to work and was awarded the right in the fruits of the community (p. 24).

Thus realising how colonialism had negatively impacted on the African values, the three revolutionists saw it fit to resist it. Trough their newly formed movement, the aforementioned intellectual revolutionists claimed that the best strategy to oppose colonialism was to encourage a common racial identity for Black Africans the world-over, that is, reclamation of African self-determination, self-reliance, and self-respect. It was more of a philosophy aimed at awakening a new [black] race consciousness, particularly among the colonised Africans – a (re-)discovery of the authentic self, collective condemnation of Western imperialism and domination.

These intellectual revolutionists, through their Negritude Movement, disavowed assimilation – a strategy that was used by French colonists to encourage the Africans to destroy the nadir of all their hopes, spiritual exuberance, and confidence in a manner that in no way challenged them to disown their own cultural values. They also denounced Europe's alleged lack of humanity and rejected its domination and oppressive ideas. The overall objective of Negritude Movement was for the Black people to achieve a place in the world – a place the Black race had been denied by the European colonists. On this note, the movement emphasised the fact that the people of Africa had a worthy culture and history comparable as equal to other cultures such as those of Europe. This is why in his analysis of Negritude, Jean-Paul Sartre (1948) in his essay: *Black Orpheus*, characterised Negritude as the opposite of colonial racism in a Hegelian dialectic. For Sartre, Negritude, thus, was an anti-racist racism, a strategy with a final goal of racial unity.

However, Negritude was later criticised by some Black scholars during the 1960s as insufficiently militant. The Nigerian poet, playwright and novelist Wole Soyinka, for example, criticised Negritude for being too emotional, outspoken and defensive.

Keorapetse Kgositsile also criticised Negritude for being too much based on blackness. This overdependence on blackness, for Kgositsile, made it impossible for Negritude to define a new kind of perception of *Africanness* that would free Black people and their art from Caucasian conceptualisations.

Pan-Africanism

Pan-Africanism was (and indeed is) both an ideology and movement that encourages unity and solidarity of all Africans world-wide (see also Falola and Kwame 2013). While Pan-Africanism has its roots from a large number of slave insurrections, modern Pan-Africanism began around the start of the 20th century, evolving from the African Association to the Pan-African Association in around 1897 through the leadership of Henry Sylvester-Williams who organised the first Pan-African Conference in London in 1900, though with participants drawn almost entirely from the Caribbean, American or European Diaspora rather than Africa itself (New Internationalist Magazine 2000). As further noted by the New International Magazine, Pan-Africanism dates back at least to the 18th century and came originally from the New World (Americas and the Caribbean) rather than from Africa herself. Prince Hall, a Black cleric in Boston, for example, campaigned unsuccessfully in

1787 for help from the State Assembly in returning poor Blacks to Africa. Another Black Bostonian, Quaker shipbuilder Paul Cuffe, took matters into his hands in 1885 by setting sail in one of his ships with 40 other Black Americans and founding a settlement in Sierra Leone, which the British had established as a refuge zone for freed and runaway slaves in 1787. In fact, having been squashed by the brutality of slavery in the Americas and the Caribbean, people of African origin (including those born in captivity) naturally yearned for their ancestral homeland (Ibid).

Modern Pan-Africanism as a movement was prompted by the 1884 Berlin Conference which partitioned Africa into smaller states which European imperialists divided amongst themselves. This scramble for Africa yielded new urgency to the Pan-African response. Later, African politicians and icons like Kwame Nkrumah, Haile Selassie, Sekou Toure, Jomo Kenyatta, and Muammar Gaddafi together with grassroots organisers such as Malcom X and Marcus Garvey, and academics such as Du Bois rallied together to form the Pan-Africanism movement as is known today (Waters 1997; Falola and Kwame 2013). With the 5th Pan-African Congress in 1945 with Dubois as its honorary chair and Amy Ashwood, Marcus Garvey's first wife, presiding its first session, the torch of Pan-Africanism was passed on to the new generation of Pan-Africanists, now from the continent of Africa itself, including Kwame Nkrumah and Jomo Kenyatta. The former [Nkrumah] soon became the chief proponent of Pan-Africanism, who at independence of Ghana in 1957 worked thick and thin towards uniting the continent of Africa.

The movement was formed pretext that only unity and solidarity among Africans will reverse the losses of colonialism while fostering self-reliance, socio-economic development, and political stability. As Agyeman (1998) Pan-Africanism was formed with the objective to lead power consolidation in Africa which in turn would compel a reallocation of global resources as well as unleashing a fiercer psychological energy and political assertion that would unsettle social and political power structures in Europe and the Americas. It was a movement meant to oppose external political, social, and economic involvement on the African continent as this had been perceived, especially during colonialism, to be unproductive and exploitative.

As a philosophy, Pan-Africanism was an expression of the aggregation of the cultural, historical, spiritual, artistic, scientific, economic, and philosophical legacies of the African people from past times to the present (Falola and Kwame 2013). It was a product of African civilisations and the struggle against slavery in its all forms, racism, colonialism, and neo-colonialism. This means that Pan-Africanism shared almost the same vision with Negritude.

While the dream of Pan-Africanism had always been that of uniting Africa, to form the United States of Africa, the movement through its Organisation of African Unity (OAU) formed in 1963, later transforming itself to the African Union (AU), has been largely ineffective. Though it still retains in its Constitution the ideals of Pan-Africanism, in practice, the AU is proving to be ineffective especially in the face of reprehensible avalanche waves of westernisation and globalisation. No clear structures have been created so far to enable the realisation of a United States of Africa.

Conclusion

This chapter has discussed selected philosophical genres and movements on the continent of Africa with a view to enhance the reader's grasp of African philosophy and buttress the argument that African philosophy is a philosophy worthy studying. With the hope to demonstrate the richness of the continent of Africa in both material resources and ideas, the chapter has discussed a number of philosophical traditions pervasive on the continent.

Also, tracing the development of prominent ideological and philosophical movements on the continent such as Negritude and Pan-Africanism, the chapter has shown how movements (as with struggles against independence) were inspired by the African principles of unity, self-reliance, and sharing, while sometimes influenced by both external and local philosophical traditions at the same time.

Chapter 5

Ubuntu/Unhu/Vumunhu: A Principal Moral Compass for the southern African World

As the Black Conscious Movement leader, Steve Biko (1970), declared: "The great powers of the world may have done wonders in giving the world an industrial and military look, but the great still has to come from Africa — giving the world a more humane face" (p. 46).

Introduction

Archbishop Emeritus Desmond Tutu, allegedly the biggest advocate of ubuntu, gave a quite exciting contribution to the "traditional" philosophy of ubuntu. His conceptualisation of ubuntu is rooted in the belief that in African cosmology, ubuntu symbolises the backbone of African spirituality and moral conduct. He based his argument on the understanding that while it is generally accepted that the Western world gave the world economic stand points like capitalism, Africa has not been able to contribute that much to the economy. Instead, the social ethic of ubuntu has been Africa's largest contribution to the world (Tutu 2000: 88). Taking it from Tutu, we argue that although Africa was and is still being alleged to be lagging behind the global north technologically and economically, it is far ahead of the global north insofar as its social and political philosophies and systems are concerned. These epistemological systems, which by and large, revolved around communal relationships, had developed a deep respect for human values and the recognition of the human worth based on a philosophy of humanism that was far more advanced than that found in the European philosophic systems at that time (Ramose 2002). The rejuvenation of the philosophy of ubuntu is, therefore, important because it provides Africans with a sense of self-identity, self-respect and achievement. Fundamentally, it enables Africans to deal with their problems in a positive manner by drawing on the humanistic values they have inherited and perpetuated throughout their history (ibid).

Drawing from all human societies across the globe, it is undeniable that in an endeavour to survive, societies evolve philosophies and or social ideologies of life informed by their existential circumstances. In the process thereof they define their own being, identity, and selves in ways that become manifest in their daily activities and societal operations. For societies to develop in a sustainable manner, it is imperative that they should first and foremost take stock of their own fundamental and unique values which are the lifeblood of any human community. These unparalleled values which more often than not, shape, influence, and guide human contact and relations are normally expressed in people's beliefs and thinking. In Southern Africa, for instance, and the rest of Africa by extension, the philosophy of ubuntu is at the centre of all human realm, whether economic, religious, political or cultural. In conformity with the above, Olinger *et al* (2007), point out that ubuntu has informed politics, business, corporate governance, restorative justice and conflict resolution among many other human spheres. As enshrined in the philosophy of ubuntu, it is the group and not individuals that motivate daily endeavours, design, and behaviour (see Khoza 2005; Nyamnjoh 2015; Ramose 2009, van Stam 2014). Interestingly, the concept of ubuntuhas also been appropriated in a wide variety of literatures beyond its usage in African philosophy, ranging from research on management and business practices in Africa (Karsten and Illa 2005) to South Africa's Truth and Reconciliation Commission (Murithi 2006). Besides, ubuntu has also become an issue in relation to government policy. Moreso, while ubuntu exists in many variations within different African cultures and languages, each conceptualisation retains the same core of meaning that is both a goal and a guide for humanity. The representation across widespread African cultures, unified by a common message represents a duality that is in itself the foundation of ubuntu. The concept runs through a range of other cultures, often combining the concept of generosity with genuine humanity (Oppenheim 2012).

In view of the preceding discussion, the main thrust of this chapter is that all societies are guided by some philosophy of life. It is the philosophy of life that informs members of the community in their plans, activities, attitudes, beliefs and thought patterns and education. In fact, Ubuntu philosophy, in its different settings, is at the base of the African philosophy of life and belief systems in which the peoples' daily-lived experiences are reflected. In the case of the African communities; they are guided by the philosophy of *hunhu/ubuntu*. Furthermore, it is maintained that it is this philosophy that informed Africans' socio-cultural, political and educational institutions. Regarding the Zimbabwean context in particular, and indeed, Southern and Central Africa in general, the major contention in this chapter is that anything contrary to the dictates of the philosophy of ubuntu risks being thrown away as irrelevant to the people concerned. Be that as it may, the present chapter will attempt to show some of the areas and disciplines influenced by the philosophy of ubuntu.

Interrogating the philosophy of *ubuntu/unhu/vumunhu*

Gade (2011) remarked that although ubuntu has been written about for over a century; this has not made the definition of the concept less problematic as the various terms in which it has been described indicate. That said, ubuntu is a complex and polysemous concept as its definitions run the gamut from the denotative, connotative to constitutive dimensions. Words have their origins in language; therefore the place to begin the exploration of the definitional complexity of ubuntu is the languages of east and southern Africa – the people of which are believed to have originated from Niger-Congo (Shillington 2000) –that birthed the concept. Ubuntu derives from Nguni and Bantu languages of southern Africa. In Zulu language of South Africa the word symbolises being human. This meaning is also expressed in other languages. In Shona, for example, a Zimbabwean language, the word *unhu* means the same thing as being humane (Samkange and Samkange 1980). The same meaning is expressed by *ubuthosi* in Ndebele, another Zimbabwean language. In Botswana, the word *botho* expresses the same meaning whilst in Tanzania it is *bumuntu*. Congo, Angola, Malawi, Mozambique and Uganda use the words *bomoto, gimuntu, umunthu, vumuntu* and *umuntu* respectively (Binsbergen 2001; Magumbate and Nyanguru 2013: 85).

The concept of ubuntu though, has gained tremendous prominence in intellectual discourse over the years in Africa and beyond, is peculiarly difficult to define with precision. This is because the concept "is elastic and pragmatic as it is employed to inform almost all spheres of the Bantu world-views; it is used in numerous contexts and situations" (Mawere 2012: 2). Mawere underscores this on his understanding that ubuntu is a fundamental human attribute hinged on cultural and philosophical intelligence which value collectivity, respect for human rights and responsibility, as well as equality and interdependence. This resonates with Ramose's (1999) understanding of ubuntu as a multifaceted philosophical system that involves logic, metaphysics, epistemology and ethics. For him, ubuntu, thus, is a philosophy of life that is concerned with the reinforcement of unity/oneness, respect and solidarity among the Bantu people–the so-called humanness. What this means is that through ubuntu, individual identity is replaced by the social such that the identity of an individual is lost, at least in principle, due to its valuing of collectivity, social conduct, high value of sharing, and social security. This means that it is the distinctive elasticity and practical nature of ubuntu that makes it applicable in almost all facets of human life. As such, the concept has been wisely exported as an underlying philosophy and code of conduct into business, legal system, education, theology/religion, healthy and academic disciplines such as African philosophy and ethics (Mawere 2012: 2). It has also been applied in theology by the likes of Archbishop Desmond Tutu (Tutu 2000), in politics by the likes of anti-apartheid icon former South African President Nelson Mandela (Mandela 1994), in management by the likes of Lovemore Mbigi (Mbigi 1997) and in the field of computer science, Linux has developed a software named "Ubuntu" which is developed and shared free of charge. Historically, the concept of ubuntu ('unhu/hunhu/humunhu,' vumunhu, bunhu, umunthu, utu, ubuntuin Shona, Shangani, Tsonga, Xhosa, Swahili, Zulu/Ndebele and 'humanness' in English respectively) or rather the philosophy of ubuntu is intergenerational, that is, it has been spontaneously passed on from one generation to the other mainly through oral tradition and practices (ibid). This is aptly echoed by Ramose (1999) who notes that African philosophy based on 'Ubuntu' is a living philosophy, based on their recognition of the continuous oneness and wholeness of the living, the living-dead and the unborn. For Ramose, and rightly so, it is commonly believed that in pre-colonial African societies, the concept of ubuntu was instrumental in maintaining social cohesion, administering peace and order for the good life of everyone in the society and even strangers (Mawere 2012).

The central concept of ubuntu translates as'humanity', 'humanness', or even 'humaneness'; importantly, it is not merely afactual description of human nature, but constitutes also a rule of conduct and socialethic (Louw 2001: 15; cf. Ramose 2003b). We underline that ubuntu is the powerhouse for the destination of [southern] Africa as it has three main dimensions namely spiritual capital, physical capital, and ideological capital. It is on the basis of this understanding that ubuntu is also known as the collective respect for human dignity (Gade 2012), or that which reinforces the nature of a person's being (Tutu). This means that as far as African cosmology is concerned, ubuntu is that which gives people their humanity (Mandela 1994). Ubuntu, thus, is both cultural and philosophical intelligentsia that respects values of community beyond personal interests, inclinations, and other such biased values.

In terms of its genesis, the word 'ubuntu' derives its name from the Bantu language noun word: u-+ -bu- + -ntu, of which 'u' is the prefix of class 14 nouns and 'bu' that of class 1 nouns while 'ntu' refers to a person. In relation to societal relations, ubuntucanbe understood as a metaphor that describes the significance of group solidarity, on survivalissues, that is so central to the survival of African communities, who as aresult of the poverty and deprivation have to survive through brotherly groupcare and not individual self-reliance (Mbigi and Maree 1995: 1).Scholars have not fared much better in defining ubuntu. One scholar who sets out to address the question, "What is Ubuntu?" noted at the end of his exposition that there is no "definitive answer to the question" (Praeg 2008: 384). Simply put, ubuntu lacks a simple and a generally agreed upon definition.

Just like in the Western thought where we have normative moral theories such as virtue ethics, Kantian deontology, and teleology, particularly utilitarianism, the African philosophy of ubuntu falls within the amphit of Normative ethics which focuses on classifying actions as right and wrong. It seeks to develop rules governing human conduct, or provide a set of norms for action (Nicolaides 2014: 18). From a broad perspective, ubuntu is many things to many people including social scientists, historians, philosophers, software developers, politicians and community members. It is also different things to different people. That said, ubuntu is also considered as an African worldview, doctrine, ideology (McAllister 2009), philosophy, ethic, community-based mind-set (Olinger *et al.* 2007), and culture among others. For Tambulasi and Kayuni

(2005: 147), ubuntu is said to be the "basis of African communal cultural life."In South Africa, ubuntu is the major philosophy that underlies politics, business, corporate governance, justice, conflict resolution and reconciliation (see Olinger *et al.* 2007) hence, it is considered as both an ideology of justification and an aspirational idea. Samkange and Samkange (1980) highlight the three maxims of what he considered as hunhuism or ubuntuism. The first maxim asserts that to be human is to affirm one´s humanity by recognising the humanity of others and, on that basis, establish respectful human relations with them. And the second maxim means that if and when one is faced with a decisive choice between wealth and the preservation of the life of another human being, then one should opt for the preservation of life´. The third maxim as a principle deeply embedded in traditional African political philosophy says that the king owed his status, including all the powers associated with it, to the will of the people under him´.

According to Ramose (2002), ubuntu is a wellspring that flows within African existence and epistemology in which the two aspects *Ubu-* and *-ntu* constitute a wholeness and oneness. As such, ubuntu expresses the generality and oneness of being human. It is also worth noting that ubuntu as an ancient philosophy or worldview has its roots deeply anchored in traditional African life. In this sense, the philosophy of *hunhu/ubuntu* is dialectical, that is, it informs African practice and is in turn enriched by the same practice. For Bhengu (1996: 10), it can also be defined as the "art of being a human being". Apart from that, ubuntu is characteristically viewed as a community friendly philosophy that accentuates virtues such as compassion, open-mindedness and harmony. Supporting the same view, Nussbaum (2009: 100) says that ubuntu 'is the capacity in African culture to express compassion, reciprocity, dignity, harmony and humanity in the interests of building and maintaining community'. In the same understanding, Broodryk (2002: 32) avers that the 'core' and 'associated' ubuntu values include the following aspects: Humanness: warmth, tolerance, understanding, peace, humanity; Caring: empathy, sympathy, helpfulness, charitable, friendliness; Sharing: giving (unconditionally), redistribution, open-handedness; Respect: commitment, dignity, obedience, order; Compassion: love, cohesion, informality, forgiving and spontaneity. The ubuntu philosophy, deals with the reinforcing of concord, oneness and cohesion amongst southern African people in particular. It has been, however, suggested that it is indeed applied in the entire sub-Saharan region of Africa (Ramose 1999). It is fundamental to note that although the concept of ubuntuis African in origin it is not necessarily limited by biological ancestry, nationality or actual place of residence' (van Binsbergen 2001: 60) as people from Europe have also adopted the same philosophy. Though the philosophy of ubuntu has been appropriated to other cultures, the concept mainly refers to 'African humanness' (see Broodryk 2002) and, especially southern African expression of humanness. In light of this, there are a wide range of perspectives and interpretations of what precisely ubuntu entails. As such, ubuntu is a multi-faceted African philosophical system that includes logic, metaphysics, epistemology and ethics (Nafukho 2006: 409-411). For Ramose (1999: 50), ubuntu is not only a moral notion, but is more importantly 'the fundamental ontological and epistemological category in the African thought of the Bantu-speaking people'. Explicitly, the cardinal goal of ubuntu is harmonious relationship among peoples and generations for the good of all. This is in line with Murithi (2007) who categorically stated that ubuntu aims at building the community as well as bonding people in a network of reciprocal relationships. It is, therefore, apparent that ubuntu is a value system which governs societies across the African continent. Loosely defined, ubuntu is a system against whose values the members of a community measure their "humanness." These values, like the ubuntu system from which they flow, are not innate but are rather acquired in society and are transmitted from one generation to another by means of oral genres such as fables, proverbs, myths, riddles, and story-telling. We can surmise from this definition that ubuntu is a standard of measure by which the members of a community evaluate individual and collective behaviour or conduct in the dimension of humanness, and that, it is an acquired or learned value (see Idoniboye-Obu and Whetho 2013).

That said, ubuntuis a concrete manifestation of the interconnectedness of human beings: it is the embodiment of African culture and life style. It acknowledges that facts are relational/contextual, and incorporate many components, and transfers everything into an embodiment in people (holism). Ubuntu is a metaphor that embodies the significance of human solidarity and stands explicitly against inequality or isolating individualism (van Stam 2014). Within ubuntu, all interactions are oriented towards the common ground, the community, the family, the birthed relationships, and in relation to the physical land. The latter is congruent with African Science, where three facets of existence are taken into account: the physical, the spiritual, and the interaction between the two (Chimakonam 2012).

In short, *Hunhu/Ubuntu* has the potential to "rescue African people from their loss of identity: to let them regain their cultural and social values and to let them experience themselves as human beings with dignity" (Sebedi quoted in Venter 2004: 152). It is only then that it will result in the production of *munhu ane hunhu* (a complete, educated person with values) or as the Nziramasanga Commission Report (1999: 61) puts it, "a human being in the fullest and noblest sense", one who is "caring, humble, thoughtful, considerate, understanding, wise, generous, hospitable, socially mature, socially sensitive, virtuous and blessed" (Venter 2004: 150). It is being argued here that *hunhu* is not an imported but an indigenous philosophy rooted in the experiences of the indigenous Africans that should permeate the epistemological, axiological and ontological underpinnings of

Zimbabwean education systems. It is a philosophy that valorises being human and the interconnectedness of human beings and, therefore, affirms life (ibid).

Ubuntu as Africa's moral compass

The African way of life is hinged on the philosophy of ubuntu. In fact, ubuntu transcend all the spheres of African life. It is virtually impossible to talk of African philosophy, without talking about ubuntu. This is largely because the two are intricately linked, hence, they are two sides of the same coin. Since time immemorial, the ideals of ubuntu have shaped and still continue to shape and guide the African worldview in its entirety. For this reason, ubuntu has been considered as the moral compass of Africa. Interestingly, all the branches of African philosophy are in one way or the other influenced by ubuntu. In other words, ubuntu is the major moral aspect in Africa.

We should underline that ubuntu, having largely drawn from [African] culture, has two main aspects, that is, the core and the periphery. The core of ubuntu represents the constant expectations throughout history that ubuntu brings forth. This means that the core, though prone to changes, do so very slowly as it is the birthmark of what ubuntu as a philosophy entails. On the other hand, the periphery refers to other aspects of ubuntu which are more flexible and always in the process of becoming depending on the needs of the society.

In pre-colonial [southern] African society, ubuntu sustained social unity, by managing peace and order for the good life of everyone, including even strangers (Nicolaides 2014). Ubuntu, as suggested by Samkange and Samkange (1980) is reflected in leaders who lead with their subjects. Such leaders are selfless and do not impose their will. A leader who has *unhu/ubuntu* is selfless and consults widely and listens to subjects. Interestingly, the great African statesmen espoused the values of ubuntu. The fight to liberate Africa was in itself a value based on ubuntu, that is, the need for equality and justice. Motivated by black academic Marcus Garvey, Kwameh Nkrumah talks about consciencism – a philosophy that relates to ubuntu. He also talks about humanism being impulsive for African socialism. He argues that egalitarianism was going to be achieved through humanism (Nkrumah 1963). He further argued that the Union of African States, was the best way forward for Africa's progress, and declared in the first constitution of Ghana that the nation was going to surrender its sovereignty to such a union (ibid). In the same vein, Julius Nyerere referred to *ujamaa*, a community building concept based on villagisation. Based on the Arusha Declaration, Nyerere believed in Africa communal living and familyhood (Mugumbate and Nyanguru 2013).

Similarly, in Zambia, former President Kenneth Kaunda talked about Zambian humanism based on African values of mutual aid, trust and loyalty to the community. Kaunda wrote several books promoting African humanism. The reconciliatory tones by President Robert Mugabe at the end of the war of liberation in Zimbabwe in 1980 are attributable to ubuntu (ibid). There is no doubt that his beliefs in fair distribution of wealth are a result of this philosophy. Even in Libya, Maamar Gadhaffi insisted on African collectivity, which he promoted through his ideas on the formation of the United States of Africa. On the other hand, Nelson Mandela has also contributed to the building of ubuntu. At the end of apartheid in South Africa, the former President talked of liberating the oppressor. He is of the view that an individual belongs to the whole (ibid).

In view of the above, Higgs and Smith (2000) made the observation that the central ethical idea in traditional African thought is 'ubuntu' and the concept of 'communalism'. In the African culture and philosophy an individual person is an integral part of society and individuals can, thus, only exist corporately. Counter to the individualist view of many western philosophies, man in Africa is inseparable from the community

(Teffo 1996: 103; Schiele 1994). However, it should be emphasised that individuality is not negated in the African conception of humankind. What is discouraged is the view that the individual should take precedence over the community. The cardinal point in the African view of mankind is 'I am, because we are, and since we are, therefore I am' (Mbiti 1969 in Teffo 1996: 103). As a philosophy *ubuntu* has the central premise of connection where different beings are united as beings. It is all about relationships in the same community; it is the link binding individuals and groups together; the ultimate meaning not only of the unity in multiplicity, but of the concentric and harmonic unity of the visible and invisible worlds (Blankenberg 1999). Interdependence, collective consciousness and a communalist worldview are of utmost importance in an African philosophy of life. Humankind is seen in its relationship with others. The "ideal person according to the African worldview [...] is one who has the virtues of sharing and compassion. The individual has a social commitment to share with others what he has. The ideal person will be judged in terms of his relationship with others, for example, his record in terms of kindness and good character, generosity, hard work, discipline, honour and respect, and living in harmony" (Teffo 1996: 103).

The philosophy of ubuntu differentiates Africans from the rest of humanity. This view is supported by Mugumbate and Nyanguru (2013) who argue that ubuntu as a philosophy is attributable to blacks of Africa, especially sub-Saharan Africa. However, its application is now worldwide (Wichtner-Zoia 2012 and Hailey 2008). In computer science, the ubuntu software, a Linux based application developed in the USA, is open source software that has been widely distributed. The software is based on the sharing tenet of ubuntu. Western culture has not been spared by the influence of ubuntu. Besides the Linux example, ubuntu has also been applied at various levels. Madonna, named her film *I am because we are* on Malawian orphans, a reflection of ubuntu influence. Bill Clinton used the term "ubuntu" to call for people centeredness in Labour Party policy when he addressed the party's conference in 2006. Ubuntu diplomacy has been introduced by the United States of America Department of State which says it 'will be a convener, bringing people together from across regions and sectors to work together on issues of common interest'. Even the American Episcopal Church had the theme ubuntu for its 76th Convention (Magumbate and Nyanguru 2013: 87-88).

Applicability of ubuntu philosophy

Ubuntu and business

Consequently, it is suggested that the indigenous phenomenon of ubuntu should be informing business activities such as the codes of ethics that are created to maintain a moral compass in business activities. Ubuntu is, thus, predominantly required to offset what are often cosmetic Western business practices which neither effectively infuse ethical conduct in business nor consider societal needs in a meaningful manner. So in a nutshell, business ethics generally includes the practices and behaviours that are considered by society to be good or bad, or ethical or unethical (Nicolaides 2014). Porter and Kramer (2006) call on businesses to be guided by what they term the 'moral imperative' since this ultimately leads to sustainability and also enhances the organisations reputation while affording it a 'license-to-operate'. Ubuntu is a vehicle that can assist in creating such an organisation.

Ubuntu, metaphysics and religion

Metaphysics is part of the ubuntu philosophy and is very much at the centre of reconciliation in conflict situations. This is because, like all human beings, Abantu live in a world of uncertainty. The world of uncertainty includes the reality of death, which all human beings must suffer. But for most Africans, like Christians, death does not mean the disappearance of the dead from beingness. Africans believe that the dead continue to exist in a spirit form and as such they are recognised as the "living-dead" or ancestors (Savage and Sonkosi 2002). African philosophy holds that the `living dead' can, when called upon by the living, intercede and advise them in certain circumstances. Such intercession is crucial in reconciliation rituals in which the ancestors, invisible beings, play a significant role. In addition to the "living-dead," there are also the "un-born" who are recognised to exist in the future. As such the living are required to ensure that the un-born are brought into the world and provided for. This also conforms to the law of creation, which the Ubuntu philosophy also takes account of (ibid).

Thus, the transformation of the living from the un-born and the living to the "living dead" occupy a continuous space, which Professor Ramose has calls "the ontology of invisible beings" or African metaphysics (Ramose 2002). It is a discourse about the unknown from the standpoint of the living. However, the fact that the unknown is unknown does not mean that it is unbelievable. The Africans, in this understanding, therefore, believe in the existence and beingness of the unknown, which has a direct influence on their own being. It is this existence of the invisible beings that is the basis of ubuntu metaphysics and the belief in the supernatural that play a role in African processes of reconciliation (ibid). This, according to Ramose, explains why Ubuntu philosophy and religion have no separate and specific theologies. Through these invisible forces Africans seek explanations to certain happenings, which cannot otherwise be explained by 'normal' or 'rational' means (ibid).

Conflicts are part of these uncertainties of existence and hence the role supernatural beings play in the reconciliation process in which the ancestors are implored to sanctify whatever is decided upon through rituals (ibid). Religion provides another arena of belief in God-the Supreme Being. It is a belief in the immanent and the transcendental. Many Africans believe in one

God, while others believe in a variety of gods and spirits. All have the same objective, which seek to explain where we come from and where we are going (ibid). Thus the insistence by Africans to uphold certain metaphysical relationships to religion enables them to 'straddle' worldly situations, including the embracing of different religions and invisible forces, without losing meaning in life. At the same time by adopting these different religious traditions to their own belief systems, they are able to synthesise them into one belief system that is coherent in their own understanding of the world around them (ibid).

Ubuntu, politics and law

Ubuntu principles have been applied in a range of disciplines in recent times including the legal services (Sloth-Nielsen and Gallinetti 2011). The act of reconciliation is based on African understanding of politics and law as they unfold in real life. As already indicated above, Umuntu is the maker of politics, religion, and law. In the philosophical domain, ubuntu is the basis of law and politics (Fortes and Evans-Pritchard 1940). This is what makes the act of reconciliation, whenever it occurs, to have the full force of recognition, legitimacy and sovereignty of the people. This is because African legal philosophy only recognises the human subject to be a living and lived experience with full authority to regulate life on earth (ibid). As a subject, Umuntu-the subject-makes the law and at the same time commands its obedience by all persons including him/herself. There is no one above the law. This explains why in ubuntu political philosophy royal power is expected to spring from the people (expressed in Sotho dictum to mean "*kgosi ke kgosi ka batho*") or in modern parlance "power belongs to the people." Therefore, all laws pronounced by the king or chief must express the will of the people who must respect and obey it in their own name since they make it together with the king in council. This is why the British Jurist, Dr. Arnold Allot, commenting on Basuto law insists that Sotho law is linked to morality, reasonableness, and justice. Another Western jurist, J. H. Driberg, has also said of African law:

> African law is positive not negative. It does not say: 'Thou shalt not,' but 'Thou shalt.' Law does not create offence, it does not create criminals; it directs how individuals and communities should behave towards each other. Its whole object is to maintain equilibrium, and the penalties of African law are directed, not against specific infractions, but to the restoration of this equilibrium (ibid).

Therefore African law based on ubuntu is a living law, based on their recognition of the continuous oneness and wholeness of the living, the living-dead and the unborn. These laws are combinations of rules of behaviour, which are embodied in the flow of daily life (ibid). In short, the African renaissance must lead to power being returned to the people if the renaissance is to be a reality. Without the empowering of the African people through their cultural heritages, which include the heritages of Ubuntu philosophy, political life in post-colonial African states can never bring about true reconciliation and lasting peace to the people of the continent. The process of historical memory should, therefore, contribute towards the re-empowerment of people so that they can face one another in dismantling ideologies of superiority and dominance that lead to conflicts and wars (ibid).

Ubuntu and management
Ubuntu has also been applied in management. Professor Lovemore Mbigi, a writer on African management, in his book ubuntu, *The African Dream in Management*, argued that service quality is not only determined by what we do for the client but also by the spirit in which we render the service. Mbigi further explored the use of ubuntu in affirmative action and marketing management. In African management ubuntu represents the

essentialist perspective of African culture, a homogenising concept tying Africans together (Magumbate and Nyanguru 2013: 90). Mbigi and Maree (1997) argued that Africa must draw on indigenous cultural practices in order to improve their management, effect transformation and make themselves more competitive. They noted that some of ubuntu values like collectivity, solidarity, acceptance, dignity and hospitality are very crucial in managerial success.

The perceived negative side of ubuntu

Ubuntu has had its own share of criticism. The major criticism that can be levelled against ubuntu/unhu/vumunhu is that it cannot be universally applied across cultures. Hailey (2008), for importance, questioned whether ubuntu can be universally applied across cultures. He argues that since ubuntu is not homogenous, it may not be universally applicable. This challenge is made worse by the fact that ubuntu has no solid framework, what it means and what makes it up cannot be theorised. But sympathisers have pointed out to the fact that globally accepted practices, like democracy, are by no means universally applied but they have found their way into most communities (ibid). It is in the same vein that ubuntu must find its way into every society. Another criticism has been on the strengths of ubuntu values. It has been argued that some of the values weaken societies. For example, respect for authority and openness to new ideas has often been cited as a contributory factor to colonisation in Africa which promoted disenfranchisement, culture erosion and dependence (Mugumbate and Nyanguru 2013). The weaker tenets of ubuntu may be used to make Africans submissive and dependent. Reference can be made to the divide and rule tactic used by colonialists in Africa.

Besides, ubuntu can be misunderstood as a new gospel of racism given the genesis of the word 'ubuntu' itself and its emphasis on the indigenous people of southern Africa. In fact, it is commonly argued that ubuntu separates Africa, and in particular southern Africa, from the rest of the world. One may, for example, wonder what could be the fate of other races such as Europeans, Chinese, and Americans living in Africa. How the humanity of such people could be determined and determined if ubuntu is appropriated and considered as the moral foundation of the so-called Bantu people? Also, where the humanity of other such entities as wild animals in this whole discourse of ubuntu? All these are questions that could be raised against the philosophy of ubuntu.

More so, those preying on African resources may emphasise the values that make Africans dependent. A case in point is how ubuntu has been used to celebrate South Africa's reconciliation efforts. This has led to South Africans remaining without economic resources despite the availability of an all embracing constitution and a welfare system based on ubuntu (ibid). On the other side, Presidents like Robert Mugabe of Zimbabwe are derided for taking back the country's land from former colonisers. This act, together with an empowerment exercise meant to economically empower indigenous people, is regarded by outsiders and other fellow Africans, including other Zimbabweans, as ubuntuless (ibid). Yet equality is a strong ubuntu tenet. Lastly, it has also been argued that ubuntu may give people a very strong identity, resulting in herd mentality. Often, xenophobia attacks in South Africa are cited as an example. However, Africa requires a strong identity that ogres well with its culture. In true ubuntu, Africa will be able to protect its culture, beliefs, economic interests and its future (ibid).

Conclusion

The philosophy of *ubuntu* is encapsulated in most philosophies of life, although it is articulated and actualised in different ways. Although ubuntu literally means African humanism, it shares values with the human race in general.

Values such as respect, dignity, empathy, co-operation and harmony between members of society are not exclusively African, but comprise the human race as a whole. In short, ubuntu is a way of life that positively contributes to the sustenance of the wellbeing of a people. It is a philosophy that promotes the common good of society. This philosophy is transcultural and, if embraced, would enable Africans to inculcate a spirit of togetherness in a world that is severely plagued by individualistic mannerisms.

Chapter 6

Pan-Africanism and the Search for Africa's Framework for Sustainable Development

Introduction

Pan-Africanism as a concept and ideology despite generating intense debate more than any issue, has had a very profound impact on the unity and development of the entire African continent. It is indeed true that this kind of an ideology has helped and informed the development and articulation of a philosophy for the global engagements of the post-colonial African states (see Okeke and Okechukwu 2011). Historically, Pan-Africanism as a unique cultural and spiritual movement for the promotion of the black race became first used among the black Americans and West Indians of the 19th century (Legum 1962). As that may be, Pan-Africanism was born out of a realisation that the African people were a downtrodden group and that they are not only culturally related but also share similar problems and aspirations (Word 1967; Akintoye 1976; July 1992). The philosophy and ideology behind this approach is seen as a part of the quest for African approaches to African problems (Francis 2006: 126). The underlying epistemological ethos informing Pan-Africanism continues to guide and influence African thinking in general and the African Union (AU) in particular (Moyo and Ramsamy 2014).

The concept of Pan Africanism is premised on the understanding that Africa cannot meaningfully and sustainably develop fully from foreign support. Rather, Africa needs to be self-sufficient and self-reliant in order to develop in transformative ways (Machel 2012). It is vital to note that African development has been a central concern of Pan-

Africanism since the early 1950s. This is reflected in the thinking of former Pan-Africanist thinkers and philosophers who proposed models of development which are firmly grounded in African philosophical ideology (see Martin 2011). Julius Nyerere, for instance, believed that in order for Africa to meaningfully develop it needed to depend upon its own resources as well as to develop policies based on collective self-reliance (see Nyerere 2000, cited in Martin 2011). It is this realisation that ignited the desire and the quest for eventual unity for all the Africans, and even the coming together of the black people in diaspora. Precisely, as a philosophical ideology, Pan-Africanism encourages the solidarity of Africans, based on the belief that unity is vital to economic, social, and political growth and that the fate of all African peoples and countries are intertwined as they share not merely a common history but also a common destiny (Kanu 2013).

This chapter is about how Pan-Africanism can be utilised as the foundation and paradigm for transformational sustainable development in Africa. The chapter seeks to position Pan-Africanism at the heart of Africa's sustainable development trajectories. This is largely because for development to be transformative and sustainable it should be firmly grounded and anchored in African epistemological systems. Unfortunately, the opposite is true as the conceptualisation of sustainable development as well as the theories and strategies for achieving sustainable development in Post-Colonial Africa have remained a territory traversed predominantly by non-African scholars. Against this backdrop, the present chapter will provide a theoretical reflection and conceptual framework of an African-led sustainable development, anchored in principles and values enshrined in Pan-Africanism. The chapter further argues that sustainable development cannot be achieved in Africa outside the parameters of Pan-Africanism. The chapter furthers the idea that the various African sustainable developmental initiatives should be firmly anchored in the philosophy and ideology of

Pan-Africanism despite the militating challenges threatening the unity of the continent. While the author is aware of the fact that there will be challenges, such as lack of political will, inadequate resources, competing agendas, and incapacities; these need not be an excuse for not getting on with the agenda of sustainable development in Africa (see also Moyo and Ramsamy 2014). In view of this, it is the contention of this chapter that it is time to revisit the link between Pan-Africanism and sustainable development given the urgent need for solidarity in resolving conflicts and the opportunities for sustainable development in the current economic, social, cultural, and political trends in Africa. It must be clear right from the onset that the chapter is not arguing for a type of Pan-Africanism that ignores the various fundamental differences in history, culture, societal systems, and values across the continent; rather, whilst the chapter recognises diversity, it therefore strongly argues for its utilisation as a unifying force for sustainable development in Africa.

An exposition of Pan-Africanism

Pan-Africanism is a recognition that Africans have been divided among themselves, that they constantly compete with each other, are deprived of true ownership of their own resources, and are inundated with paternalistic external actors (Murithi 2007: 2). Modern-day paternalism takes a sophisticated form, manifesting as a kind and gentle helping hand with benign and benevolent intentions. In reality, however, it perpetuates a 'master-servant' relationship and resists genuine empowerment of Africans and independence of thought in Africa. The net effect is disempowerment of Africans, so they do not decide for themselves on the best way to deal with problems and issues unique to them. Pan-Africanism recognises that the only way out of this existential socio-political crisis is by promoting greater solidarity amongst Africans (ibid).

It is axiomatic to posit that despite the flood of books and articles on Pan- Africanism in recent years the study of the phenomenon is still in its babyhood. Scholars and politicians alike tend to bury its aspirations and dynamics in minutiae of fascinating but largely irrelevant details. Not surprisingly there is still no consensus on what Pan- Africanism is all about. As a concept, the term "Pan-Africanism" is credited to Henry Sylvestre-Williams, and Marcus Garvey, amongst others, renowned for organising the largest Pan-African movement in history (Dieng 2005). The ideal of unity for all peoples of African descent have found resonance globally, attracting intellectuals, writers, artists, leaders of religious and cultural movements, and politicians of varying renown. Pan-Africanism has inspired scholarly traditions that privilege African-centred knowledge production, epistemologies and perspectives that challenge perceived Euro-centric (mis-)representations of Africa and people of African descent (Obenga 2001). Ndabaningi Sithole (1968: 71), a former participant in the Kwame Nkrumah Ideological Institute at Winneba as a freedom fighter with the African Nationalist Congress of Southern Rhodesia now Zimbabwe, defined Pan-Africanism as the common identification of the peoples of African descent who have discovered their common destiny and who demand to be treated as equals with men of other races. Fundamentally, Pan-Africanism is a revolt against the doctrine of racial inferiority which centuries of oppression and humiliation have rammed down the throats of the dark-skinned peoples and is a reaffirmation of the equality of the dark-skinned peoples with the peoples of any race (ibid).

Broadly conceptualised, Pan-Africanism is an ideology and movement that encourages the solidarity of Africans worldwide. It is based on the belief that unity is vital to economic, social and political progress and aims to "unify and uplift" people of African descent. At its core, Pan-Africanism is "a belief that African peoples, both on the continent and in the diaspora, shares not merely a common history, but a common destiny" (Chime 1977: 12). As a philosophy, Pan-Africanism represents the aggregation of the historical, cultural, spiritual, artistic, scientific and philosophical legacies of Africans from past times to the present (ibid). Interestingly, Esedebe captures the multiple and often contradictory understandings associated with Pan-Africanism when he writes that it is impossible to give an accurate definition of Pan-Africanism in a short sentence. He rather poses a list of major concepts and ideas which characterise Pan-Africanism.Rather, he captures the essentials of Pan-Africanism in seven major interrelated ideas; "First, is the conception of Africa as the homeland of Africans and persons of African origin. Second is reflective and organic solidarity among all peoples of African descent. Third, is collective and individual pride in African personality. Fourth, is the rehabilitation of Africa's past.Fifth, is the pride in African culture. Sixth, is the idea of preserving Africa for Africans at political and religious planes. Seventh, is the hope of emergence of a united and glorious federation of African states" (Esebede 1982: 45-6). He went on to state that Pan-Africanism is a political and cultural phenomenon which regards Africa, Africans and African descendants abroad as a unit. It seeks to regenerate and unify Africa and promote a feeling of oneness among the people of the African world. In fact, it glorifies the African past and inculcates pride in African values. Thus, Pan-Africanism demands the unity of all Africans, regardless of social and political differences on the basis that African peoples on the continent and in the diaspora have a common history and destiny (ibid).

For Anyidoho (1989: 2), Pan-Africanism means talking about the black world, the various areas where blacks live, how they got there, but also and above all, the current conditions in which black live, all the world over. Anyidoho's definition of Pan-Africanism is centred on the daily living conditions and mental-psychological-state of Blacks wherever they are and the same notion is at the core of Kwame Nkrumah's treatment of the theme of Pan-Africanism. First of all, he was advocating the union of all African states for better conditions for Africans, but he was also and above all concerned by the connection between continental Africa and the black Diaspora (Traore 2015). Nkrumah started by stressing political independence, economic emancipation, while recommending the strategies that can counteract the colonial imperialistic powers and he calls for the alliance of colonial territories.

Apart from that, the Columbia Encyclopaedia (2008: 1) refers to Pan-Africanism as the general term for various movements in Africa that has as their common goal the unity of Africans and the elimination of colonialism and white supremacy from the continent. Thus, it is apparent that one key element in the philosophy of Pan-Africanism is the prescription of African unity as an inevitable framework for both emancipation of the continent from colonial rule for its rapid socio-economic transformation. In conformity with the above understanding, Pan-Africanism represents the totality of the historical, cultural, spiritual, artistic, and scientific worldviews of Africans from past times to the present, in order to preserve African civilisations and to struggle against slavery, racism, colonial and neo-colonialism (Okeke and Okechukwu 2011). Add to that, Badejo (2008) gives a similar meaning by articulating that Pan-Africanism is 'a socio-political worldview, philosophy, and movement, which seeks to unify native Africans and those of African heritage into a 'global African community. Despite those differences in the meaning of Pan-Africanism, there is a uniting factor, that is, all the authors 'believe in some form of unity or of common purpose among the people of Africa and the diaspora' (Adi and Sherwood 2003).

Ideological and philosophical development of Pan-Africanism

Pan-Africanism as a search for dignity by African peoples has gone through many different iterations in the past five-hundred years. At the time of enslavement, Pan-Africanism meant freedom from slavery, freedom from bondage. And at the time of colonialism and the partitioning of Africa and the Pan-African Congress, Pan-Africanism meant independence, the struggle against Jim Crow discrimination. At the time of apartheid, Pan-Africanism was the struggle for the dignity of the African people. And at that moment, the leaders of Africa articulated a vision of Pan-Africanism leading to the unification of the continent of Africa (Campbell 2005). Historically Pan-Africanism- the perception by Africans in the diaspora and on the continent that they share common goals- has been expressed in different forms by different people. Rather than a unified school of thought, Pan-Africanism is a movement with its common underlying theme as the struggle for social and political equality and freedom from economic exploitation and racial discrimination (Murithi 2007).

By and large, the global dispersal of persons of African descent is partly responsible for the emergence of the Pan-African movement. As Hakim Adi and Marika Sherwood observe 'Pan-Africanism has taken on different forms at different historical moments and geographical locations' (Adi and Sherwood 2003: vii). They also note that the underpinning of these different perspectives on Pan-Africanism is 'the belief in some form of unity or of common purpose among the peoples of Africa and the African Diaspora' (ibid). The movement also emphasises a celebration of 'Africaness', resistance to the exploitation and oppression of Africans and their kin in the diaspora as well as staunch opposition to the ideology of racial superiority in all its overt and covert guises.

Moreover, it is generally agreed that the history of the Pan-African movement has its origins among black expatriates living in Europe, the USA, Latin America, parts of South Asia, the Middle East, India, Australia, New Guinea and the Caribbean etc. (see Nyamnjoh and Shoro 2011). Indeed, as a movement, Pan-Africanism originated not in Africa, but in the West Indies, amid feelings of nostalgia about and occasional dreams of an eventual return to a lost home land – mother Africa (ibid). The concept of Pan-Africanism in general came into being in the 18th century when Prince Hall and Paul Cuffe initiated the movement to repatriate Blacks from the USA to Sierra Leone (Traore 2015). The theory of Pan-Africanism was originally conceived by Henry Sylvester Williams, a Trinidad barrister who organised the first meeting of Africans and Africans of the Diaspora at the London Conference in 1900. Sylvester-Williams coined the term "Pan-Africanism" for what had previously been called "the African movement" (Moyo and Ramsamy 2014). Dr W.E.B. Du Bois, an African-American scholar and a promoter of the London Conference, applied the term "Pan-African" to a series of six conferences that he convened in the capitals of European colonial empires from 1919 to 1945 (ibid). Africa at that time, as is the case today, was confronted with the problems of colonisation and slavery. Between the years 1919-1945, Dr Du Bois organised intensively for the broadening of the Pan-African movement idea and its perspective. The key actors who are associated with the early initiatives of the Pan-African Movement are W.E.B. Du Bois; Marcus Garvey; George Padmore and many others (ibid).

It was these black intellectuals who came together at the turn of the 20th century to give voice to the aspirations of black people around the world. A number of important congresses were held by them to mobilize people in the African Diaspora in Europe and elsewhere in the world behind the banner of Pan-Africanism. These early founding fathers of the Pan-African Movement were later reinforced by newly arrived African students, who were studying in Europe and the USA. Thus, the 1945 Congress of the Pan-African Movement held in Manchester, UK, was attended by many African delegates, including George Padmore, Du Bois; Kwame Nkrumah from Ghana; Nnamdi Azikiwe from Nigeria; Jomo Kenyatta from Kenya, just to mention a few.There is no doubt that the increasing number of African students in Europe and the USA during those years helped to awaken the attention of the world to the cause of African emancipation. These African students and their associates were able to highlight the plight of black people in Africa. Pan-Africanism is also associated with the growing opposition to British imperialism in the wake of the Berlin Conference of 1884, and it finds expression in Marcus Garvey's Universal Negro Improvement Association, or the UNIA during the 1920s and following decades (see Omi and Winant 1986).Historically, Pan-Africanism has attempted to integrate the mosaic of newly independent African countries and has reflected the complex relations between continental Africans and Diaspora Africans (Lemelle and Kelley 1994).

As a philosophy, Pan-Africanism represents the aggregation of the historical, cultural, spiritual, artistic, scientific and philosophical legacies of Africans from past times to the present. As an ethical system, Pan-Africanism traces its origins from ancient times, and promotes values that are the product of the African civilisation and the struggles against slavery, racism, colonialism and neo-colonialism (Adi and Sherwood 2003). This understanding made some scholars such as Harris to arrive at the conclusion that Pan-Africanism is usually seen as a product of the European slave trade. For Harrisson (1993), enslaved Africans of diverse origins and their descendants found themselves entrenched in a system of exploitation where their African origin became a sign of their servile status. Understood from this perspective, Pan-Africanism set aside cultural differences, asserting the principality of these shared experiences to further solidarity and resistance to exploitation.

123

As an intergovernmental movement within Africa, Pan-Africanism was launched in 1958 with the first Conference of Independent African states in Accra, Ghana. Thereafter, as independence was achieved by more African states, other interpretations of Pan-Africanism emerged, including: the Union of African States in 1960, the African States of the Casablanca Charter and the African and Malagasy Union in 1961, the Organisation of Inter- African and Malagasy States in 1962, and the African-Malagasy-Mauritius Common Organisation in 1964 (see Sherwood 2003).Campbell notes that, "Pan-African identification has taken many forms, but it has been most clearly articulated in the project of achieving the liberation of the continent of Africa and the dignity and self-respect of all Africans" (Campbell 1994: 205). It emerged from the experiences of slavery and colonialism on the continent and the Diaspora and the legacy of racism and discrimination that followed (Lemelle 1992: 12; Campbell 1994: 285-286).

Mazrui (1977: 8-9) and Ali (2005: 433) have distinguished five levels and phases of Pan-Africanism. According to the former, these are the sub-Saharan, trans-Saharan, Trans-Atlantic, West Hemisphere and global (see Mazrui 1984: 68). Sub-Saharan Pan-Africanism- limits itself to the unity of black people or black countries south of the Sahara. It could take the form of sub-regional unification, like the East African Community or the experimental Economic Community of West African States. Or it could be a commitment to limit solidarity to black African countries, excluding both the Arab states and the black people of the Americas. Trans-Saharan Pan-Africanism- extends solidarity to those who share the African continent across the Sahara desert – the Arabs and Berbers of the North. Trans-Saharan Pan-Africanism insists on regarding the great desert as a symbolic bridge rather than a divide, a route for caravans rather than a deathtrap. Trans-Atlantic Pan-Africanism is the third level of solidarity, encompassing the peoples of the Black Diaspora in the Americas as well as of the

African continent. One form of trans-Atlantic Pan-Africanism limits itself to black people and excludes the Arabs of North Africa. Under this version Afro-Canadian, Jamaicans, black Americans, black Brazilians and others find common cause with Nigerians, Zimbabweans, Namibians and Ugandans, but find little in common with Egyptians, Libyans and Algerians.

However, there is another version of Trans-Atlantic Pan-Africanism, under which Stokely Carmichael of the Black Diaspora was a hero in Algiers, and Colonel Gaddafy of Libya extends financial support to black Americans. West Hemispheric Pan-Africanism encompasses West Indians, black Americans, black Brazilians and other black people of the Western Hemisphere. Within this version of Pan-Africanism the strongest links so far have been between black Americans and English-speaking West Indians. This has included movements of population. In the first thirty years of this century alone, 300 000 people from the Caribbean moved to the USA, taking humble jobs in coastal towns and gradually becoming part of the racial mosaic of the United States. At the outside, one out of every twenty black Americans today is descended from a West Indian male who moved into the United States some time since emancipation.

One important bond of West Hemispheric Pan-Africanism lies in the fact that almost all black people in the Western Hemisphere are descended from slaves. This contrasts with trans-Atlantic Pan-Africanism which includes descendants of slave dealers both north and south of the Sahara. Trans- Saharan Pan-Africanism emphasises the quality of having been jointly colonised; West Hemispheric Pan-Africanism finds solidarity in having been jointly enslaved; while the trans-Atlantic idea encompasses the broader concepts of having been jointly exploited by the Western world. As for global Pan-Africanism, this brings together all these centres of black presence in the world, and adds the new black enclaves in Britain, France and other European countries, which have come partly from the

Caribbean and partly from the African continent itself. Potentially these black enclaves in Europe are the most radicalisable of them all because of a combination of their demographic smallness and economic weakness, and the fluctuations of the European economies themselves.

According to Alli (2005: 433) Pan-Africanism has passed through four phases as articulated below:

- The colonial phase, from 1900 to 1957 when Ghana won her independence. The independence phase, from 1957 to 1963, when majority of African states won their independence up to the formation of the OAU;

- The national liberation phase, from 1963 up to the independence of Zimbabwe in 1980;

- The anti-Apartheid and Economic Development Phase, from 1980 when all focus of Pan-African national liberation struggles were directed at removing the apartheid regime, from the continent up to the collapse of the apartheid regime and the election of Nelson Mandela as President of the Republic of South Africa in 1994. The period also cover the period of economic-awakening and refocusing of attention on economic issues, the introduction of the Lagos Plan of Action (LPA) in 1980 and the African Economic Community (AEC) in 1991; and lastly,

- The globalisation phase, from 1994 to date, including the transformation of the OAU in 2000 to the African Union (AU), the introduction of the NEPAD initiative and other efforts to overcome economic decline and achieve more rapid economic development in Africa, institutionalise more participatory and more democratic governance and resolve the remaining national questions.

In the postcolonial era, the nature of Pan-Africanism and the problems facing Pan-Africanist projects changed dramatically. For the first time, Pan-Africanism became a broad-based mass movement in Africa and enjoyed its greatest successes as an international liberation movement in the first two decades after the war.

Objectives of Pan-Africanism

At the dawn of independence, it was obvious that Africa's development lies in the unity of her people. Indeed, it was the quest for unity that fired African nationalism and led to Pan-Africanism as a guiding ideology upon which the battle for de-colonisation was fought with vigour, strength and determination (Olu-Adeyemi and Ayodole 2007). Essentially, Pan-Africanism is recognition of the fragmented nature of the existence of Africans, and their marginalisation and alienation both on their own continent and the rest of the world. In fact, Pan-Africanism seeks to respond to Africa's under development and exploitation and the culture of dependency on external assistance that unfortunately still prevails on the continent (Murithi 2007: 1). Fundamentally, the goals of Pan-Africanism are a re-examination of African history from an 'African perspective' and a return to traditional African concepts about culture, society and values.In the twenty first century, the new Pan-Africanism movement is still committed to the 'long aspired-to African unity and solidarity', but with an unprecedented new level manifested in the recognition that development, peace and security and democracy in Africa are intertwined and interdependent. This new understanding of Pan-Africanism explains the termination of the OAU and the birth of its successor, the AU (Da Costa 2007). Below are some of the major objectives of Pan-Africanism;

- **Unity and solidarity**
One of the core objectives of Pan-Africanism, since 1958, has been African unity. Pan-Africanism emphasises African unity beyond identities confined by geography, primordialism and narrow nationalism, and champions socio-political

inclusiveness for all those who willingly claim or are compelled to identify with the "Black" race and a place called "Africa" (Fanon 1967; Senghor 1977; Mkandawire 2005; Bah 2005; Biney 2011). As a quest for a global Black or African community, Pan-Africanism is an aspirational project towards a world informed by solidarities and identities shaped by a humanity of common predicaments. It is the glue to hold together the dreams and aspirations of Blacks divided, inter alia, by geography, ethnicity, class, gender, age, culture or religion (Nyamnjoh 2009). Nkrumah presented three objectives for the unification of Africa. They included an overall economic plan (now called NEPAD), the establishment of a unified military and defence strategy, and the adoption of a unified foreign policy. He concluded:

> Proof is therefore positive that the continental union of Africa is an inescapable desideratum if we are determined to move forward to a realisation of our hopes and plans for creating a modern society which will give our peoples the opportunity to enjoy a full and satisfying life (Nkrumah 1963: 217; see also Museveni 1997: 18).

In arguing for solidarity, unity, and relational existence Kwame Nkrumah (1963: 34) further argued that; "No sporadic act or pious resolution can resolve our present problems. Nothing will be of avail, except the act of a united Africa."

To buttress his point, Nkrumah argued that independent African countries should suspend pursuit of economic development until all African countries were free from colonialism. This meant that African independent countries would provide support to any African country seeking independence, by postponing economic development. In substantiating this argument, Makgoba maintained that this principle of the union of African states was enshrined in the constitutions of some African countries, and now called for legitimate and selfless leaders to implement it (Makgoba 1999: 8). In an endeavour to demonstrate its commitment to the materialisation of this objective, Ghana under Nkrumah was among the first African countries to include in her constitution a willingness to surrender her sovereignty voluntarily for the "furtherance of African unity" (see Nkrumah 1963: 85). Had the African leaders taken Nkrumah's vision of unification seriously, Africa would have made positive achievements in social and economic development in the first few decades following the independence of some African countries. There were of course some external interferences which delayed economic development. For instance, the Cold War and the policies of International Monetary Fund (IMF) and the World Bank made the situation worse as they openly rejected some of the initiatives that were meant to economically capacitate African countries. For Kwesi Kwaa Prah n.d: 269), "the ideal of African unity is premised on the notion that the emancipation, development and prosperity of people of African descent can be achieved only through the unity of the people." Supporting the afore-mentioned view, Nkrumah, believed that in unity lay the solution to African problems (see also Biney 2011).

Sadly, there is no agreement as yet on the constituency for the much desired unity. Some, like Nkrumah, Padmore and Diop, have advocated a unity of the entire continent of Africa, a unity that would include the Black Africans and the Arabs in the African continent. Some like Azikiwe and Museveni have advocated a unity of all who now reside on the African continent—Blacks and whites, including the Arab and European colonial settlers. Yet, others want the unity to be between the Black Africans and their Diaspora in the Americas; and still others want the unity, whatever its form or forms, to be between the Black Africans in Africa and the Blacks world-wide, excluding the European and Asian settlers on the continent (Kwesi Kwaa Prah n.d). The ideal of African unity is premised on the notion that the emancipation, development and prosperity of people of African descent can be achieved only through the unity of the people (ibid). What is certain, however, in the words of Fanon (1967: 276) is that there cannot be "one Africa that fights against colonialism and another that attempts to make arrangements with colonialism."

- **Economic integration**

The second objective arises from the first one: Africa's unity, which overcomes artificial racial, national, or ethnic conflict, is creating stability conducive to the enhancement of Africa's economic potential (see Makgoba 1999: 8). Makgoba reiterated some of the benefits of this economic integration. With the strengthening of democratic structures, peace, and stability, economic development would follow (ibid: xviii). Economic integration creates a "self-centred power base" in the emerging regional interstate economic groupings such as the Economic Community of West African States (ECOWAS); the Southern African Development Corporation (SADC), and the East African Community (EAC).

Unpacking sustainability

Sustainability is simply able to be maintained or ability to endure. Today, the term is used to "describe community and economic development in terms of meeting the needs of present without compromising the ability of future generation to meet their needs" (Park 2007: 439). That is, the ability to find or put appropriate measures in place to ensure the continuous use of a society's natural endowment to improve the standard of living of the people without compromising that of future generations. In other words, it refers to the society's ability to achieve economic development and improve the quality of life for its people, now and for future generations (Awuah-Nyamekye 2015).

Understanding development

The concept of development is multidimensional. Development has many construals. Eliot (1971) observes that there is no agreement as to what development is. In the words of Haynes (2009: 5), the term "development' has long been vague yet predictive; struggling to acquire a precise meaning." No wonder it has been defined differently across disciplines. For Sibanda (2009), development refers to improvement in a country's economic and social conditions. Quoting the World Bank, Sibanda (2009) says, 'when referring to a country, it will be taken to mean reaching an acceptable standard of living for all people. It means people have the basic things they need to live.' From the above, one can posit that the term 'development' is seen in materialistic or economic terms but in actual fact the concept is conceptualised by different people at different times as development may be relative to time and space (see Awuah Nyamekye 2012). In the indigenous African worldview, the term development is not limited to material and economic terms but it is viewed in a holistic way. For them, development is a process and in fact, a means of ensuring a holistic well-being of humans utilising judiciously the total environment of the people from both the sacral (religious) and secular point of views but not where there is economic growth at the cost of greater inequality, high unemployment rate, loss of cultural identity, consumption of foreign goods and depletion of resources needed by future generations (ibid).

What is sustainable development?

Several definitions and explanations are attributed to Sustainable Development today. Sustainable Development basically means working toward ensuring descent living conditions for the current generation of human beings without jeopardising the living conditions of future generations (Traore 2015). Bill Hopwood *et al.* (2005) in their article titled, "Sustainable Development: Mapping Different Approaches" clearly shows that Sustainable Development certainly has the potential to solve fundamental challenges for humanity now and in the future. They stress that sustainable development has to be understood as a notion which concentrates more on the sustainable livelihood and well-being, rather than well-having which is an attitude created and encouraged by the capitalist worldview. Fowke and Prasad (1996) as quoted by Williams and Millington (2004: 99) for instance, have listed 'at least eighty different, often competing and sometimes contradictory definitions' of sustainable development. This implies that the term defiles unanimity among scholars. It is against this backdrop that William and Millington (2004: 99) concluded that: "sustainable development is a notoriously difficult, slippery and elusive concept to pin down."

The World Commission on Environment and Development (1987) explain: "Sustainable development as *development* that meets the needs of the present without compromising the ability of future generations to meet their needs". Sustainable development, according to the Brundtland Report (2008) is "Balancing the fulfilment of human needs with the protection of natural environment so that these needs can be met not only with the present but in the indefinite future". The International Institute for Sustainable Development (2008) also defines sustainable development as that: "development which meets the needs of the present without compromising the ability of future generations to meet their own needs". This simply infers that the concept of sustainable development operates on the principle of need fulfilment both for the present generation and the generations unborn. Hattingh (2002: 19) argues that the meaning and interpretation of sustainable development is informed by various philosophical and ethical interpretations. He says that sustainable development is strongly associated with "a *moral imperative* that apparently no one can ignore or reject, without having to provide a very good reason for dissent ... even though there is ... little consensus about the content, interpretation and the implementation of this imperative".

Pan-Africanism as a driver of sustainable development in Africa: Successes and failures

The vision of African unity dates from the dreams of the first Pan-Africanists. The founding fathers of Africa's independence were fierce optimists. Freed from the shackles of colonial rule, they believed fervently in the promise of a unified continent following concurrent paths of economic and political integration. For them, unity was the means to achieve dignity, prosperity and security (Senghor 2009). More importantly, the goal for the unification of Africa has not changed. As it was for Nkrumah's time, so it is now. Makgoba redefined it as rebuilding Africa as a self-centred power, based on the principles of autonomy and efficiency through democratic and ethical governance that can meet the needs and aspirations of the majority of Africans (Makgoba 1999: 8).

Some of the successes of Pan-Africanism
The Pan-African movement evolved into a political entity with a clear agenda of eradicating all forms of oppression, slavery, and colonialism. It also sought to end racism, the dehumanising treatment of Africans, and aimed at political and socio-economic emancipation of Africa. The ensuing section, is a response to the question whether it possible for Pan-Africanism to be the framework and foundation of sustainable development? In furtherance of the quest for new paradigms a number of "homegrown" development strategies and paradigms have emerged.Significant amongst these are the Lagos Plan of Action (LPA), and The New Partnership for African Development (NEPAD).

- **Creation of the Organisation of African Unity**

Headquartered in Addis Ababa, Ethiopia, the Organisation of African Unity (OAU) was founded to bring African nations together and strengthen their independence from European rulers. Factually, African states' elites had not been short of development agenda. First, having realised that Pan-Africanism was a sine qua *non* for the continent's progress, they formed the OAU in May 1963 (see Bukarambe 2004), and second, the establishment of the African Development Bank in 1964. With these twin institutions in place, African leaders, though divided, believed that their region was on the path, of growth (Cervenka 1977). Indeed, during the first decade of independence, the African economies showed modest growth as investment and savings ranged from 15% to 20% of the Gross Domestic Product-GDP (Chisinga 2010: 10).

Honestly, the creation of the OAU marked the launch of a formal Pan-African project for regional integration. The OAU charter stated that member states would 'coordinate and harmonise their general policies' in sectors then dominated by government (Senghor 2009). In practice, most of the OAU's attention was focused in its early years on building solidarity with Africa's remaining liberation struggles. The anti-apartheid movement was a dominant concern, as the OAU expressed Pan-African support for the African National Congress in exile and its campaign against minority rule in South Africa. The OAU lobbied member states, foreign governments and international organisations to boycott the apartheid regime (ibid).The OAU now renamed the African Union (AU), has been advocating for unity and cooperation among African nations since its establishment in 1963. The philosophy and ideology behind this approach is seen as a part of the quest for African approaches to African problems (Francis 2006: 126).

The AU came into existence in July 2002, in Durban, South Africa. It was supposed to usher in a new era of continental integration leading to a greater unity and resolution of its

134

problems. The underlying purpose of the AU is to promote solidarity, cooperation and support among African countries and peoples in order to address the problems of the continent as a whole (Murithi 2007). A number of historians and political analysts believe that the creation of the AU and its predecessor, the OAU, was a manifestation of the rise of the Pan-African movement in the 21st century. In addition, the establishment of the AU was a desire by African leaders to unite all people of Africa in order to face new realities of globalisation, including the role of emerging powers that are shifting the power relations between the North and the South (Adi and Sherwood 2003).

- **The Lagos Plan of Action**

It was adopted by an Assembly of Heads of State and Government of the OAU in April 1980. The goal of economic integration was formally adopted in the LPA for the Economic Development of Africa. The plan set a 20-year time frame to create a single unified African economy for the next millennium. Self-reliance was a recurrent theme of the LPA. Industrialisation and regional trade were encouraged as a means to reduce dependence on foreign markets (Senghor 2009). The LPA mapped two phases for implementation. In the 1980s, priority would be given to harmonising trade within existing regional economic communities. New regional blocs would be created spanning all five sub-regions of the OAU, as a precursor to an African Common Market. In the 1990s, the second phase would lay foundations for a unified African Economic Community. In reality, both decades witnessed a loss of momentum – and further deterioration in conditions for the poor (ibid).

- **The Abuja Treaty**

The Abuja Treaty came into effect on May 12th 1994. The treaty outlines the steps to create a unified African Economic Community by 2027, including: a single currency, full mobility of capital and labour as well as free trade among the 53 member countries. It sets out a six-phase timetable for integration spanning 34 years, from 1994 to 2027(Senghor 2009). In the first stage, to 1999, Regional Economic Communities (RECs) were to be strengthened or new ones created. In the second stage (1999-2007), member states were to encourage integration through two processes. The initial goal was to rationalise existing tariff and non-tariff barriers to trade, including customs duties and internal taxes. The next goal was to coordinate RECs, in order to harmonise their activities in trade, agriculture, transport and finance (ibid). A third stage (2007-2016) requires the abolition of internal tariffs and non-tariff barriers to intra-regional trade. This stage, in which RECs are to become free trade areas and customs unions, also requires member states to set a common external tariff on imported goods and services from third states. In the fourth stage (2017-2018), RECs are to eliminate all intra-regional tariffs and other non-tariff barriers to create a single Pan-African customs union.

The fifth stage (2019-2022) sets out criteria for the creation of an African Common Market. Member states are to adopt common monetary, financial and fiscal policies, with free movement of capital, labour and people, without restrictions on rights of residence. The sixth stage (2023-2034) inaugurates the African Economic Community and the free movement of capital and labour within a single African market (Ibid). Pan-African economic and monetary union will introduce a single currency administered by a common central bank.The Abuja Treaty vested political decision-making within the OAU Assembly but anticipated the creation of a Pan-African parliament, elected by the entire African population. Other institutions would follow, including a Court of Justice, a Secretariat, an Economic and Social Commission and various specialised technical commissions (ibid).

- **The New Partnership for African Development (NEPAD)**

In October 2001, African Heads of State and Government meeting in Abuja endorsed the New Partnership for Africa's Development (NEPAD) the main development agenda for Africa presently (NEPAD 2001). NEPAD purports to constitute a 'partnership' at two levels. Firstly, it is a partnership of African countries with the governments and owners of capital in the Western world. Success at this trans-continental partnership is desirable for two reasons. First, it is envisaged that it would change the historical relationship between Africa and the West in order to dispense with the "dependency through aid" that underpins it (ibid). Next, this type of partnership is desirable to the extent that it holds the prospect of generating "capital flows to Africa, as an essential component of a sustainable long-term approach to filling the resource gap" (ibid). Secondly, NEPAD aspires to build a partnership among African countries principally for the purpose of implementing 'the Programme of Action'. This programme essentially seeks to derive maximum gain from the anticipated capital flows (ibid). The NEPAD document diagnoses the challenge for Africa to be one of understanding the fact that development is a process of empowerment and self-reliance. Africans must not be wards of benevolent guardians; rather they must be the architects of their own sustained upliftment (ibid). Consequently, NEPAD assumed the status of an "African-owned and African-led development programme" and, on this basis, claimed difference from all previous initiatives and approaches to Africa's development (ibid).

The document recognises that Africa's "malaise of underdevelopment and exclusion in a globalising world" stems from "centuries of unequal relations between Africa and the international community, especially the highly industrialised countries" (ibid). This relationship has occasioned "the credit and aid binomial" which underlies the logic of African underdevelopment. Section (v) of the document then outlines a 'Programme of Action', for restoring the integrity of Africa in its relations with the world, and stipulates the objectives, goals and strategies for achieving these. The main objective of the programme is to enable the continent catch up with developed parts of the world (ibid); and its goals are:

- To achieve and sustain an average GDP growth rate of above 7 per cent per annum for the next 15 years;
- To ensure that the continent achieves the agreed International Development Goals (IDGs) (ibid).

Agenda 2063

The Agenda 2063 also called, 'the Africa we want', was adopted on 26th May 2013 at the 50th anniversary of the African Union (AU). The agenda is "a shared strategic framework for inclusive growth and sustainable development for Africa's transformation over the next 50 years" (African Union Commission 2014: 10). It is both an endogenous continental vision, as well as, a global action plan for a more united, prosperous and peaceful Africa (Udah 2015). The agenda is anchored on the principles of participation and inclusivity of all stakeholders including the African Diaspora. It is also based on Africans shared values and a common destiny and focuses on the following eight key areas: African identity and renaissance, decolonisation and the right to self-determination, unity and integration, socio-economic development, peace and security, democratic governance, Africa's destiny and Africa's place in the word (ibid).

The Africa of 2063 is expected to play a more significant role on the global stage and be able to overcome what Moyo (2009: 151) calls, "the four horses of Africa's apocalypse – *corruption, disease, poverty and war.*" Thus, Agenda 2063 provides a road map for Africa's sustainable development. It builds on existing strategic frameworks, such as the Monrovia Declaration of 1979 for a self-sufficient Africa, the Lagos Plan of Action for Africa's economic development in 1980, the 1991 Abuja Treaty for African for an African Common Market by the year 2000 and NEPAD in 2001. The agenda outlines new strategies to bring about high levels of socio-economic and cultural transformation in Africa. Some of the concrete plans outlined in the Agenda 2063 Draft Framework include: free movement of people within Africa by 2015, free trade by 2017, Common Market by 2023, foreign-aid independency by 2028 (ibid).

By 2063 (when the AU will be marking centenary celebrations), Africa is envisioned to be prosperous, economically vibrant and well established, culturally progressive, democratically governed, socially united, secured and peaceful (ibid). It is expected that by 2063, corruption, disease, poverty and war will be a history and women and the youths will be empowered. By 2063, it is expected that Africa will catch up with the rest of the world in technology and infrastructure in size and quality. By 2063, it is expected that opportunity will abound to end the horror illegal migrations of African youths in search of greener pastures elsewhere. It is expected that by 2063, Africa will be attractive and favourable for anyone to live, work, study and settle. Therefore, for a continent such as Africa with nations which have a protracted history of corruption, poverty and underdevelopment, the Agenda 2063 is a long-term strategic plan and a blueprint on how to achieve the desired future we want for Africa (ibid).

Taking stock of the failures of Pan-Africanism

Africa's development challenges and its marginal role in the international political economy have generated heated and continued debate for quite some time now. The history of regional integration in Africa is a story of frustrations. The struggle to reform policy within the regions, and at Pan-African level, has been long and often bitter. The ambitions of the first Pan-Africanists remain salient. Regional integration has not fulfilled their vision. Good intentions, expressed incountless treaties and 'plans of action', have been hampered by poor leadership and inadequate resources (Senghor 2009). The lack of political will among national governments has frustrated attempts at cooperation. The prospect of successful continental integration has arguably suffered a loss of political drive with the absence of authoritative, clear minded political leadership. There is a dearth of energetic leadership with the drive to promote integration – and arguably an even greater dearth of strong and viable institutions on the continent. In barely half a century, Africa has slipped from parity with much of East Asia tolanguish at the bottom of the world development rankings (ibid). Among the greatest obstacles to effective integration is the plethora of regional institutions – the 'spaghetti bowl'. According to NEPAD, institutions tasked with building African unity adopted an 'ossified, static, protected-fortress approach to integration' (ibid).

Although the LPA provided for African integration, it did not adequately address the crucial elements for African development discussed above, namely, capacity, autonomy and partnership. While concentrating on sectoral programmes, the Lagos Plan did not adopt a detailed strategy for building the capacity of domestic institutions in African countries. The plan also dealt with the African development predicament as a mainly, if not purely, economic crisis; corruption and clientalism were not major concerns (Basiru 2011). However, the Bretton Woods institutions and the West refused to accept the approach of the Lagos Plan, which had stated that "Africa was directly exploited during the colonial period and for the past two decades; this exploitation has been carried out through neocolonialist external forces which seek to influence the economic policies and directions of African states" (OAU 1982). The rejection, though not explicitly stated, constituted in the West's ignoring the Plan and "refusing to re-orient their economic relations with Africa so as to connect with and address the programmes and policies of the Plan" (Ake 2001).

Apart from that, NEPAD, as the name suggests, places great emphasis on developing partnerships with external actors. NEPAD is certainly a document open to many criticisms. First, for a document which claims to be African-owned and African-led, it is surprisingly oblivious of the role African culture can play towards development. Although it acknowledges "Africa's rich cultural legacy", the only role it assigns to this culture is that it "should serve both as a means of consolidating the pride of Africans in their own humanity and of confirming the common humanity of the peoples of the world" (NEPAD 2001). As that may be, it is startling to realise how individuals and groups of persons in one country may feel culturally distant. While declaring the existence of African values and the spirit of *ubuntu* there has hardly been a coherent debate of what it means to be African. Is it just the *skin colour* and the *needs* that distinguish Africans from people in other continents? What is it about the African culture that can be coherently defended, imparted and understood by kids and adults alike everywhere? Clearly, this is scarcely congruent with "a rich cultural legacy". Secondly, theoretical underpinning of the programme is clearly neo-liberalism, whose policy prescriptions have repeatedly been shown not to work in Africa. Its neo-liberal orientation includes its endorsement of opening up African economies to external investors and securing the property rights of foreign capital. Further, neoliberal democratic politics is not consistent with the social theory and organisation in the indigenous African setting.

Sadly, NEPAD's emphasis on integrating Africa's economy into the globalisation process, free markets and free movement of capital were rejected by Nigeria and other countries at the World Trade Organisation (WTO) meeting at Doha, Qatar. This greatly undermines its ability to address local needs and therefore secure local ownership and support (Lehulere 2003). Furthermore, NEPAD distinguishes itself from all previous plans and initiatives by conceiving itself as an agenda reached through participatory processes involving ordinary Africans. However, it does not seem that the African leaders who proclaimed this ideal of participation meant to practice it, as they did not deem it necessary to consult the African people before formulating and adopting the programme. In fact, this disregard for the people's participation is consistent with the document's conception of democracy which states emphatically: "Africa undertakes to respect the global standards of democracy, which core components include political pluralism, allowing for the existence of several political parties and workers' unions, fair, open, free and democratic elections periodically organised to enable the populace choose their leaders freely" (NEPAD 2001). That an "African-owned and African-led development programme" committed to the self-reliance and sustained upliftment of Africa (ibid) should affirm the philosophy, aims, and processes of globalisation, is rather perplexing. As indicated in section (1) clause (4.1). This is precisely because the aims and philosophy of globalisation vary from the African perspectives on the human being and society. Finally, the supposition that a 'partnership' with the West could be achieved to rectify the existing unequal relations borders is fantasy. The Akan maxim, that 'the hand that receives is always beneath that which offers' succinctly explains why such a supposition is illusory, for if one takes the philosophy of capitalism seriously, one would hardly come to the conclusion that capitalists will offer someone resources in aid to enable the person ascend to the position where you can compete with them.

On the other hand, Francis argues that despite women's activism against colonialism and apartheid in many African countries, Pan-Africanism has remained a male-dominated ideology. Its narratives and discourses give credit to men and ignore women's contributions (Francis 2006: 14). Bineta Diop, founder of *Femmes Africa Solidarité* (FAS), in Senegal notes that the OAU was created without having women in the centre of

142

the debate, and as a consequence, women's issues were not adequately addressed" (African Union 2013). However, the OAU was not as effective in monitoring and policing the affairs of its member states when it came to the issues of violent conflict, political corruption, economic mismanagement, poor governance, infringement of basic human rights, lack of gender equality, and eradication of poverty (Murithi 2007: 2).

It is paradoxical that African leaders proclaim and rehearse the beauty of African Unity meanwhile African students, researchers and business men from various sub regions cannot move freely from one country to the next (Kingah n.d). On the economic side, all the figures from the World Trade Organisation (WTO) and the United Nations Conference on Trade and Development (UNCTAD) indicate that Africans engage more in formal commercial relations with non-African states (Kingah n.d). One of Africa's economic challenges in the 21stcentury is that there is little intra-African trade. Much of the trade in Africa has been between African countries and the Europeans, Americans and the emerging economies. The share ofintra-African trade has declined from 22.4% in 1997 to around 12% in 2011 (UNCTAD 2013, in Zonke, 2014: p. 89). It is argued that trading within Africa is more costly than trading outside Africa given the fact that many African countries are beset by very poor infrastructure, and destructive tariffs, among others (Zonke, 2014). For so long, African countries have been urged to develop strong trade relations between and among them as a means of shielding themselves from the vagaries of the world commodity markets (Zonke, 2014; Moyo, 2009) though this is yet to be heeded to. According to Haas (1971), regional integration is a process of combining separate economies into larger political communities. To the extent that political and economic forces are inextricably intertwined, any discussion of integration must encompass both economic and political variables.

Conclusion

Pan-Africanism as a flexible, inclusive, dynamic and complex aspiration in identity making has been an important by-product of colonialism and the enslavement of African peoples by Europeans. Though it has taken a variety of forms over the two centuries of its fight for equality and against economic exploitation, commonality has been a unifying theme for many Black people (Sherwood 2003: viii). The chapter has shown that Pan-Africanism is at the heart of Africa's developmental frameworks that can create an enabling environment to redress past injustices and imbalances. The chapter has also demonstrated that the different developmental paradigms pursued by African leaders though better intentioned are failing to materialise because they are modelled on the European Union and, thus, not homegrown. It is evident that the issue of development for Africa should be primarily the responsibility of Africa's theoreticians.

Chapter 7

Nyerereism:
A Blend of African Communalism and Socialism

Introduction

Mwalimu Julius Kambarage Nyerere, one of the first crop of political thinkers to emerge from Africa as well as the first President of the United Republic of Tanzania, is arguably one of the prominent Pan-Africanist leaders who was very passionate about African ways of perceiving society while at the same time very vocal about the impositioning of Western exploitative ideological systems and dogmas on the African soil. Nyerere also occupies a privileged place in the pantheon of Africa's leading political philosophers and theoreticians (see Mazrui and Mhando 2013). Besides being the founder of the Organisation of African Unity (OAU) in 1963, Nyerere is one of the few African leaders of the late twentieth century whose name has remained unsullied by accusations of corruption, and who retained a life-long allegiance to socialism (Sherwood 2003). He also played a pivotal role in African Affairs in the 1970s and his contribution to the Pan-African movement cannot be underrated; like Amicar Cabral who added a revolutionary dimension to Pan-African movement and put the working class at the forefront, Julius Nyerere's Pan-Africanism has its own special features which add up to that of Nkrumah and Cabral (Traore 2015). Influenced by his humble yet inspiring upbringing which was grounded in African communalistic ethos and realities, he was convinced that there is no other sustainable and befitting developmental paradigm that fits the African context other than African socialism. For him, African socialism was the only practical and equitable systems that he perceives as capable of promoting positive development within the African framework in comparison with other individualistic and exploitative ideologies such as capitalism. Nyerere was vehemently against a capitalist system that encouraged individualism at the expense of the community. Nyerere noted that, "capitalism fosters excessive individualism; promotes the competitive rather than the cooperative instinct in man; exploits the weak; divides the society into hostile groups and generally promotes inequality in the society" (Akinpelu 1981: 115). He believed that capitalism regarded some individuals as superior (the rich) and others as inferior (the poor). He further asserted that the major aim of capitalism was the production of goods and profits, not human satisfaction or the interest of the consumer. According to Nyerere, these capitalist ideas could not be reconciled with African values; therefore, he advocated for African Socialism on the basis that it benefits all members of the society (Nyerere 1968b). His socialist experimentation was lumped under a single name, *Ujamaa* which in Swahili means "familyhood". Ujamaa was to help restore the cooperative spirit that the African people had before the colonisers introduced the idea of individualism. Nyerere's African socialism is a blend of economic cooperation and racial and tribal harmony, a policy of the type advocated by Kwame Nkrumah. Although Nyerere and Nkrumah were towering figures of Pan-Africanism, one cannot fail to see that they arrived at Pan-Africanism through different intellectual and political routes (Traore 2015). Mulenga (2001a: 17) categorically stated that, "Nyerere's aim was to transform the colonial value system which had alienated Africans from their past into one group of attitudes based on past African values and attitudes of self-esteem, cooperation, and family." In short, Nyerere put forward his thesis that socialism was the only rational choice of economic and social system for the Third World countries given their recurrent common problems.

In the same vein, Kwame Nkrumah espoused the ideology of socialism on the basis that it is the only suitable developmental framework that can accelerate the economic growth of Africa without destroying social justice, freedom and equality, which are central features of African traditional life (Nkrumah). Basing on their similar conceptualisation of socialism, Nyerere and Kwame Nkrumah have been considered as the two most notable exponents of African socialism. Against this backdrop, Nyerereism is regarded as a blend and or a synthesis of communalism and socialism. That is, it heavily borrows from these two ideologies which more often than not are intricately related. In reviewing Nkrumah and Nyerere, Hallen (2002: 73) points out that the vision of these two leaders was that "socialism in the African context was to be a formalised, (economically and politically) institutionalised expression of indigenous humanitarian social moral values." The philosophical underpinnings enshrined in African socialism is to build a society in which all members have equal rights and equal opportunities; in which all can live at peace with their neighbours without suffering or imposing injustice, being exploited, or exploiting; and in which all have a gradually increasing basic level of material welfare before any individual lives in luxury" (Nyerere 1968: 340). As a result, Nyerere advocated for a kind of socialism that is deeply rooted in familyhood. The adoption of African socialism by Nyerere as a developmental philosophical compass was an endeavour to pursue an independent, authentic, and hence nonaligned political, social, and economic framework for development. Thus, he looked back to precolonial Africa to find guide posts and inspiration toward an authentic African philosophy, if not ideology, for social organisation and economic development (see Mkapa 2008). This, however, formed the basis of his philosophy called *Ujamaa*. For Nyerere, *Ujamaa*, as the practical expression of the doctrine of African socialism, means first and foremost the building of society on the traditional African value of familyhood.

It is worth noting that Nyerere's *Ujamaa* and African socialism were a confident rebuttal to the colonial project, which was intellectually founded on the arrogant presupposition of African inferiority and European superiority. The *Ujamaa* policy rejected that intellectual presupposition and presumption. The kernel of African socialism relates to the fact that traditional African peoples were socialist by nature and therefore there is no need to dissipate energy on arguing for a socialist ideology as a fitting ideology for the African continent. The essential features of this socialism include: equality among the peoples, the idea of sharing, which include burdens and privileges, community ownership of land and identification of the individual with the community. Contrary to Western socialism, Nyerere's philosophy of *Ujamaa* was rooted in traditional African values and had as its core the emphasis on familyhood and communalism of traditional African societies. At the same time, it was influenced by a mix of Fabian socialism and Catholic social teachings (Ibhawoh and Dibua 2003).

Stoger-Eising (2000: 134-5) has argued that there are close parallels between Nyerere's political ideas and those of Rousseau. She further noted that Nyerere's ideas represented an attempt at fusing European concepts deriving from Kantian liberalism with the ethos derived from his more communitarian native African society. On this basis, Nyerere's socialism may be considered as a blend of African socialism and communalism. Nevertheless, *Ujamaa* was founded on a philosophy of development that was based on three essentials - freedom, equality and unity. The ideal society, Nyerere (1967: 16) argued, must always be based on these three essentials. According to him, there must be equality, because only on that basis will men work cooperatively. There must be freedom, because the individual is not served by society unless it is his. And there must be unity, because only when society is unified can its members live and work in peace, security and wellbeing (Nyerere 1967). These three essentials, Nyerere further contended are not new to Africa; they have always been part of the traditional social order.

Interestingly, Socialism in indigenous African societies has become a common theme in most discourses on African Philosophy. As such, this chapter critically examines Nyerere's *Ujamaa* philosophy in order to advance the argument that *Ujamaa* is not just a development theory, but is also a philosophical ideology (Cornelli 2012). In order to achieve this, the chapter first presents the basis of Nyerere's ideology which ultimately influenced his ontology and phenomenology of African socialism as a form of social organisation in traditional African societies. Before winding up, the chapter will also discuss about some of the pitfalls of African socialism especially in a post-colonial Africa setting.

Unmasking Nyerere's ideological background

Julius Kambarge Nyerere was born in 1922 at Butiama, a small rural village in northwestern Tanzania near Musoma.Born in a polygamous family, Nyerere's father had eighteen wives that bore him twenty-six children. Out of the twenty-six children, Nyerere's mother, Mugaya had six children. Nyerere's childhood, in the words of William Redman Duggan in his book Tanzania and Nyerere, was "much like that of other African children in a rural tribal set ups. When he was a small boy he used to herd the family livestock. When he was of school going age, he sought permission from his family to attend school (Duggan 1976: 44). He was granted permission and to this end young Nyerere was sent to boarding school in Musoma, which was located on the eastern shore of Lake Victoria. After quickly rising to the top of his class at Musoma, Nyerere's outstanding academic performance enabled him to be enrolled at Tabora Government Secondary School in 1937 (Duggan 1976: 44). It was during this period that Nyerere became intensely interested in the Catholic faith, and consequently, he was officially baptised in 1943. That same year after completing his secondary education, Nyerere began his studies at the prestigious Makerere University in Kampala, Uganda, where many of the British East Africa's elites were schooled (Adi 2003: 147). After completing two years at Makerere University, Nyerere returned to Tabora in Tanzania where he got a teaching post at St. Mary's Catholic Boys' School. It was at this school that Nyerere got inspiration from Father Richard Walsh, who proved to be a guiding and influential figure during this period of Nyerere's life (see Adi 2003: 148). In 1949 with the assistance and unwavering support of Father Walsh, Nyerere left Tabora and went to Edinburgh University in Scotland to study for a Masters Degree. By and large, it was Father Walsh who assisted Nyerere in getting the necessary financial backing.

More importantly, it was at Edinburgh University that a major impact on Julius Nyerere's political, economic, and social views were recorded. As Duggan states, "Nyerere claimed that he evolved most of his political philosophy while at Edinburgh" (Duggan 1976: 45). While at Edinburgh, Nyerere became increasingly active with the Scottish Council for African Questions, a group that was formed in 1952 with the intent of coordinating efforts of various committees whose goal was the equitable distribution of economic and political power in the British African colonies. One of the group's main concerns, and a large personal concern for Nyerere himself, as his future actions would show, was the increasing White domination of the Central African Federation. At Edinburgh, Nyerere also became influenced by Fabian socialism, a brand of socialism that advocates achieving the socialist agenda by gradual and reformist, rather than revolutionary, means (Cole 1961: 7). Nyerere returned to Tanzania in 1953 with a wealth of new information, and policies and beliefs formulated much more fully. When Julius Nyerere returned to Tanganyika from Edinburgh University, he took up a position as a history professor at St. Francis' College, near Dar-es-Salaam. It was not long before Nyerere began to meet intellectually stimulating people who would later become very important to the independence movement. Among these men were Amir Jamal and Fraser Murray, men who would have a positive influence on Nyerere's burgeoning political activism. The Tanganyika Africa Association (T.A.A.) was at the time one of the most important organisations in Tanganyika. After his victory and appointment to the T.A.A.'s leadership, Nyerere and his group of friends and advisors determined that the only way to turn the T.A.A. into an effective agent for independence and change was to transform it into a political organisation (Listowel 1968). The process of transforming the organisation also entailed a name change, and it was then that the famous name by which the Tanganyikan independence movement would go down in history was formed—the Tanganyikan African National Union (T.A.N.U.).

The ideology of Nyerere's Party (T.A.N.U) had much in common with Kwame Nkrumah's Convention People's Party of Ghana. On July 7, 1954, T.A.A. had its Annual General Meeting in Dar-es-Salaam, and Nyerere's group took the opportunity to announce the official transformation of the organisation into T.A.N.U. In 1959, T.A.N.U resoundingly won the elections and thereafter Nyerere formed his first responsible government in September 1960. The main thrust of Julius Nyerere's economic policies in office was the development of the rural areas of Tanzania. "Mwalimu," as Nyerere was commonly referred to, believed that the success of Tanzania rested not in rapid industrialisation and growth of the cities, but on developing the nation as a whole. He was given the title "Mwalimu" as a mark of honour for being a teacher. As Donatus Komba put it, "this was to be achieved through rural development based on agricultural transformation. To develop towns and neglect rural areas, where over 80 per cent of the population lived would be tantamount to a betrayal of all who had fought hand in hand for independence in the hope that their living standards would improve" (Komba 1995: 32). Nyerere's broad plan for developing the villages was called *"Ujamaa"* socialism. It reflected a Tanzanian government policy where the emphasis would be on agricultural development before industrialisation. *Ujamaa* socialism was not an imported philosophy: It was the adaptation of development to the traditional communal ties that Nyerere believed Tanzanians were most effective in using. In this sense, it bore little resemblance to either free-market capitalism or doctrinaire Marxism. The emphasis was not on material gains, but on uplifting the people. As Komba describes it, "Hard, intelligent and cooperative work was, therefore, the root of development. In other words, self-reliance meant an emphasis on the people, their land, and agriculture as organised and fused together under the guidance of the policies of *Ujamaa*, self-reliance and good, democratic leadership" (Komba 1995: 37-38). At this juncture, let me hasten to point out that the ideological upbringing of Nyerere paved way for his future philosophical theories of development which were anchored on African traditional values and ethos premised on *Ujamaa*.

Socialism: Conceptual analysis

The concept of socialism, academically, is traceable to George Bernard Shaw for whom socialism meant —absolute equality in money incomes (Cole 1961). It is from the sense of equality and collective ownership of means of production and of distribution of goods, that socialism has been variously defined as an economic and political system based on public or collective ownership of the means of production. Thus, central to the meaning of socialism is common ownership of production and equality.Socialism is also associated with communalism, which signifies belief in or practice of communal ownership, as of goods and property (Ibid). To determine the validity of Nyerere description of socialism as a concept, it is necessary first to establish the legitimacy of the meaning attached to the word "socialism'. What exactly is socialism?

Basing himself on the concrete historical manifestations of socialism and on the 'observable traits' of socialism as it has been existing in various countries, Kornai (2000: 29), has identified three fundamental characteristics. The first is the absolute power of the communist party, next is state ownership of property (the major means of production), and finally state coordination of economic activities.

Kornai (2000: 29), states that, socialism in its concrete historical manifestations is characterised by "undivided power of the Marxist-Leninist Party." A Marxist-Leninist party is a communist party, a communist party is a vanguard party and a vanguard party is a party of workers and peasants that has absolute control of state power which it consolidates after overthrowing capitalism (Shivji 1973). According to Kornai (2000), the second attribute of socialism, state ownership of the major means of production, calls for dominance of public property but not absolute dominance. Private property and profit making organisations can play a secondary role. The essential factor is that private property must not prevail. In short, the minimum that socialism requires from the political sphere is to discourage the private property market and any acts hostile to the institution of the public property. The third and final essential attribute of socialism is the "preponderance of bureaucratic coordination" (Kornai 2000: 297). This term indicates that in socialism, the main mechanism of economic coordination does not occur through the market, regulated by the laws of supply and demand, but through state intervention, which plans and coordinates all economic activities.

African socialism: In search for a definition

Since the attainment of independence by most African countries there has been much talk about African socialism. Moreover, there has been no individual or country which has at any time defined this socialism nor has there been any common ground among the leaders as to what they meant when they talked of African socialism. It is in the seminal thoughts of Julius Nyerere that people glean an organised and systematic body of a doctrine on socialism that is indisputably anarchistic in its logic and content. Historically, the concept of African socialism emerged in African thoughts in the 1950's at a time when many of the African countries were getting ready for independence (Agbaje 1991). The major problem confronted by the first crop of political elites or leaders in their various territories was how to mobilise the values and the energies of their people, tradition and modern, for the development of their countries after independence. It was within this atmosphere that African socialism emerged as a (compass) body of ideas (ibid). Some of these African leaders and proponents of African socialism are Julius Nyerere of Tanzania, L. S. Senghor of Senegal, Kwameh Nkrumah of Ghana, Nnamdi Azikiwe and Obafemi Awolowo of Nigeria and Sekou Toure of Guinea (Olufolake 2014).

What then is African socialism? The fact that the originators and proponents of African socialism are of different temperaments and have not often spoken with one voice, makes it difficult to give a univocal meaning of the concept. African socialism was the brainchild of African ideologies or philosopher-kings in the Young African republics after wrestling power from the colonisers. It maintains that the central values of Africa are communal rather than individualistic and it is for this reason that its adherents see it as being a natural evolution of African communalism (Makumba 2007). For Nyerere (1973), its fundamental themes are threefold, that is, the problem of continental identity, the crisis of economic development and the dilemmas of control and class formation. The aim of African socialism as its protagonists understood it, was "to reconsider African society in such a manner that the humanism of African traditional life reasserts itself in modern technical community (Nkrumah 1973). In fact, African socialists sought to create a social synthesis between traditional African human values and modern technology for the development of their nations. This they hoped to achieve without falling into the excesses of either capitalism or communism (Makumba 2007). However, for a working definition we may say that African socialism is an attempt to recapture and modernise the communal way of life practiced by the traditional African before the exposure to the world and values of the white man (Agbaje 1991). Also, African socialism is a search for an altogether different type of a social system with its root in African soil.Understood from this perspective, African socialism is not new to Africa as it is naturally reflected in the communitarian nature of African society. By and large, it is as an ideological orientation which is peculiarly African (Olofun 2014). Supporting the afore-mentioned view, Nyerere notes that there was no need for Africa to sacrifice its cherished traditions, values, and cultural identity on the altar of policies, doctrines, and theories of development that came from some other societies (see, for instance, Nyerere, 1968a; 1971). As such, he strongly believed that African socialism meant building upon the foundation of the African past and building to African design (Nyerere 1962; Komba in Legum and Mmari 1995: 37).

It was in the same vein that Tom Mboya (1972) conceives of African socialism as a political philosophy which stands to restore national values, communal social practice and above all to restore the traditional values in the African socialist mentality and outlook, and to create more values in the changing world of money economy to build an economy which reflects the thinking of the great majority of people. Mboya's list of basic values and social practices of traditional African consist of the communal spirit, hospitality, hard-work, generosity, acceptance and practice of equalitarianism, communal ownership of land, equality of opportunities for all, tribal loyalty and so on. Nyerere also views African socialism or "Ujamaa Socialism" as he terms it, as more than a political system, it is a philosophy, a world view as well as a gateway to African selfhood. Nyerere asserts that African socialism is:

> Essentially an attitude of the mind which involves a change in personal attitude and a reconciliation of individuals but goes beyond these to effect structural change consistence with the socialist outlook, creating a pattern of justice in which creative and justice in which equality and freedom of all will be assured.

In view of the above understanding, Nyerere advocated for socialism with a human face, which he christened Ujamaa socialism. Ujamaa is a Kiswahili word that may be translated as familyhood or brotherhood. In his conception, family is understood as ultimately embracing the whole human society. That is why he says: "The foundation and objective of African socialism… regards all men as his brethren – as members of his ever-extending family" (Nyerere 1973). It is thus important to highlight that Nyerere made Ujamaa the bedrock of his socialism, a socialism that was rooted in African communalism. Yet, Nyerere had its similarities with Nkrumahism especially in their conception of the scope of African socialism. They both saw it as extending beyond the narrow boundaries of their respective countries and encompassing the entire continent. For this reason, modern African socialism can draw from its traditional heritage the recognition of society as an extension of the basic family (Makumba 2007).

However, there were varieties in interpretation of what constitutes "African socialism". According to Sprinzak (1973: 629), the thesis regarding African socialism is that village society was traditionally communal, and that consequently the introduction of socialist regimes in newly established African states might not pose major difficulties. The kernel of African socialism relates to the fact that traditional African peoples were socialist by nature and, therefore, there is no need to dissipate energy on arguing for a socialist ideology as a fitting ideology for the African continent. The essential features of this socialism include: equality among the peoples, the idea of sharing, which include burdens and privileges, community ownership of land and identification of the individual with the community. Thus, Senghor (1959) one of the first generation of African leaders claimed that "we should learn that we had already realised socialism before the coming of the European" (ibid).

Nyerere's account of socialism is not one that scholars would accept as a measure of socialism. In practice, however, Nyerere's *Ujamaa* met all the criteria of socialism in its concrete historical manifestations; it was established by a vanguard party, which after independence monopolised state power, undermined private property, emphasised state ownership of property and planned economic activities. Thus, from a practical perspective, Nyerere's *Ujamaa* met the basic requirements of socialism and it was, therefore, valid to categorise it as such.

The nexus between socialism and communalism

It is of paramount importance to note that economic development has been central to the ideologies of postcolonial African states. In their choice of which ideological model to adopt for economic development, some states have chosen a form of socialism labelled African socialism. African socialism was a unique brand of socialism peculiarly suited to the African in his own environment. It ranged from Nkrumah's positive socialism to Senghor's existential and "negritude" socialism to Nasser's democratic socialism. Nyerere's philosophy of *Ujamaa* was rooted in traditional African values and had as its core the emphasis on familyhood and communalism of traditional African societies. At the same time, it was influenced by a mix of Fabian socialism and Catholic social teachings. Stoger-Eising (2000: 134-5) has argued that there are close parallels between Nyerere's political ideas and those of Rousseau. She further noted that Nyerere's ideas represented an attempt at fusing

European concepts deriving from Kantian liberalism with the ethos derived from his more communitarian native African society. Nevertheless, *Ujamaa* was founded on a philosophy of development that was based on three essentials – freedom, equality and unity. The ideal society, Nyerere (1967: 16) argued, must always be based on these three essentials. According to him, there must be equality, because only on that basis will men work cooperatively. There must be freedom, because the individual is not served by society unless it is his. And there must be unity, because only when society is unified can its members live and work in peace, security and wellbeing. These three essentials, Nyerere further contended are not new to Africa; they have always been part of the traditional social order.

Osabu-We (2000: 171) notes that *Ujamaa* "was supposed to embrace the communal concepts of African culture such as mutual respect, common property and common labour." And, Nyerere said: "*'Ujamaa'*, then…describes our socialism." "Our socialism" isthe recognition of society as an extension of the basic family unit; it was anattitude of mind for Nyerere that reaches back to "tribal days." But, he says, "the family to which we all belong must be extended yet further—beyond the tribe, the community, the nation, or even the continent—to embrace the whole society of mankind. This is the only logical conclusion for true socialism." Thus, Nyerere (1963) writes:

> The traditional African community was a small one, and the African could not think of himself apart from that community in which he lived. He was an individual; he had his wife-or wives and children, so he belonged to a family. But the family merged into a larger "blood" family, which itself merged into a clan or tribe. Thus, he saw himself all the time as a member of a community, but he saw no struggle between his own interests and those of his community, for his community to him was an extension of his family. He might have seen a conflict between himself and another individual member of the same community, but with the

community itself, he saw no struggle. He never felt himself to be a cog in a machine. There could not be this all-embracing, all-powerful modern concept of a society which could use a person as a cog. . . . The African is not communistic either in his thinking or in his traditional way of life. He is, 'communitary' in thinking and in his way of living. He is not a member of a 'commune,' some artificial unit of human beings; he is a member of a genuine community or a brotherhood. Nyerere himself has urged that the same socialist attitude of mind which, in the tribal days, gave to every individual the security that comes of belonging to a widely extended family, must be preserved within the still wider society of the nation.

Nkrumah's communalist thrust and Nyerere's ethic of cooperating for the common good are two sides of the same coin of "the humanist essence of our [i.e. African] culture" (Wiredu 1980). Likewise, Kwameh Nkrumah explains African socialism through the communal life practiced by traditional African, he says; anyone who seeks the socio-political ancestors of socialism, the one must go to communalism. Socialism has characteristics in common with communalism, just has capitalism is linked with feudalism and slavery (Olofun 2014). The only system that negated capitalism is socialism, whose political ancestor is communalism, for socialism and communalism have common characteristics. Communalism is already the sort of traditional set up of African society, so the principle of communalism in a socialist society only needs to be given a centralised and correlated expression so that economic disparities due to political inequalities may not result. Therefore, socialism is a defence of the principles of communalism in a modern society (Uhanze 2011).

As that may be, Nyerere's perceived ideal state is the old African traditional society is based on humanistic principles. In this ideal state, he recognises and acknowledges the absence of anti-social effects of acquisitiveness, competition, exploitation, oppression, loiterers, parasitism among many other social vices. In fact, everybody had an obligation to work and there was co-operation and communal living. Add to that, there was a sense of security as a result of the fact that wealth was not hoarded but was collectively and equitable shared as both the rich and poor individuals were completely secured in traditional African society. In this societal set up nobody starved either of food or of human dignity because he/her would depend on the wealth possessed by the community of which s/he was a member.

The pitfalls of African socialism

The African socialism espoused by Nyerere in Tanzania was a major factor in engendering a sense of mutual respect, dignity, unity, and national identity. Though the concept of African socialism was seen as a panacea to African's recurrent and unending developmental woes by especially Nyerere, the concept has met severe criticisms. African socialism, for what it's worth, has been variously criticised for lacking theoretical coherence and clarity, and, worse still, for the questionable manner in which it seeks to isolate world socialism from that practiced in Africa (Ibhawoh and Dibua 2003). Critics of African socialism have pointed out that exploitation and oppression are universal evils, and that socialism is universal in scope and application (though it can be adapted to suit individual cultures). It is generally believed that the pursuit of African socialism, in its various hues and shades, was somehow partly responsible for Africa's poor economic record compared with Asia. Consequently, Ujamaa shared the same premise and fallacy, of developmentalism that has propelled and constrained successive development initiatives in Africa (ibid). Apart from that Nkrumah, Nyerere and others have been criticised for romanticising precolonial systems of social organisation. In any case, there was no uniformity of culture or social organisation in precolonial Africa (Mkapa 2008). On the other hand, the actual policies and the failures of "African socialist" regimes reveal the emptiness of such grandiose, self-serving rhetoric as economic performance under that framework was not too impressive (ibid). Despite socialist rhetoric, capitalist relations of production remained dominant for the most part in "African socialist" societies. Socialism in Africa, for all practical purposes, was based on the Soviet/Eastern European model, and it displayed all the essential features and characteristics of that model.

Furthermore, some commentators such as Kopytoff (1964) and Clapham (1970) have observed that the "socialist" interpretation did not square with the empirically discovered/observed reality. According to these commentators, facts on ground depicted that African peoples are diverse in several ways such that they cannot be identified with only one ideology. In addition, it is generally acceptable that there were features of individualism, which is the major feature of the capitalist ethos, among some African peoples. Olofun has also castigated African socialism. Firstly, he argued that African socialism gives the false that the African past society was free from conflict. Yet, history is replete with evidence pointing to the fact that there were cases of intra/inter-tribal wars. Also, there were criminals and exploiters in the traditional societies of Africa, as we have in the present capitalist states (Olofun 2014). Secondly, communal co-existence suggested by African socialism is not plausible in an over populated geographical area as the African states, except if sanctions will be applied in proportions to the populations (ibid). Also, communalism is not peculiar to Africa as it is found in traditional industrial societies all over the world.

Thirdly, African socialists assert that the bond of brotherhood and unity, in the traditional society of Africa was very strong and they suggest that this brotherhood and unity should be encouraged in the modern society (ibid). This is really a good suggestion; but then if the bond of brotherhood and unity was that strong, why did Africans sell their fellow African brothers into slavery in exchange for the goods of the white man? Again, it is believed that the values extolled as African values, values such as communal spirit, hospitality, hard-work, generosity, and altruism are not peculiar to Africa, these values are human values, encouraged by human beings all over the universe, since human nature is universal (ibid). Finally, African socialists have not been able to translate their theory into practise in the present African states. Ayittey (1990) advanced the argument that African Socialism has fatally failed as a socio-economic blue-print for African countries and as such, one is tempted to say that African socialism is nothing but a myth. As such, there is need to look for another blue-print for the development of Africa and deliverance from the present quagmire.

When asked what he thought his main mistakes as a Tanzanian leader were, or what he would, given the chance, do differently, Nyerere had it that:

> There are things that I would have done more firmly or not at all. For example, I would not nationalise the sisal plantations. This was a mistake. I did not realise how difficult it would be for the state to manage agriculture. Agriculture is difficult to socialise […]. The land issue and family holdings were very sensitive. I saw this intellectually but it was hard to translate it into policy implementation (see Bunting 1999).

Conclusion

Nyerere believed that the egalitarian and communalistic nature of traditional African society as reflected by their philosophy of *Ujaama* was in line with the principle of socialism. For socialism to thrive there must be a belief that every individual man and woman, whatever, colour, shape, race, creed, religion, or sex is an equal member of society with equal rights in the society and equal duties to it (Omoregbe 1991). Nyerere believes that with these socialist principles, he will build a socialist society in which the socialist principle of equality is applied to the social, economic, and political organisation of the society. *Ujamaa* socialism means love extended to the individuals in the state as members of the same family aimed completely at the progress and *well-being* of humanity. Nyerere wishes all these ideals of the traditional African society realised in a modern African socialist state in order to make it ideal state. He believes that when these ideals are practiced or extended beyond tribes, community to embrace nation, then, we have a truly socialist state. The chapter has clearly shown that African socialism is a three-fold affirmation. It affirms Africa's 'originality', 'distinctiveness and 'personality'. Besides, it also affirms Africa's 'independence' ideologically as well as politically. In a nut shell, it affirms Africa's 'open-mindedness,' its rejection of the 'tyranny of concepts', and indeed of ideologies. Thus, African peoples had to develop their own form of socialism and had to beware, in a world divided between the rich and the poor, that they were not used as 'tools' by either.

Chapter 8

Nkrumahism:
A Search for the Logic of African Unity and Consciencism

"Africa is one continent, one people, and one nation" – Kwame
Nkrumah

The year 1957, when Ghana gained its independence from
Britain, marked and ignited the fire of independence struggles
across the continent of Africa. In all these tumultuous struggles,
Kwame Nkrumah was a central figure, a driving force that
propelled and catapulted the spirit of struggle not only in Gold
Coast (now Ghana) but the whole continent. The time that
Ghana attained its political independence was also a time when
the world was experiencing the taxing so-called Cold War with
tensions mostly between the United States on one side and the
Soviet Union on the other. The two countries were engaged in a
tension and hostility, a contest for world leadership which could
be traced to as early as the mid-40s to the late 80s. The hostility,
which is believed to have been due to the fear of nuclear
escalation, began with the end of the Second World War. The
war was called Cold War because there was no active war
between the two nations [United States and Soviet Union]. The
war ended withthe dismantling of the Berlin Wall and the
collapse [or disintegration] of the Soviet Union in 1991. And
Ghana, as with many other African countries, received a lot of
financial aid from Soviet Union in its bid to gain influence in
Ghana. The fall of the Soviet Union was, therefore, a blow on
Ghana and many other African countries that had enjoyed its
financial gains. This is to say that Ghana attained its
independence in a very tumultuous time in global politics. It was

165

also a time when many of the African countries were malnourished, languishing in abject poverty, toiling and burning in wars, and in fact inching closer to their graveyards owing to the wounds that had and were being inflicted on them by Western imperialists and African turned imperialists. But all the same, Kwame Nkrumah had to soldier on, assisting and mobilising struggles in other African countries for them to attain independence as well. But who was Kwame Nkrumah? What were his political, cultural and philosophical ideas?

One may wonder whether it is still important for us to critically examine the life and works of a long-dead nationalist, Kwame Nkrumah whose life is sometimes associated with substantial amounts of debauchery. In response to this we argue with Charles Abugre, head of policy and advocacy at Christian Aid in the UK (cited in Biney 2011: 2) that:

> Dead politicians are different things to different people. Both their good and their wrong define the goal posts and hence the playing fields upon which the survivors take their positions in society. Their good is usurped, their failures exhumed and magnified as appropriate and in accordance with creed. It is in the nature of humanity to review the past, for in doing so we not only define our own essence but also seek to learn lessons if we genuinely desire to do so.

We agree that dead politicians just like dead authors are not dead. They are true heroes and heroines who have simply passed on to continue living in another world, a world beyond the comprehension of the corporeals. Their history, their names and works will always touch the lives of humanity in copious ways, good and bad. The good thing in this is that whether good or bad, lessons will always be derived from their works and histories. This reality, thus, cannot escape the nationalist and giant of African history, Kwame Nkrumah.

Profiling Kwame Nkrumah

Kwame Nkrumah was born in Nkroful, Gold Coast (now Ghana). Nkrumah (Born: Francis Nwia Kofi Ngonloma), was born on the 21st of September 1909. Between 1935 and 1945, Nkrumah studied at several Universities in the United States of America earning degrees in theology, Masters in science education and Masters in philosophy. He taught for some time at Lincoln University in Pennsylvania before he travelled to London in 1945 where he founded the West African National Secretariat to work for the decolonisation project of Africa. After working for the pan-African movement in England, Nkrumah returned to Ghana in 1947, where he was appointed General-Secretary of The United Gold Coast Convention before he entered parliament in 1951.

Nkrumah died of prostate cancer in Bucharest, Romania in 1972 after living in exile in Guinea since his overthrow through a coup in 1966. Nkrumah was overthrown for many reasons ranging from autocratic/dictatorial rule to a clinging on socialist ideology and mismanagement of the economy. The multi-million questions are: Why would Africa celebrate a man whose leadership was criticised for his socialistic stance? A man who was criticised for being an elitist and for his controversial policies? What was so special about the legacy of a politician whose political ideologies were perceived as the exact opposite of his people's will? What role and contribution did Nkrumah made to ensure that Ghana and Africa at large invest in African development initiatives?

Nkrumah was one of the twentieth-century's most important nationalist philosopher leaders in Africa as he believed Ghana could only be considered totally independent if and only if the whole of Africa was independent. Nkrumah demonstrated that he wanted Africans to develop an African personality with a typically African identity as he announced to his nation on the eve of independence that: 'We are going to see that we create our own African personality and identity. We again rededicate ourselves in the struggle to emancipate other countries in Africa; for our independence is meaningless unless it is linked up with the total liberation of the African continent.'

To ensure that the African struggles are directed towards emancipation and total independence of the African nation-states, Nkrumah suggested the need for education of the youth across the continent.

In the *African Concord,* Kofi Hadjor (1986: 8-9) describes Kwame Nkrumah as a Pan Africanist, theoretician and realist, thus: 'It is Nkrumah the theoretician and practitioner of Pan-Africanism who continues to provide interest and respect' now and in the future.

Amilcar Cabral, the Guinea-Bissau leader (1979: 115) in his: *Unity and struggle* describes Kwame Nkrumah as 'the strategist of genius in the struggle against classic colonialism.' For Cabral, as with many other Pan-Africanists, Nkrumah was no doubt a political and philosophical genius who merged theory and practice in his executions.

Similarly, Cooper (2002: 161), commenting on the personality and contribution of Nkrumah to the world of politics and the history of the African struggle for socio-economic, political independence and recognition had this to say:

> There is a particular poignancy to the history of Ghana because it was the pioneer. Kwame Nkrumah was more than a political leader; he was a prophet of independence, of anti-imperialism, of Pan-Africanism. His oft-quoted phrase 'Seek ye first the political kingdom' was not just a call for Ghanaians to demand a voice in the affairs of state, but a plea for leaders and ordinary citizens to use power for a purpose – to transform a colonised society into a dynamic and prosperous land of opportunity.

What Cooper is saying is that Nkrumah was a distinguished political leader, an Afrocentrist opposed to Afro-pessimism associated with Africa during his time. He wanted the African people to be proud of their own, history, culture and themselves too. For Cooper, Nkrumah was in fact not only a leader of Ghana but an activist, a critical pedagogist, progressivist, and great leader for the entire continent of Africa. He was very optimistic of Africa's future such that even though many other African countries' attainment of independence was belated as compared to that of Ghana, Nkrumah never lost hope on Africa. He knew one day the whole of Africa will be set free.

Ghana was the first sub-Saharan African nation (excluding Ethiopia) to gain independence with its first independent administration inaugurated on 6 March 1957 with Kwame Nkrumah as Prime Minister. This was some 5 years after the first nation on the African continent, Egypt, gained its independence in 1952. Ghana was declared a republic on 1 July 1960 with Nkrumah as its president.

Kwame Nkrumah's philosophical political ideas

Some heroes are born, others created to respond to particular situations as every situation has a response to it. Colonialism in Africa, for example, was responded to by revolutionary struggles for independence. Apartheid in South Africa, which no doubt was centred on race, was responded to by counter radical force of Black consciencism which centred itself on countering white supremacism. Africanist scholar, Magobo Moore (2004) explains the relationship between oppressive political ambiance and how such situations create equally strong forces to resist it when he says: "Just as Karl Marx was 'created' by capitalism; Lenin by the Russian aristocracy, Gandhi by British imperialism, and Fanon by the colonised 'Wretched of the Earth' who were victims of white oppression, Biko was created by apartheid racism" (p. 86).

Likewise, Kwame Nkrumah was created by an oppressive colonial regime in Gold Coast (now Ghana). He saw how his people and many others across the African continent suffered in the face of foreign domination and exploitation. The situation Nkrumah happened to witness required a force from within to deal with and unshackle the people of Africa from chains of oppression.

In terms of personality and talent, Nkrumah was a polymath, charismatic, theoretician, influential thinker and accomplished scholar of global proportions, but ambivalent and controversial at the same time. His controversial character resulted in his political ideas, most of which are philosophical, to be received differently domestically, continentally and even globally. Ama Biney (2011: 1) aptly captures the ambivalence and controversial nature of Nkrumah's political ideas when he says:

> Nkrumah's historical reputation is shrouded in considerable ambivalence and controversy. His performance as independent Ghana's first leader and his policies on the domestic, African, and international stage have continued to generate lively debate within African studies and in popular forums. African listeners to British Broadcasting Corporation (BBC) Focus on Africa reflected the popularity of Nkrumah in a poll in December 1999. Nkrumah was voted as "Africa's Man of the Millennium."

Yet, while some of his philosophy and policies remain controversially perceived, Nkrumah's ideas on Africa are well respected by many even today. He is widely honoured in Africa as an Africanist, a political leader who encouraged the African people to dispel the Eurocentric idea that Africans could only progress by copying European models and practices. On this important note, there is no doubt that Nkrumah contributed significantly to the social, political, philosophical, and cultural thought of Ghana and indeed the whole of Africa. In the section below we discuss Nkrumah's contribution to the political arena both to Ghana and Africa at large.

Nkrumah's philosophy of unity

Some critics described Nkrumah as a dictator but others are quick to note that Nkrumah just like Gaddafi was a dictator who had the well-being, consciousness and prosperity of his people at heart. Many of Nkrumah's grand plans were of a pan African nature hinging on Africa's economic growth, need for the upholding of African consciousness, and Africa's political independence.

He argued that socialism was the only system that would best accommodate the changes that capitalism had brought forward, while at the same time continues respecting African values. Nkrumah (1965: 6), thus, wrote:

> We know that the traditional African society was founded on principles of egalitarianism. In its actual workings, however, it had various shortcomings. Its humanist impulse, nevertheless, is something that continues to urge us towards our all-African socialist reconstruction. We postulate each man to be an end in himself, not merely a means; and we accept the necessity of guaranteeing each man equal opportunities for his development. The implications of this for socio-political practice have to be worked out scientifically, and the necessary social and economic policies pursued with resolution. Any meaningful humanism must begin from egalitarianism and must lead to objectively chosen policies for safeguarding and sustaining egalitarianism, hence, socialism and scientific socialism.

Nkrumah was a self-proclaimed Marxist as far back as 1957 when he wrote his magnum opus: *Ghana: The Autobiography of Kwame Nkrumah* though it is questionable how many of his ministers were. He attempted to instil socialist doctrines and values especially the need for a United States of Africa by his establishment of the Ideological Institute in 1962 and his socialist tone in his numerous speeches to civil servants and the Ghanaian public. This idea of a United States of Africa was adopted by Nkrumah from Marcus Garvey who in 1924 coined the term "United States of Africa" in his poem: *Hail, United States of Africa*. From his student days to the end of his life, Nkrumah, like his contemporaries such as Hailie Selassie (Ethiopia) and Sekou Toure (Guinea), was totally committed to his ambitions for socio-economic and political unification for Africa. For him, the scramble for Africa by the Western colonialists had parcelled and created many artificial states which were non-existent before. As such, Nkrumah saw Pan-Africanism as a force that would allow Africans to re-shape the political geography of their continent on their own without basing on outsiders' interests. He clearly envisioned a supranational entity, an African continent with a common united front which, taking it from Garvey, he named United States of Africa. For him, this supranational entity would be created through the African Investment Bank, the African Monetary Fund, and the African Central Bank. Nkrumah, unlike any other African leader of the time, gave much thought to the future of both guerrilla forces and professional armies in Africa especially in the event of it united to form a supranational state. When Africa was fully unified under a single African government, Nkrumah thought Africa's professional armies would be replaced by people's militias, under African political control. The only purpose of the militia would be to maintain law and order (see Browne 2007). As further revealed by Browne, Nkrumah also believed that in an African continent strong and united, there would be neither more internal strife, and African killing African nor was there likely to be a foreign threat as the people of Africa could defend themselves in the unlikely event of any outside power either daring or wanting to attack.

To this grant project, Nkrumah wanted Ghana to emerge as a microcosm with all qualities for other African countries to follow suit. His idea of unifying Africa grew even stronger when he experienced first-hand racism during the civil rights movements in the United States of America. Upon his return to the Gold Coast (now Ghana), Nkrumah refused to be a second class citizen ruled by colonialists in his own country. He demanded 'self-governance now.' Yet his idea of unifying Africa did not die with his country's attainment of independence in 1957. After achieving independence for his country on 6 March 1957, Nkrumah declared "The independence of Ghana is meaningless unless it is linked up with the total liberation of Africa." Unfortunately, many of Nkrumah's contemporaries misunderstood and mistook Nkrumah to be an opportunist. Henry Kam Kar (2012) in his paper *'Africa Must Unite': Vindicating Kwame Nkrumah and Uniting Africa Against Global Destruction,* aptly captures the lack of impetus to the idea of a United Africa by many self-seeking African leaders right from the start:

> Many self-seeking African leaders described Kwame Nkrumah as a dreamer of impossibility. A few decades after his clarion call, some European countries created the European Union (EU) for their greater unity, collective benefit and for providing global leadership. Since then, American and Asian states have also come together, challenges notwithstanding. Africa is yet to make any meaningful progress towards a union government in spite of public acknowledgement of this need by some of its leaders (p. 26).

Yet, Nkrumah saw African unity as the only precondition and means by which Africa could develop socially, economically and politically through harnessing of its many resources for the betterment of its people. While the European countries mobilised other African leaders to go against the idea of a united

Africa, they interestingly copied that idea of Nkrumah and went on to create the European Union in 1993, a union that is similar to the union (of African states) proposed by Nkrumah some nearly four decades down the line. As visionary as he was, it was in fact ludicrous to Nkrumah how each African nation-state could make socio-economic and political progress in isolation without coordinating strategies on a continental level.

It is through this line of thinking that we see Nkrumah (together with other fellow contemporaries, Hailie Selassie and Sekou Toure, among others) being instrumental in the establishment of the Organisation of African Unity (OAU) on May 25, 1965 with the signing of the OAU Charter by 32 countries in Addis Ababa, Ethiopia. Though the OAU Charter was signed in 1965, OAU was founded in 1963 in Addis Ababa, as an attempt to transform Africa and as a framework for Africa's future socio-economic and political development; a framework that would promote unity and solidarity among states of the continent of Africa. It was, of course, not a body intended on creating one unified federation of African states with a common government for the whole of Africa. However, it was also interested in exterminating colonialism completely from Africa, promoting economic cooperation, and ensuring that Africa spoke with a common voice on the international scene.

In July 2001 in Lusaka, Zambia, OAU changed its name to the African Union (AU) in imitation of the European Union, mostly as a result of Libyan Col. Muammar Gaddafi's latest brainstorm and voicing of the organisation's leaning on Western principles. The 'new' body also decided to establish a continental Central Bank, Court of Justice, parliament, and, in the future, a single currency that would be adopted by all African countries on the continent.

As alluded to above, Nkrumah, in 1963, made strenuous diplomatic efforts to mobiliseAfrican heads of state to accept his concept and proposal of a continental union government for

Africa. The OAU frustrated his aspiration of a greater economic and political integration of the African nation-states, as it respected the notion of the non-inviolability of the colonially inherited borders. He was even surprised as to why African heads of state kept on clinging on the colonially created boarders. In 1964, his contemporary heads of state also rejected his proposalfor an African High Command. His proposed African High Command was targeted to combat what he considered instability in the African continent and neo-colonial Balkanisation. Underpinning these rejections was the belief among some African heads of state that Nkrumah's proposals were too colossal, kitschy and impracticable. Some of the heads even went a step further to think that by tabling these proposals, Nkrumah was in fact demonstrating his own untamed desire for self-enhancement and strategic positioning on the African political stage. Worse still, it is clear that many African leaders during the time of Nkrumah considered African unity as a loss of territorial sovereignty. They believed that such a unity would give rise to an internal interference. Nyerere (1997: 4) revealed of Nkrumah inhis 1997 address on Ghana's 40[th]anniversary, that Nkrumah miscalculated 'the degreeof suspicion and animosity which his crusading passion had created among a substantial number of his fellow Heads of State.'

Besides Nkrumah's writings, his vision of a united Africa is confirmed by other prominent African statesmen like Julius Nyerere. In 1997, Nyerere was invited in Ghana's capital Accra to mark the 40th anniversary of Ghana's independence. He made a very important speech about Kwame Nkrumah's vision on Africa:

> Kwame Nkrumah was the state crusader for African unity. He wanted the Accra summit of 1965 to establish Union Government for the whole of independent Africa. But we failed. The one minor reason is that Kwame, like all great believers, underestimated the degree of suspicion and animosity, which his

crusading passion had created among a substantial number of his fellow Heads of State. The major reason was linked to the first: already too many of us had a vested interest in keeping Africa divided (p. 4).

The grand proposal above was the same as that Murmur Gaddafi had in mind for Africa. He, like Nkrumah, envisioned totally independent pan African financial institutions. His Libyan Investment Authority and the Libyan Foreign Bank were important players in setting up these important institutions. Through the Libyan Foreign Bank and the Libyan Investment Authority, Gaddafi was indeed instrumental in setting up Africa's first satellite network, the Regional African Satellite Communication Organisation (RASCOM) to reduce African dependence on external powers.

Like Nkrumah's proposed grand ideas, Gaddafi's institutions were treated with animosity, umbrage, and resentment by the former European imperialists and institutions such as European Union, International Monetary Fund and the World Bank, which all viewed the union of Africa as a blocking blow to their [European] exploitative tendencies since the trans-Atlantic slave era. These proposed grand ideas were in fact a bitter pill for the rest of the global north especially the capitalists. It was a bitter pill that would possibly reduce Europe to a pauper, poor than what most African countries are conceived today. This is because even after colonialism from which the global north benefitted directly from Africa's resources, it [global north] continues to do so even today through interest gains and exportation of finished products to Africa. And with this realisation, who can ever imagine Europe and the United States accepting to have a test of it?

While the question of African unity has been a major concern of some African political leaders, especially during the period immediately after political independence of several African countries in the late 50s and early 60s, it is unfortunate

176

that many of these leaders had distracted from the idea by the time the whole of Africa was politically independent. In fact by the decade 80 through 90, many of those African political leaders who supported the idea of a United States of Africa now seemed to have changed their minds. At the extraordinary summit meeting held in Libya in September 1999, the members of the then Organisation of African Unity (OAU) discussed methods of increasing the effectiveness of their organisation. Gaddafi suggested the need to establish a United States of Africa there and then but the idea was rejected. As Tieku (2004: 252) argues:

> It came as a surprise to the 33 African leaders attending the Sirte Summit when Gaddafi opened the summit with a presentation of the 'United States of Africa' plan. Equally shocking was his insistence that the plan, which entailed the creation of a continental presidency with a five-year term of office, a single military force, a common African currency, be approved 'there and then.'

Nkrumah's consciencism

The rise of national consciousness in Ghana developed largely in the twentieth-century in response to colonial policies in the country. Nkrumah's vision on African consciousness is quite clear in his lobby of African-centred institutes such as his 1961 established Institute of African Studies in Ghana. Commenting on Nkrumah's visionary dream of an Africa that is conscious of its own being, Ameyaw Debrah (2014: 1) cites Ngugi wa Thiongo who commented:

> The Institute of African Studies, established in 1961 and formally opened in 1963 by the late Dr. Kwame Nkrumah, first president of the Republic of Ghana, is undoubtedly one of the earliest institutes and centres of African centres on the African

continent [...] That Congress aimed to galvanise Africanists, researchers, scholars, and activists in the coordination of energies and resources – material and intellectual – towards the study of the continent and its people, and chart a course for the discipline of African studies.

Emphasising the same point, Ama Biney (2011: 143), one of Britain's outstanding Nkrumah's scholars commented:

> In the course of 1960, Nkrumah felt the need for a "new style secretariat" to deal with Ghana's increasing responsibilities in Africa. This led Nkrumah to set up the BAA, the African Affairs Centre (AAC), and the African Affairs Secretariat (AAS) as institutions parallel to the Ministry of Foreign Affairs. They were considered appropriate agencies for fulfilling his foreign policy objectives. At the same time, there was a rapid expansion in the setting up of overseas diplomatic missions.

Fulfilling his foreign policy objectives, Nkrumah for instance, was instrumental in creating an Institute of African Languages and Culture at the University of Pennsylvania, one of the eight of America's Ivy League institutions of higher learning. Through the parallel institutions he set, Nkrumah could now support liberation struggle movements across Africa. Yet his diplomacy and intellectual legerdemain was not only displayed in politics but even in academia. In 1945, the Lincolnian, a Lincoln University newspaper, voted him the "most outstanding professor-of-the-year."

Nkrumah (1964) believed that African history through the centuries has accumulated much of confused teachings and orientations from external influences: colonial imperialists, Islamic and Euro-Christian elements which resultantly produced equally confusing and conflicting vision of what Africa is and should be. As Nkrumah understands, this situation has been aggravated by the deceptive writing and presentation of African history as a story of Western adventure mainly by the Eurocentric scholars and explorers. This, for Nkrumah, had always negative impact on Africa and the African people such that the need to undertake fully the venture of the unification and liberation of Africa called for totally reformed and revolutionarised philosophical system which he calls *Philosophical Consciencism*. This philosophical system would serve as a "body of connected thought which will determine the general nature of our action in unifying the society which we have inherited, this unification to take account, at all times, of the elevated ideals underlying the traditional African society" (p. 78).

As could be seen from the quote above, Nkrumah was one such visionary leader who called for leaders and ordinary Ghanaians and indeed Africans to demand a voice in the governance and political affairs of their time. In fact, his call for [self-]consciousness was more of a plea for Africans to use the power and reason vested in them for a purpose, the purpose of which was to bring real peace to the world, transform their colonised tainted society into a dynamic, productive, and prosperous one with varied opportunities. To demonstrate his commitment towards peace building and his passion to use power and reason for good purpose, Nkrumah initiated *The Accra Assembly —The World Without the Bomb* as part of the initiatives for peace in this world.

The power and reason for a purpose that Africans were supposed to deploy was unity and consciencism as he believed nothing better than the reason and power to unite and to be conscious of oneself as an African would open up opportunities for Africans. As revealed by Kofi Bentum Quatson (2015), Former National Security Co-ordinator, on 12 April 1962, Kwame Nkrumah made a profound statement to a CPP study group: 'Friends and comrades, Africa needs a new type of man: A dedicated, modest, honest and devoted man: A man who submerges self in the service of his nation and mankind. A man who abhours greed and deters vanity. A new type of man, whose meekness is his strength and whose integrity is his greatness. Africa's new man must be a man indeed.' He called for a socio-political revolution in the emergent independent African nation-states. This revolution was meant to instil a critical thinking approach in Africans with the ultimate goal of redeeming the African humanist society of the past from the vagaries and prejudices of the colonial predators. Nkrumah believed that his notion of consciencism was best placed to achieve this goal. He defined his consciencism as 'the map in intellectual terms of the disposition of forces which will enable African society to digest Western and Islamic and the Euro-Christian elements in Africa, and develop them in such a way that they fit into the African personality. The African personality is in itself defined as 'the cluster of humanist principles which underlie the traditional African society' (Nkrumah 1970: 79). This means that Nkrumah's consciencism was concerned with the broader issue of African personality and African society to ensure that there was progress and permanent peace among all groups of people who were and in fact identified themselves as Africans.

Nkrumah's consciencism and philosophy of only wane with his death in 1966 but was not obliterated to the root. The idea of consciencism, for example, was still greatly needed in many other countries that were still in the bondage of colonialism. Indeed, there was need for Africans in the bondage to realise who actually were they as a people – be conscious of their selves as Africans – and why they were in the situation they were – be conscious that they were under the insult of colonialism – in order for them to stand against imperialism. This was important because as long as Africans did not realise that the ghost of colonialism needed total eradication from the African soil, they would forever remain subdued mentally though might perhaps be physically independent.

It is this realisation that prompted the South African black consciousness leader and one of the greatest martyrs of the anti-apartheid movement, Steve Biko (1946 – 1977) to assert that 'the most potent weapon of the oppressor is the mind of the oppressed' (Biko reprint 2002: 92). He was the principal force behind developing Black Consciousness in the then apartheid South Africa, as a coherent pragmatic philosophy and organising it as a revolutionary movement to dislodge racism and apartheid. Yet, Biko's philosophy did not develop in vacuity. Consciencism had been used to function as the dialectical opposition to colonialism and neo-colonialism in Ghana. Ghana's first president and Africanist intellectual, Kwame Nkrumah (1964: 56) explains the dialectical relationship between environment and ideas when he avers: 'Social milieu affects the content of philosophy and the content of philosophy seeks to affect social milieu, either by confirming it or by opposing it' (p. 56).

Biko, like Nkrumah, strongly believed that political freedom in South Africa and Africa at large could only be achieved if blacks stopped feeling inferior to whites. And for this to be achieved, Biko believed that psychological liberation should precede political liberation. This philosophy which is a philosophy of black consciousness attracted enormous international attention such that it is considered by many to be the turning point in the demise of apartheid. Just like Nkrumah who discontinued his studies in London to pursue the struggle against colonialism in Ghana, Biko gave up studying medicine to devote himself to the struggle against apartheid in South Africa. He founded the Black Consciousness Movement in 1969. But what did Biko mean by his Black consciousness? Biko (2002) defined Black Consciousness in an article for a student leadership seminar as "the realisation by the black man of the need to rally together with his brothers around the cause of their operation – the blackness of their skin – and to operate as a group in order to rid themselves of the shackles that bind them to perpetual servitude [...]. It seeks to infuse the black community with a new found pride in themselves, their efforts, their value systems, their culture, their religion and their outlook to life" (p. 49). In his paper titled: 'The Definition of Black

Consciousness' went on to explain the relationship between consciousness and his emancipator project when he asserts that: "The interrelationship between the consciousness of the self and the emancipatory programme is of paramount importance" (see Biko: ibid).

As Germana (2014) rightfully puts it, central to the project of consciencism, particularly as it applies to Biko, is also the influence of Georg.W.F. Hegel's "lord – bondsman dialectic" and how Biko applied the dialectic to the situation of blacks under apartheid. The lord – bondsman dialectic, introduced by Hegel in the *Phenomenology of Spirit*, involves a struggle for recognition when two independent self-consciousnesses meet. As Hegel himself explains, the consciousness that succumbs to fear of death becomes the bondsman, while the consciousness that overcomes this fear becomes the lord as it conquers fear. The lord desires recognition of his freedom through the bondsman's consciousness. However, this desire is self-defeating because the lord's consciousness cannot be recognised by a consciousness that has no freedom of its own. Biko's principles of Black Consciousness, just like Nkrumah's consciencism, drew [directly or otherwise] from Hegel's concept as he viewed psychological liberation as the first step towards black South African freedom.

This African consciousness we see in Biko had been demonstrated in Ghana by Nkrumah who viewed the colonised African people's consciousness as a means of developing an African way of thinking that would be unique and instil pride not contingent upon the colonialist recognition.

The fall of Kwame Nkrumah

Kwame Nkrumah is dead but alive. He only fell down to rise later. Although dead physically, Nkrumah continues to be revered as the founder of modern Ghana to Ghanaians across the ideological spectrum and beyond.

On 24th February 1966, the government of Kwame Nkrumah was overthrown through a military and police coup d'état. The key figures in this coup d'état were Colonel E.K. Kotoka, Major A.A. Afrifa, and Inspector General of Police J. W. K. Harlleywith Kotoka on the front (Nani-Kofi 2013). When news of the coup reached him, Nkrumah was in Peking (today's Beijing) en route to the Vietnamese capital, Hanoi, with plans to end the American war in Vietnam. He was too far away for a quick return to Ghana where he may have been able to end the military action. Leaders of four African countries sent Nkrumah immediate messages of support and invitations. They were the presidents of Egypt (Gamal Abdel Nasser), Mali (Modibo Keita), Guinea (Sekou Toure), and Tanzania (Julius Nyerere). Nkrumah decided to accept Sekou Toure's invitation as he had a brotherly bond with the later. Nkrumah was even made an honorary co-president of Guinea where he was declared "a universal man." While in Guinea, Nkrumah lived in Conakry. The government of Guinea shared Nkrumah's Pan-African objectives, encompassing the liberation of the African people from all forms of social injustice and economic exploitation (Browne 2007).

However, Ghana's coup had a trail of history that followed it. At local level politics (in Ghana), by the time of his overthrow, Ghana had become a one-party state in which the colours of the one party – the Convention People's Party (CPP) – had become the nation's colours, replacing the national colours. Besides, the coup of 24 February 1966 led to the release of more than 2,000 political detainees, including many long-time detainees with five or six years in prison without trial. The creation of the one-party state – CPP – had been effected through one of the first, if not the first, of the 90% plus "referenda" that came to characterise the results of "referenda" in post-colonial Africa (Otchere-Darko 2014).

On the international stage, it is widely known that in 1965, after a failure of the All Africa Peoples' Conferences due to disturbances at Bamako, Mali, in 1964, to discuss the prosecution of the struggle against neocolonialism, Nkrumah had gone further to write his critical book: *Neo-colonialism – The Last Stage of Imperialism* published the following year, 1965. The book received a serious protest from the USA government. This was then followed by the US Central Intelligence Agency (CIA) influenced coup d'état to overthrow Kwame Nkrumah in 1966 (Seymour 1978; Figueira 2007; Nani-Kofi 2013).

The files of the US Central Intelligence Agency declassified in 1999 show that USA has been trying to influence people to overthrow President Kwame Nkrumah since 1964 (Seymour 1978; Figueira 2007; Nani-Kofi 2013). It is further alleged that the CIA backed coup in Ghana was part of the Cold War conflict of the time as Nkrumah was seen as an ally of Soviet Union and Eastern Europe, both of which were adversaries of the USA during the Cold War. The1966 Coup was an event that affected, in many ways negative, the politics in Ghana thereafter. It marked the first step towards a total shift from all theAfrocentric structures and institutions that Nkrumah worked tirelessly to establish on the continent and beyond.

Yet the question on whether Nkrumah's downfall in 1966 could be linked to his own mismanagement of the economy, his clinging on to power, his dedication to Pan- African unity, and the controversial policies he effected to achieve Ghana's economic growth and Africa's unity remains highly debatable both locally [in Ghana] and beyond. With his grandiose vision for Ghana and Africa, it appears Nkrumah's ideas were far beyond the heads of many of his contemporaries such that he could be easily misread and misunderstood.

From his own understanding and analysis, Nkrumah believed the cause of the coup was totally work of the imperialists and neo-colonialists who, like a crocodile that has tested human blood, did not want to lose their grip on Africa. For Nkrumah, Africa was already a casualty with would inflicted by the crocodile – European colonialists – and the coup was meant to ensure that the wounds of the casualty would never heal. Ghana under Nkrumah's government was one among what Young (1982) characterised as "African Socialism group" or "populist socialism," and Friedland and Rosberg (1964) also characterised as the "first wave" of socialist regimes in the 1960s with many other countries such asTanzania, Algeria, Guinea, Mali, Libya, Egypt,and Tunisia falling in the same category. Nkrumah, thus, did not consider his dictatorial style of political leadership, ambitiousness, and his economic and political miscalculations as having been largely the contributing factors towards his demise. Instead of sitting down and reconsider his socialist stance that had costed him his presidency, Nkrumah believed he had not pursued socialism fast and meticulous enough. Thus, Nkrumah went to his deathbed in 1972 a committed socialist, Pan-Africanist, revolutionarist, internationalist, and self-proclaimed first brand Marxist.

The continued relevance of Kwame Nkrumah's philosophy to Africa

While during the hey days of decolonisation in Africa, the proponents of Nkrumah's philosophy of African unity considered imaginable prospects of various forms of supranational federation in Africa, this realisation died a natural death as time went on. In fact, after Nkrumah was toppled by a coup d'état, forced into exile and eventually died in 1972, the leaders of the independent African states were left without any clue as to who would lead a potential United States of Africa. The major reason for the failure of this grand idea was political will among the African political leaders especially after independence from the Western colonial powers. Most of the leaders that emerged after Africa's political independence found themselves in a comfort zone. They easily forgot or ignored what the proponents of African unity in the 1960s such as Nkrumah envisioned for the good of Africa and the African

185

people. As Cooper (2002: 161) notes "Nkrumah's hopes for a United States of Africa achieved little support from African leaders' intent on protecting the sovereignty they had so strenuously fought for."

The idea of uniting Africa remains more urgent now than ever considering the experience that African nation-states have failed to maximise their national economic development in isolation over the years. There is need to ensure that Africa's raw materials and human resources/brains circulate around the continent. This is because as long as Africa continues allowing its human and natural resources tapped out by the global north capitalists, the continent will be remain impoverished. No wonder while some critics believe that the 1966 coup that ousted Nkrumah from power opened Ghana's doors to democracy, others think otherwise. They think that the coup was a side-blow kick and setback not only to Ghana but to Africa's socio-economic and political progress. June Milne, the former research and editorial assistant to Kwame Nkrumah and later his literary executrix describes, in her blog, the coup as a big drawback to the continent, a coup that set Africa back: 'It is not difficult to imagine the greatly improved condition of the African people today if Nkrumah had continued in power in Ghana to lead the pan-African movement' (Browne 2007).

Nkrumah's ideas against European capitalism and exploitation of Africa continue echoing in the minds of many concerned Africans decades after the publication of Nkrumah's *Neo-colonialism: The last stage of imperialism*. In this book, Nkrumah denounces the exploitative nature of multi-national companies of the West. He also notes that the West's gimmick of making Africa its dependent through foreign aid, debt and exploitation of its natural resources was to impoverish Africa and to ensure that Africa will continue limping and nurturing its colonial wounds for quite some time to come. Ali Mazrui (2004) concurs with Nkrumah as he comments that Nkurumah's *Neo-colonialism: The last stage of imperialism* like Lenin's infamous *Colonialism: The*

186

last stage of capitalism criticises unbridled capitalist expansion and the negative side of Western promulgated globalisation on Africa. Nkrumah, thus, wrote in the introduction of his *Neo-colonialism: The last stage of imperialism* that 'The essence of neo-colonialism is that the State which is subject to it is, in theory, independent and has all the outward trappings of international sovereignty. In reality its economic system and, thus, its political policy is directed from outside' and with the objective to extend the gap between the capitalists and the ordinary or that of the colonialist and the colonised.Part of Nkrumah's project was to see to it that equality between ethnic groups, African nation-states and all other nations are at par without one imposing her values on the other. On this, Nkrumah, like the *Negritude* poet Aime Cesaire's (reprint 2013: 95) verse from *Notebook of a Return to the Native Land* would reason that: "And no race has a monopoly on beauty, on intelligence, on strength and there is room for everyone at the convocation of conquest."

Nkrumah's emancipatory project and his stance against globalisation and its sister forces: colonialism, capitalism and neo-capitalism, are also expressed in his pamphlet he wrote in 1945. In the famous pamphlet entitled: 'Towards Colonial Freedom,' Nkrumah (1962) laid bare his problems with capitalism, colonialism, and neo-colonialism when he wrote:

> The duty of any worthwhile colonial movement for national liberation, however, must be the organisation of labour and of youth; and the abolition of political illiteracy. This should be accomplished through mass political education which keeps in constant contact with the masses of colonial peoples. This type of education should do away with that kind of intelligentsia who have become the very architects of colonial enslavement (p. 41).

Yet Nkrumah's critical treatment of globalisation and other such 'forces' should not be mistaken to mean that Nkrumah was conservative. He was in fact a progressive pedagogist and

187

politician as Cooper tells us. Besides, he was a man with powerful theoretical temperament. In his attempt to forge national unity among different ethnic and religious groups, for example, he advocated the abandonment of tradition and the upholding of modernity and tolerance in both Ghana and many other newly independent African nation-states. Nkrumah, for example, was involved in taking the steps towards the formation of first the African Asian People's Solidarity Organisation (AAPSO) in 1957 and was involved in is expansion to the Organisation of Solidarity with the People of Asia, Africa and Latin America and Latin America in January 1966 not long before his overthrow (Nani-Kofi 2013). Nkrumah, thus, demonstrated that he was not only an Africanist but an internationalist committed to the total liberation of Africans and the African world.

Conclusion

Most of Kwame Nkrumah's political and philosophical ideas have been characterised as controversial, impractical and theoretical by some critics. This means Kwame Nkrumah was not only misunderstood, misread and misinterpreted by his contemporaries. Even scholars today continue discussing his ideas in many spheres ranging from political science to philosophy, culture, history, sociology and African studies.

While misunderstood in many quarters, what seems universally agreeable among scholars even the most unapologetic critics of Nkrumah is that his contribution, at least, to the liberation struggles for independence [or the so-called decolonial project in Africa], identity and self-consciousness of the African peopleas a people remains critical to the African world. Nkrumah personally embodied his philosophical outlook in the struggle against colonialism and neo-colonialism, displaying a consciousness determined to unite and educate Africa and its people. The inclination towards the self-consciousness, identity and the need for a decolonisation [anti-imperialism] process in Africa is evident in many subsequent scholars writing from Africa or in the diaspora. These include, but not limited to, Ngugi wa Thiongo, Walter Rodney, Steve Biko, and Francis Nyamnjoh, among others. Though the works by the aforementioned scholars are not necessarily about Kwame Nkrumah, it remains clear that they touch on the same issues that Nkrumah grappled with, hence the later ignited a flame that will remain shining on the continent for a long time to come.

Chapter 9

African Philosophy, Cultural Identity and Globalisation:
Confronting Fear, Terror, and Uncertainty

"If anything, modern globalisation, which I call 'glo-thwartilisation', in Africa is a bitter pill that one takes with a crinkle face. It has brought more harm than good, more suffering than happiness, more problems than solutions" (Munyaradzi Mawere 2013).

The way that globalisation as a process has attempted to promote unfettered international market of ideas, goods and services among the people, companies, and governments of different nations, is not only associated with positives but also negatives. This has resulted in globalisation being understood as a controversial if not a typically notorious process.

While proponents of globalisation generally argue that it allows developing countries and their citizens to develop socially, economically, and politically to raise their standards of living, the opponents of globalisation have claimed that the process has always benefitted multinational corporations in the global north at the expense of local enterprises, local cultures, and ordinary people in the so-called developing countries. In many countries in Africa, the effects of globalisation have impinged and impacted negatively on the African philosophy and cultural identities of the African people. Put differently, globalisation has instilled fear of the unknown, uncertainty and sometimes terror as some people feel that their cultures are being supplanted and replaced with foreign values and philosophies. This realisation has resulted in the resistance to globalisation taking shape both at local and governmental levels as well as continental level as the African people and their

191

respective governments try to manage the flow of ideas, goods and services that constitute the current trend and package of globalisation.

This chapter examines the matrix existent between African philosophies and cultural identity as the African people respond to the effects of globalisation. The chapter tries to suggest how the degree of uncertainties and fear of the unknown among those cultures, especially in Africa that feel their values and philosophies are being undermined by the process of globalisation, could be averted or at least minimised.

African philosophy as the birth-bed of African cultural identity

In the previous chapters, we have discussed at length what philosophy and African philosophy are all about. We have tried to demonstrate that African philosophy is the birth bed of African cultural identity while African culture itself is the birth bed of African philosophy. But how is this possible and indeed the case?

In response to the question raised above, it could be noted that any philosophy is drawn from a particular cultural orientation. There is no philosophy without elements of culture from where it is rooted. Similarly, cultural identity emanates from the general philosophy of a society where it is drawn from. This means that the baseline of cultural identity of a particular people is their philosophy of life. It can therefore be noted that there is a relational network between culture and philosophy vis-à-vis cultural identity.

The relational amity of culture and philosophy is made possible by the fact that all humans are endowed with the powers to experience the world from a particular orientation, to imagine, think and reason. In fact no reasoning being can exist without a culture and therefore a philosophy as the latter is dependent and achieved through experience and reasoning. This entails that no human society can be denied a culture. Neither can it be denied a philosophy as racist thinkers like Kant, Hume and Hegel, among others, believed of other societies such as those of Africa.

The denial of philosophy to the people of other societies was a crime against humanity that should not only be condemned but challenged now and forever. It is not only denial of a people of their philosophy but of their cultural identity. It is a crime with the same gravity as denying a child his/her parents. That child will grow like a tree in a desert where nourishment is always a problem. The tree will not take long before it succumbs to death as a result of lack of nutrients and water besides the scorching heat.

As reasoned here and other chapters of this book, the fact that African people have a philosophy as has been proven beyond doubt in writing and verbal debates by African philosophers mean that they also have a cultural identity based on their cultural orientation. This characteristic is not only unique to the African people but to people of other cultures such as those of Europe, Asia and America. African culture, for example, is the birth bed of African philosophy while the later plays a fundamental role in enriching African cultural identity. The latter is definitive and unique to the people of Africa such that it can be used to distinguish them from people of other societies. The distinction of one people from another, thus, is possible not only on the basis of differences in their biological make-ups or physical appearances that may exist between them. Let us give another example to illustrate this point. The cultural identity of the Ndebele people of Zimbabwe can be used to distinguish them from the Shangani of Mozambique regardless of the fact that the two groupsshare similar physical appearance besides that they both originated from the Nguni of the South before they established their chiefdoms in different geographical spaces. These people have different cultural identities based on their perceptions, physical environment, belief systems and experiences as a people.

By identity we mean the fact of being what or who one is.In the Western philosophical tradition, the idea of identity is accredited to John Locke. For Locke (1999: 311), identity consists in:

> When we see anything to be in any place in any instant of time, we are sure that it is that very thing, and not another which at that same time exists in another place, how like and undistinguishable so ever it may be in all other respects: and in this consists identity, when the ideas it is attributed vary not at all from what they were that moment wherein we consider their former existence, and to which we compare the present [...] when, therefore, we demand whether anything be the same or not, it refers always to something that existed such a time in such a place, which it was certain, at that instant, was the same with itself, and no other.

Basing on this understanding, Locke (1999) distinguishes between qualitative and numerical identity. For him, a thing's qualitative identity comprises its defining properties, that is, properties that one must mention in a fullanswer to the question "Who am I?" or "What is it?"

Though it has some elements of choice, identity is normally something to do with our consciousness of what and who we are as well as why we are what and who we are. Besides, when related to human beings, it is the essential or quintessential aspects that make human beings what they are (and not trees for example) as distinguished from other beings or things. It is one with itself, consistent and divided from others. As underlined above, identity makes it possible to ask and answer one of the most important metaphysical questions: "Who are we/ Who am I? What do we have in common – making this person look the same as myself – and different but different at the same time?" The latter question tries to capture and explain the fact that identity marks differences between things or people but can also be shared: identity is marked by both difference and similarity. This is why we also have what Oliver (2011) calls diachronic identity, that is, identity of the same thing, X, across time as opposed to numerical identity over time which is what makes X at one time the same person as Y at another. In human beings, the differences and similarities in identity could be in terms of language, skin colour, biological, cultural, and sexual orientation, among others.

The foregoing implies that all things have, in some ways, different identities that distinguish them from others. For instance, the qualities of matter, referred to in traditional metaphysics as accidents, such as size, colour, shape etcetera, distinguish one being from the other (Njoku, 2002).In the case of human beings, they have for example, moral/spiritual identity, physical identity and cultural identity. This means that identity can be both personal and collective. It is personal when it is about oneself by virtue of him/her being a human being. It often means some sort of immaterial subject of consciousness – the self – observable when the question "Who am I" or that of personhood is raised. This is in line with the first principle of being which states that every being is determined in itself, is one with itself and is consistent with itself. The knowledge of identity of things is important not only in metaphysics as a philosophical discipline but even in real life. It helps us to understand and know what a thing in question really is and what can legitimately be (not)-attributed to it at any given time.

On the other hand, identity is collective when it is shared among a group. For example, if certain norms, values and traditions are shared by a group, the end result is cultural identity, that is, identity that will be shared by a group of people based on their cultural orientations.

As underlined above, cultural identity differs from society to society based on the society's culture and philosophy – way of life. Similarities between groups, therefore, should be treated as coincidence not universality of culture. Thus, we have African cultural identity that is distinct from Asian, European or American cultural identity. It is important to note that this identity should be defined and maintained. Failure to do so will result in people risking being indescribable actors such that naming them becomes impossible. In fact without identity *zvose zvinenge ava madirativhange* meaning everything will be everything. This is why in many societies processes such as globalisation are negatively conceived as threatening the cultural identities of their people.Benjamin (2010) observes that for centuries, there have been systematic and ruthless attempts to deny Africanpeople the fundamental human right of self-determination and self-identity.This denial gave rise to the birth of the so-called "Black Consciousness Movement" in the Pan-African world as a serious attempt towards the reaffirmation and restoration of the identity of Africa and the African people.

In many contemporary subaltern societies of the world, for example, cultural identities are perceived as being threatened in one way or another mainly as a result of what we call 'modern' globalisation. By modern globalisation, henceforth referred to as globalisation, we mean the process of globalisation as initiated and propagated by the global north – Euro-America. Yet not only is the realm of cultural identity of the subaltern societiesthat is feeling the heat. Many other sectors such as politics and economics of societies are also affected, either negatively or positively. In the section below, we explore this matrix further in relation to Africa.

Globalisation and Africa

Globalisation, both as a concept and as a process, has been notoriously understood. This diverse understanding of globalisation has resulted in it being positively accredited by some while negatively conceived by others.

Those who look at globalisation with positive lens perceive it as a process that connects all people across the world; a process that leaves out no one outside. Roland Robertson (1992), for example, understands globalisation as the compression of the world and the intensification of the consciousness of the world as a whole. Martin Albrow and Elizabeth King (1990: 8) conceptualise globalisation as "all those processes by which the peoples of the world are incorporated into a single world society." For them [Albrow and King], advances in transportation and telecommunication infrastructure, including the rise of the telegraph to the development of internet are the major strides that globalisation as a process has made over the years. For Andre Gunder Frank (1998), such developments are positive in that they generate further interdependence of economic and cultural activities. Thomas Larsson (2001) also views globalisation from a positive perspective. For him, globalisation "is a process of world shrinkage, of distances getting shorter, things moving closer. It pertains to the increasing easiness with which somebody on one side of the world can interact, to mutual benefit, with somebody on the other side of the world" (p. 9). In short, globalisation shortens distance, directly or indirectly, between actors around the world.

Other scholars who view globalisation from the narrow perspective of economics also perceive globalisation as a positive process. Jagdish (2004: 3), for example, sees globalisation as a typically economic process, thus, as: "the integration of national economies into the international economy through trade, foreign direct investment, capital flows, migration and the spread of technology." Similarly, Ihuah (2006) views globalisation largely but narrowly from an economic perspective thus:

> Globalisation may be said to be the process of integrating scientific technology across borders with the intention of increasing productivity and high returns. Expectedly, globalisation is becoming the society's main productive force and the decisive

factor of the increase in labour and productivity for transnational corporation (TNCs). Thus, globally intertwined and connected, humanity is today living an e-life (p. 37).

However, other scholars who have, over the years, witnessed the 'negative' effects of globalisation scrunch their faces as soon as they hear about globalisation. Ekwuru (1999), for example, describes globalisation as cultural atrophy or forced acculturation whereby some cultures are being swallowed-up by others. He notes that the cultures that tend to swallow-up others are those from the global north which normally consider themselves as superior to other cultures especially those from the so-called third world countries. This means that for Ekwuru, one of the greatest consequences of globalisation is that it is spelling doom of the "weaker" indigenous cultures the same way colonialism did. Viewing it this way, Ekwuru sees no benefit associated with globalisation especially as far as the so-called third world countries are concerned. There is no symbiotic relationship as far as the equation of integration and sharing of values, goods and services is concerned.

Ekwuru is not alone in this camp. Others like Aborishade (2002) describe globalisation as Western imperialism that seeks to impose its hegemony on nations once subjugated by colonialism; what Waters (1995) describes as the direct consequence of the expansion of European culture across the planet via settlement, colonisation, and cultural mimesis. For Aborishade as with Waters, globalisation, thus, is an extension of Western colonialism perpetuated in the guise of passion for international connection. Understood as such, globalisation is no doubt inherently bound upwith capitalistic development pattern which is also grounded and ramified through cultural and political subjugation. On the basis of an understanding as this enunciated here, Aborishade goes a step further to criticise globalisation for being an under-current with the hidden agenda of widening the gap between the rich and the poor to the extent that the rights of the latter end up being thwarted and invisible from the global stage.

Yet, there are others who view globalisation as neither a positive nor a negative process. For these scholars, the goodness or badness of globalisation depends on how it is conceptualised, translated, and practically implemented in societies. Munyaradzi Mawere (2014), for example, who talks about what globalisation ideally should be, understands it as a "process of *equal* international interactions of all kind whereby societies or nation-states *fairly* share their cultures, goods, capital, services, and information among themselves" (p. 8). Mawere is, thus, underlining that if globalisation is to be understood as a fair, equal and neutral process, the integration process of societies into a common system should be done with the consent of all the societies involved and with the ultimate goal of achieving equal benefit for all stakeholders or actors involved. As long as there is no consent, fairness, and equality between actors involved, the process, for Mawere, no longer fits to be considered as globalisation but "glo-thwartilisation" (see for instance, Mawere 2013). It is glo-thwartilisation because some cultures/societies especially those perceived as inferior are not afforded equal opportunities but forcibly have their values subjugated, engulfed and erased from the global scene by those perceived as superior. By glo-thwartilisation, Mawere thus, mean the process aimed at silencing or erasing other cultures from the global stage in the false name of globalisation: it is globalisation by exclusion or elimination; a process that started in the modern times with its apparent indicators manifested during trans-Atlantic slave trade and colonialism. Such observations have also led Mawere (2015: 1) to argue that "globalisation is attractive and sometimes beautiful. It is, however, no proof against imperialism. It is no proof against foreign domination. It is no proof against cultural atrophy." This is in sync with his earlier observation that modern "globalisation is a bitter pill that one takes with a crinkle face. A bitter pill has a double effect: It may (or may not) heal the ailing body but at the same time pains the body that takes it" (Mawere 2013; see also Mawere 2015: Ibid). No wonder some other scholars like Maduagwu (1999: 6) believe that "Africa seems to have no place in the globalising New World Order." Yet understood ideally, globalisation as a process is neither good nor bad as its goodness or badness depends on how the process takes place and shapes the society in question. It remains good as long as it leaves in the hands of other cultures to choose what to take from it, and becomes bad as soon as it seeks to universalise certain values at the detriment of others by forcing, directly or otherwise, other cultures to replace what belongs to them with foreign values.

But when did globalisation as a process started? Is it a new phenomenon that started in the so-called modern times or it has always been there? These questions like the conceptualisation of globalisation itself are problematic and confusing.

While some scholars ascribe the origins of globalisation in Africa to the so-called modern times, others like Mawere (2014) trace its history, at least in Africa, to the period long before the European Age of discovery, expeditions and adventures came to the scene. In fact, for Mawere, globalisation is not new to Africa besides its increased scale in terms of intensity, velocity and impact in the modern times: globalisation has always been taking place well before the coming of Europeans to Africa given that there has always been human interaction, intermarriages, and trading between the various African ethnic groups/societies across the continent. Besides, trading between Africa, Asia and India started well before the 15th and 16th centuries when Europeans made important discoveries in their exploration of the oceans including the trans-Atlantic travel to the "New World" of the Americas that was historically marked by the accidental landing and "discovery" of Christopher Columbus of the latter [America] in 1492 on his way to Asia (the Indies). The overland Silk Road that connected Asia, Africa and India suffice to substantiate the claim that globalisation took place in the Old

World Africa. Also, the existence of Africans known as the Jarawa in the Island of Andaman in India is a clear testimony of the existence of globalisation in Africa, as elsewhere, prior to the European contact with Africa. The Jarawa people are believed to have been stranded in the Andaman Island and stayed there forever, but nobody knows how these people got there. Other scholars like Frank (1998) even trace the origins of globalisation to the third millennium BCE. No wonder scholars such as Anthony Giddens (1991: 64) understand globalisation as "the intensification of worldwide social relations which link distant localities in such a way that local happening are shaped by events occurring many miles away and vice versa."

However, large scale globalisation is believed to have started in the 19th and 20th centuries through technological development of new forms of transport and later electronic communications such as mobile phones and the internet (see O'Rourke *et al.* 2000). In the 19th century, globalisation grew faster than has ever been imagined through the intersection of four interrelated sets of "communities of practice" namely, academics, journalists, publishers and libraries (James and Steger 2014). This resonates with the International Monetary Fund's (IMF) (2000) findings that identified four basic aspects of globalisation namely, trade and transactions, capital and investment movements, migration and movement of people, and the dissemination of knowledge. We should underline, however, that not only positive movements are associated with globalisation. Environmental challenges such as global warming, air pollution, pollution of trans-boundary rivers, and over-fishing are all connected to globalisation (see also Bridges 2002).

Now in view of African philosophy, questions bordering on African identity arise as soon as we examine globalisation visa-a-vis cultural identity. These are: What is Africa? What does it mean to be an African? Who qualifies as an African? How can an African be distinguished from a person from other continent?

A quick note of these questions seems to tell one that answers to these questions are obvious. Surely, one can say everyone knows what Africa is, who an African is, and what distinguishes an African from a person of other continents. The answer to these questions, however, becomes less obvious once we factor in the issue of globalisation, particularly what we call in this book 'modern' globalisation as initiated and promulgated by the global north. Technological developments in the past few decades have stimulated increases in migration, international investment in the so-called developing countries, and cross-border trade, among other indicators. As revealed by Suny Global Workforce Project (2015), the volume of world trade has increased by 20 times since the 1950s, and from just 1997 to 1999, flows of foreign investment nearly doubled, from $468 billion to $827 billion. This increased wave of globalisation has provoked scholars like Friedman (2005) to describe current globalisation as farther, faster, cheaper, and deeper.

What is perturbing and most unsettling, however, is the fact that the current wave of globalisation has been driven not only by policies that have opened economies domestically and internationally but also international politics. In the past three decades, for example, many African governments have been "forced" to adopt free-market economic systems such as the Economic Structural Adjustment Programmes (ESAPS) with the view that these will vastly increase their productive potential while creating new opportunities for their people. Through these economic policies adopted in the name of globalisation and liberalisation of economies, many African governments have negotiated thespian reductions in hitches to commerce and set-up international agreements to foster trade in goods, services, and investment. These policies have, however, impacted negatively on many African countries such as Zimbabwe, South Africa and Mozambique, among others, as they have resulted in massive retrenchment and/or loss of jobs and abject poverty among the masses. Instead of benefitting African people, the policies seemed to have worked in favour of the global north that duped African countries to adopt the nefarious policies. The envisaged opportunities were capitulated by the global north, which on realising the escalating poverty levels and cataclysmic downfall of African economies as a result of the policies, were quick to move into dumping their processed and second-hand goods to Africa. Due to the impoverished state of the African governments as a result of the ESAPS, it also became easier for the global north's firms to build foreign factories and establish production and marketing arrangements with Africa thereby increasing the dependence of the latter on the global north.

As enunciated by the Suny Global Workforce Project (2015), technology has been the other principal driver of globalisation across the world. Advances in information technology, for example, have dramatically transformed the world economic life of all stakeholders—governments, consumers, investors, business corporations—enhancing them with valuable new approaches and tools for reaching out and pursuing different economic opportunities around the world. Unfortunately, countries that seem to have benefited more and continue to do so are those from the global north. This has instilled some fear and a sense of uncertainty on the part of societies such as those of Africa. Most of these societies have tended to view globalisation as another terrorising wave of imperialism with the same venom as that of trans-Atlantic slave trade and colonialism. We focus more this in the ensuing sections.

Globalisation: Fear, terror and uncertainty

As underlined in the preceding discussion, globalisation is a deeply controversial process. Proponents of globalisation argue that it allows poor countries and their citizens to develop economically and raise their standards of living, while opponents of globalisation claim that the creation of an unfettered international free market has benefited multinational corporations in the global north at the expense of local enterprises, local cultures, and common people in global south (see also Suny Global Workforce Project, 2015). The latter view is adequate to generate fear and cultivate a sense of uncertainty in the hearts of people in the global south. They remain suspicious of globalisation as a process initiated especially by actors from the north. Nicely put in the words of Isawa Elaigwu (1997: 7), "the Western values, politics and business culture are being powerfully transmitted across nations; while their concepts of democracy, human rights, market economy and life styles are being disseminated around the world as models." This massive transmission of the Western values, politics, cultures and models in the name of globalisation is understood by many critics as a form of terrorism; a purely an attempt to spread Western culture with its attendant capitalist socio-economic political tinge to thwart other competing cultures. Malcom Waters (1995: 3) captures this brilliantly when he argues:

> Globalisation is the direct consequence of the expansion of European culture across the planet via settlement, colonisation and cultural mimesis. It is also bound up intrinsically with the pattern of capitalist developments as it has ramified through political and cultural arenas.

Waters's argument makes it crystal clear that Western culture, just like American culture, is terrorising other cultures in so far as it is increasingly establishing itself as the measuring yardstick in which all other world cultures must be either viewed or standardised. In fact, the Western world mistakenly and falsely perceives itself (and imposes the same perception on others) as the most developed of all cultures. We argue with Kwasi Wiredu that even the West is underdeveloped when considering its social, moral, and political structures. In his famous essay entitled, "How Not to Compare African Thought with Western Thought," Wiredu suggests that "development," in its most fundamental sense, is measured by "the degree to which rational methods have penetrated thought habits" (Wiredu 1995: 163) and not the technological and scientific advancements as is the case today. If we think of development in these terms, Wiredu further argues, it becomes crystal clear that the West remains underdeveloped, perhaps the most underdeveloped continent in the world, in many key areas of thought, despite its advanced state with respect to knowledge ofthe natural world. Summarising his position, Wiredu (1995) thus says:

> The Western world is "developed," but only relatively. Technological sophistication is only one aspect, and that not the core, of development. The conquest of the religious, moral and political spheres by the spirit of rational inquiry remains [. . .] a thing of the future even in the West. From this point of view, the West may be said to be still underdeveloped (p.163).

Following this line of thinking, we argue that globalisation is nothing other than power politics at play as was with the case of colonialism: it is a political game played in the name of science and technology which are often considered as the barometer of success in the global world. This scientific and technological barometer of success is also evident in the often repeated observation that it was science, after all, that allowed a relatively small number of Europeans to colonise a much larger number of Africans (Owomoyela 1991: 162-63). No wonder Aluko, Akinola and Sola (2004) perceive globalisation as the renewed attempt to consolidate the re-colonisation process of formerly colonised societies. The trio further observes that every element of the current crisis (in many African countries) of collapse of industries, educational and health facilities, infrastructure, public security, environmental degradation, inflation, escalating debt bill, weakening of the currency, is traceable to the renewed attempt to consolidate the re-colonisation process by the West and the Americas. Aluko *et al*, thus, agree with Waters that Euro-American culture, thus, is promoting "global identities" which we challenge in this book as imprudent given that they result in unfounded and baseless individuals who believe to be progressive when in actual fact they are trapped between ignorance and self-denial. This disrupts traditional identities in many cultures especially the once marginalised and subjugated ones such as those of Africa. We argue that such a scenario is more of dogmatic naiveté that sends signals of a chilling quiver to all non-Western cultures such that for the latter, globalisation requires a counter-force to neutralise its venom as we never know where its impacts are heading us to. From an empirical perspective, there have been undoubtedly clear observable changes in African cultures especially among the young generation, most of which are negative. The negative aspects surrounding these changes especially among the youths are aptly captured by Oni (2005) who observes that African youths are rapidly losing touch with their cultural values as this is seen in the alien culture they portray; their bizarre dressing, dancing and language, which invariably affect other aspects of social life. Nicolaides (2012) makes a similar observation about South African youths:

> The younger generation of teenagers in South Africa has for the most part abandoned their African culture and language, and often religion and try to be hip by imitating their mainly American rap artist role models who for most part display an acute lack of values and act immorally on television shows and who promote promiscuous behaviour especially in the lyrics of the music they write (p. 123).

In fact, what Nicolaides argues makes a lot of sense given that youths are supposed to promote their culture while helping transmitting it from one generation to another. It becomes painful and even deplorable especially to culturalists when the youths fail to play this important role: it will a betrayal of their own culture. Bello and Adesemoye (2012: np) observed:

> Teenagers and youths generally are vital segments of the society who could be instrumental in promoting African culture and morals. But unfortunately, the mentality and lifestyle of the teenagers and youths in African societies have been grossly affected by exposure to Western films to some extent rather than promoting African cultures, they have become hardened acolytes and promoters of Western culture.

Such is the same observation that Ogunjimi and Na'Allah (2005: 36) make before arguing that peculiar African cultural values are being eroded by the pop culture, greeting norms, cuisine (appearance and dress), customs, occupations, religion, and cultural components brought about by globalisation. Leaving globalisation, as instituted from the global north, spreading its tentacles in the African soils is as good as risking sleeping around with an HIV infected person. If unchecked, it will remain a threat to cultures, politics and economies of those in the global south.

Through the realisation in many subaltern societies that it is not only individual persons who can be oppressed but also nation-states depending on their position within the global geo-political order, resistance to globalisation has begun taking shape both at a popular and at a governmental level as people and governments attempt to controland manage the flow of information, capital, labour and goods that constitute the current wave of globalisation. In their bid to resist globalisation while trying to promote unity and solidarity among Africans, African leaders have formed organisations such as African Union (AU) besides economic blocks such as South African Development Cooperation (SADC) and East African Community (EAC), among others. Singling out the formation of the AU, this was of course, a step in the right direction despite the fact that AU has done nothing much to liberate its people from the shackles of neo-colonialism, elite imperialism, and Western dependency. In fact, suffice to note, the AU has become a moribund body due to its fiasco to liberate Africa from neocolonialism and socio-economic overdependence. Besides, the AU has failed to unite Africa since its historic portioning by European imperialists in 1884.

Coming back to the question on globalisation, one continues to wonder how fear and anxiety generated by globalisation in lieu of Africa could be allayed. We argue in this book that in order to dispel fear and anxiety in African citizens, African leaders, on behalf of the people of Africa, should make sure that the continent strikes a balance between costs and benefits associated with globalisation. In fact citizens of all nations, whether in Africa or beyond, need to understand how globalisation works and should be actively involved in the policy choices facing them and their societies. This would give all stakeholders the chance to bargain, contribute and analyse possible effects of globalisation on their respective societies and make choices from an informed position. That way, fear and anxiety are dealt with before globalisation as a process is possibly declared a terrorist agent by some sectors of the world. Most importantly, globalisation will be freed from all its Western and American ideological biases and conceptual controversies currently associated with it.

African philosophy, renaissance and education: Neutralising globalisation

After the trans-Atlantic slave trade, colonialism, and subsequent independence of African nation-states from European imperialism, neo-colonialism in the form of 'modern' globalisation or what Mawere (2013) calls *glo-thwartilisation* seems to have caused importunate headache to Africa and the African people. As such, the current wave of globalisation has compelled

Africa to rethink its position in terms of geopolitics, its cultural-economic and philosophical status in the global world order. With the increasing realisation that globalisation is fast threatening African cultures, philosophies and even economies, there has been a burgeoning call by critical thinkers for Africa to redefine itself and respond accordingly to globalisation as instituted from the global north. This realisation has enlivened the spirit and talk of *African Renaissance* amongst scholars and politicians on the African continent. The African Renaissance Institute (2000) defines African Renaissance as:

> A shift in the consciousness of the individual to re-establish our diverse traditional African values, so as to embrace the individual's responsibility to the community and the fact that he or she, in community with others, together are in charge of their own destiny (p. 1).

The concept of renaissance has been subject to debate among African scholars for quite some time, with some arguing that it is borrowed from experiences unique to Europe and not Africa, therefore, rendering it out of context in Africa. Thabo Mbeki formally re-introduced the term *African Renaissance* in his address to the Corporate Council on Africa in Chantily, VA, USA, in April 1997 and later in a meeting held on September 28 and 29of 1998, in Johannesburg, South Africato address academics, politicians and business people in Africa (Mbeki 1998). As Mbeki informed attendees, the main objectives of the meeting in Johannesburg was to define "who we are and where we are going in the global community, and to formulate practical strategies and solutions for future action that would benefit the African masses" and help the indigenous systems in different sectors of African life with theoretical frameworks, definitions and objectives to resist globalisation while promoting African philosophy and renaissance (Makgoba 1999: xiii-xxi).

What is worth noting in the two meetings by Mbeki is that his speeches provided a motto of an African vision widely embraced by majority of the participants. He emphasised the need to resist globalisation by establishing and advancing development frameworks and agendas that make Africa a sturdy competitor and not a dependent in the global world economy. Mbeki like other scholars such as Stephen Ejanam (2007), thus, sees modern globalisation as counterproductive and anti-African. Ejanam recapturing the nostalgic feeling of traditional African communalism and the role it plays in societal development and promotion of justice and unity had this to say:

> With this prevalent sense of community amongst the people, all forms of greedy tendencies are shunned. Cohesion is enhanced and ensured as well as the being of the individuals through greetings, friendship, hospitality, brotherhood and co-operation. As communalism takes root in any society, justice is accorded its right place, life becomes peaceful, and the individual develops in appropriate ways in the community (Ibid: 399).

The focus of Mbeki's speech, thus, was directed at economic growth, social and human capital, modern economic and social infrastructure, the cancellation of Africa's debt, Africa and world trade, domestic and foreign investment, Africa and foreign aid, and most importantly the need to resist globalisation as instituted by the global north. He banked so much on the educated Africans to reverse Africa's situation. This is clear in his speech, set objectives, and proposed strategy Mbeki where he avers:

> I am convinced that a great burden rests on the shoulders of Africa's intelligentsia to helpus to achieve these objectives [...] we have arrived at the point where the enormous brain power which our continent possesses must become a vital instrument in helping us tosecure our equitable space within a world affected by a rapid

process of globalisation and from which we cannot escape (Mbeki 1999: xiii-xxi).

As revealed in his words above, Mbeki like many other Africans and pro-African scholars' movements such as negritude and Pan-Africanism, is concerned with the 'negative' effects of globalisation and the need for the restoration of the African dignity. While others sees the wave of globalisation as more of an unstoppable tornado, Mbeki however, remain convinced that as long as the African educated elite is committed to restore African dignity, define Africa's future and compete with the educated from other continents, the negative effects of globalisation will be easily wiped out and overcome. On this note, Mbeki saw African Renaissance as an essential ingredient necessary for African scholars to embrace in order to help reflect on how to bargain and position Africa equitably and squarely with the other continents in the world in view of politics, cultures and economics. We underscore here that the emphasis of Mbeki on the need to embrace African Renaissance should not be underestimated. It should be understood as a call to reclaim a Pan-African identity that help fostering socio-economic growth and restore the dignity of the African people. This is important as a person without identity is like a tree without roots. Ayi Kwei Armah (1973: 7) captures this aptly when he argues that "a people losing sight of origins, are dead. A people deaf to purpose are lost. Under fertile rain, in scorching sunshine there is no difference: Their bodies are mere corpses, awaiting final burial." We agree with Armah that a person who loses sight of his own origins is similar to a mere corpse that awaits burial. This resonates with Mbeki's argument that our future is in our own hands: we determine our own destiny. Mbeki, thus, is right when he argues that the future of Africa partly lies in the hands of the educated elite and everyone who is African. Education cannot be left out in the journey towards the full recognition of African identity and restoration of the

African people as it helps with reflective tools to map up the new envisioned Africa. Stressing the role and importance of education in restoring African dignity and redefining the hopes and aspirations of the African people for a new envisioned Africa, Walter Rodney (1981) had this to say:

> Education is crucial in any type of society for the preservation of the lives of its members and the maintenance of the social structure ... The most crucial aspect of pre-colonial African education was its relevance to Africans in sharp contrast with that which was later introduced (that is, under colonialism) ... [T]he main purpose of colonial school system was to train Africans to participate in the domination and exploitation of the continent as a whole ... Colonial education was education for subordination, exploitation, the creation of mental confusion and the development of underdevelopment (p. 263).

Ngugi wa Thiongo (1998: 98-99) advocates the same when he argues:

> What is needed is a revolt by all those trained in the traditions of the Macaulay system to reconnect with the dwellers of the colonial and neo-colonial caves and together develop strategies and tactics for breaking free. Such intellectuals, writing and talking in the languages that the people can speak and understand, could then bring all the wealth of their contacts with the languages of the world to enrich theirs.

As evidenced in Wa Thiong'o's advocated freedom, the interpreter should engage with other interpreters if s/he is to construct a meaningful freedom that is understandable to the marginalised, disadvantaged, and oppressed and those remained trapped in the caprices of colonialism.

One way of attaining such freedom as advocated by Wa Thiongo is to sensitise people of the need to promote the use of indigenous languages as equals or even preferred languages to foreign imperialist ones in education or what we call here the indigenisation of African educational system. Mazrui captures this aptly when he argues:

> No country has ascended to a first rank technological and economic power by excessive dependence on foreign languages. Japan rose to dazzling industrial heights by the Japanese language and making it the medium of its own industrialisation. Korea has approximately scientificated the Korean language and made it the medium of its own technological take-off. Can Africa ever take-off technologically if it retains so overwhelmingly European languages for discourse on advanced learning? (Key Note Address, 22-27 April 1996).

Mazrui, like ourselves, is concerned that in African countries' talent is thwarted and remain imperceptible as a result of the continual use of foreign languages that are far-removed from the realities of children. He encourages that children be taught in indigenous languages to promote African philosophy, African Renaissance, and pan-Africanism as well as restoration and retainment of African dignity and cultural identity, thus, argues:

> In secondary schools in Africa the literature taught to many African children issometimes still European literature. But what is more to the point is that the Africanliterature taught to African school children is almost never in indigenous languages. TheEuropean Other haunts the African Self from a young age in a post-colonial school. Have we been witnessing a clash of civilisations in African schools? Or does literature provide a cover for dependency? (Ibid).

Mazrui as with Ngugi wa Thiongo, thus, sees language as an emancipatory instrument if used to the advantage of the marginalised and the oppressed – what Frantz Fanon (1961) calls "the wretched of the earth". It enables people to develop themselves and their societies in almost all respects and aspects of life. Pixley ka Isaka Seme sums it all in his speech when he argues:

> The regeneration of Africa means that a new and unique civilisation is soon to be added to the world. The African is not a proletarian in the world of science and art. He has precious creations of his own, of ivory, of copper and of gold, fine, plated willow-ware and weapons of superior workmanship. Civilisation resembles an organic being in its development-it is born, it perishes, and it can propagate itself. More particularly, it resembles a plant, it takes root in the teeming earth, and when the seeds fall in other soils new varieties sprout up. The most essential departure of this new civilisation is that it shall be thoroughly spiritual and humanistic -indeed a regeneration moral and eternal! (*The African Abroad*, April 5, 1906).

In view of the foregoing discussion we argue that it is through a distinguished philosophy, language and education of a people that they can re-interpret their history and culture, reclaim their lost dignity, seriously contemplate and invent alternative versions of their histories and philosophies, and bargain equally and purposefully in the whole mantra of globalisation. This is germane to what Olabiyi Yai (1997: 96) calls for when he constantly declares the wish to see: "established in Africa an autonomous, theoretical and *practical* debate, which would be the master of its problems and its themes rather than simply being a distant appendage to Western theoretical and *practical* debates." Thus, there is no way Africa could be an equal partner in globalisation as long as it continues to embrace foreign languages as medium of communication, despise its own philosophies and education curricular.

Conclusion

While globalisation connects the world and makes life easier in many ways discussed in this chapter, there is no doubt that it is increasingly becoming a threat in the so-called developing world such as Africa. The threats that globalisation pose to Africa challenge Africans to adopt development policies that are largely if not wholly rooted in their cultural value systems if they are to build a strong African edifice. The threats, in fact, challenge Africans to develop their own development models and frameworks that take into account contemporary African realities as manifested in their philosophies, languages, and traditional curricula of life. It is only these truly African laden frameworks and models that would seriously eradicate poverty and underdevelopment in the continent while making Africa competitive and allowing it to globalise its philosophies and cultures in the face of increasingly globalised European and American cultures. Besides, the truly African laden frameworks and models will afford Africa with the opportunity to wean itself from European and American dependency while promoting and strengthening interdependence among African nations.

Chapter 10

Democracy and Human Rights Talk: Africa's Post-colonial Challenge

Introduction

The present chapter advances the argument that democracy and human rights are contested and highly controversial terms not only when applied to Africa. This is chiefly because they can be conceptualised from a myriad of often conflicting perspectives given the diversity that currently characterise the planet earth. A closer scrutiny at the history of these terms reveals that there is generally no common position regarding their meaning and most importantly applicability. It is the contention of this chapter to further the argument that democracy and human rights should be understood in relation to one's cultural and ideological background. This means that there is no blanket approach to democracy and human rights issues. In fact, there is no one size fits all approach to the understanding of democracy and human rights. It is not an exaggeration to point out that the way democracy is understood in the West is obviously different from the way it is understood in Africa and other parts of the world. Understood this way, the West while acknowledging the ideological gap between them and Africa, should not by whatever means necessary, impose their understanding of democracy and human rights to the rest of humanity and Africa in particular. Failure to take cognisance of the fact that Europe and Africa are separate continents with different human beings accustomed to different beliefs and values has caused the West to make the alleged claim that there are no human rights and democracy in Africa. What we mean is that, there is Western democracy in as much as there is African democracy. In short, African democracy should be understood in the context of Africa, while Western democracy should be understood in the context of Europe and America. The problem that currently obtains is that Europe and America based on their hegemonic and superiority complex; believe that their understanding of democracy should be universalised. Yet, the same people out rightly accept the existence of diversity. Diversity takes note of epistemological differences based on differential cultural grooming and upbringing. If diversity is a fact, then people should not have problems in comprehending the divergent types of democracy found across the globe. What remains certain however, is the fact that democracy does not mean the same in the Western and African contexts. Besides, varied as the types are, there is no universal understanding of democracy.

The same applies to the issue of human rights that has made headlines on both print and electronic media across the globe now than ever. Adopted on 10 December 1948 as the Universal Declaration of Human Rights (UDHR), a few years after the end of the infamous World War II to mitigate the atrocities which were perpetrated by both warring parties, the issue of human rights if not properly and thoughtfully handled, will end up being the second Sarajevo of the 21st century that will ultimately ignite the nuclear power and possibly facilitate the demise of the planet earth. We are saying this because the so-called 'superpowers' are intervening in the political affairs of weak nations under the guise of promoting democracy and protecting human rights. If all human beings are equal as purported by the Universal Declaration of Human Rights, why is it that some people and countries are more important than others? Why is it that there are superpowers? Why is it that there are First and Third world countries? This clearly shows that human rights are used as bait by the West to deceive other nations in disregarding their cultural values and unconsciously adopting Western norms and values in the false name of democracy and human rights.

As that may be, Africa is playing a game in which the West is both player and referee. No matter how skilful Africa may be, it is extremely difficult to beat the West in their own game. Considering that the West is holding the whistle, more often than not, Africa is always caught offside in the sense that it is perennially accused as the chief culprit in infringing and violating human rights. Yet, history is replete with evidence that Europe unsympathetically and purposefully abused the people of Africa in the past and now. The slave trade and colonialism are undisputable cases in point. Currently, the universalisation of democracy and human rights as well as the removal of national boundaries in the name of globalisation is a diplomatic way of interfering in the affairs of other sovereign nations. In fact, the West will always find an excuse to undermine the rights of others and instead advance their own interests. It is on record that when Europe first came into contact with Africa, Africa was at a certain stage of development. The question that quickly comes in mind and begs for an answer is how then did Africa managed to survive and progress without the 'so called-human rights?' Fundamentally, how did Africa managed to be at peace with each other in the absence of human rights? This entails that human rights are not new to Africa but were instead, repackaged and designed in a way that suit the Euro-American ideology. It is clear that democracy and human rights are universal concepts cherished in each and every society. What makes them problematic is that they should be cultivated across the globe using the West as the yardstick on which to measure and judge the entire world. Sadly, for a country to be considered as developed, it must first and foremost, be democratic in a way that satisfies the 'superpowers.' Certainly, these rights reflect Western values, which give primacy to individualism, and thus, run counter to African traditional values that are strongly embedded in the context of the community (Ibhawoh 2000). Consequently, Africa is naturally finding it extremely difficult to fit within the framework of Western democracy. Moreover, the

West's conception of democracy and human rights is now being used as the yardstick to measure and judge development (see Ake 2003). That said, the whole issue of democracy and human rights is a terrain of struggle between oppressors and the oppressed. Since the engagement between the dominated and the dominating is generally couched in ambiguous and contradictory terms, then democracy and human rights as ideological issues and artefacts of human struggles are themselves fraught with ambiguities and contradictions.

The chapter problematises the issues of democracy and human rights in post-colonial Africa. This is largely because post-colonialism on the African continent raises complex issues involving democracy and human rights. In view of this, the chapter attempts to provide a general overview of democracy in its various forms. It argues that there is confusion about the precise meaning of democracy. This confusion is more than definitional; it is analytic and ideological. The democratic aspiration of the African people is not only confined to the arena of political democracy (of elections, and granting of civil and political rights), but involves the demand for economic empowerment, better living standards, and adequate social welfare. Indeed, for the majority of the people, democracy is meaningful only when it delivers socio-economic goods. In other words, political democracy must be linked to socio-economic development. This chapter argues that whilst democracy and human rights are indeed a necessity in each and every human society now than ever, their meaning and implementation should be culture specific.

Democracy and human rights: Theoretical analysis

Democracy and human rights are ubiquitous terms which are difficult to define with precision. Part of the problem emanates from the fact that each and every society has its own understanding of democracy based on its contextual setting. If a term is moved out of its context, it loses not only its meaning but its relevance as well. This is precisely what happened to the concept of democracy. With the West imposing its democracy to the world basing on its economic and political muscles, the concept has failed to make a significant impact outside the Western framework. That said, democracy as a universal and indivisible core value and principle of the United Nations (UN), has its origins in the sixth century B.C in Greek. Etymologically, the word comes from two Greek words *"demos"* (which means people) and *"kratos"* (which means rule) (United Nations 1994). Loosely translated democracy simply means rule by the people. In other words, democracy as government by the people; is a form of government in which the sovereign power resides in the people as a whole, and is exercised either directly by them or by officers elected by them. It is often referred to as popular government. Whatever its origins, democracy has come to mean a principle or system to which most political parties of Western governments subscribe to.

The UN one of the leading international bodies defines democracy as being "based on the freely expressed will of the people to determine their own political, economic, social and cultural systems and their full participation in all aspects of their lives (ibid). In line with this, the International Covenant of Civil and Political Rights (ICCPR) lists the key principles of democracy under International Laws to include freedom of association with others, the right and opportunity to take part in the conduct of public affairs and the right to vote and to be elected at genuine periodic elections which shall be by universal and shall be held by secret ballot, guaranteeing the free expression of the will of the electors (ibid). In the same vein, the USAID Democracy and Governance (2001), defines democracy as "...programmes that promote the rule of law and human rights, transparent and fair elections coupled with a competitive political process, a free and independent media, stronger civil society and greater citizen participation in government, and governance structures that are efficient, responsive and accountable".

Apart from that, scholars have attempted to come up with *one-size-fits-all* generic definitions of democracy but these have not sufficed, especially given the dynamic and evasive political developments in the world. Yet while some scholars have portrayed democracy as "...the participation of the largest possiblenumber of those concerned with the organisation of society; majority rule; the existence of realalternative, others have expressed it as initiatives that encourage citizen participation in publicdecision-making (Paul 2005). Interestingly, there are some scholars who argue that democracy is not an end in itself but an ongoing process which should be cultivated and inculcated and be allowed to grow within a society (Gaventa 2006).

While current debates around democracy have tended to be associated with participation, Nelson and Wright (1995) have added their voice by portraying democracy as 'empowering the weakest and poorest'. On the other hand, another school of thought has based its definition of democracy on the simple principle that when making an important public decision, the majority vote should prevail because the will of the majority outweighs the wants of the minority (Leftwich 1993). Most importantly, the HSRC incorporates grassroots people in its definition of democracy by asserting it as "... a government by consent, giving all citizens (including grassroots people) an equal chance to influence the process of government, and entails the participation of everybody in whatever decision is taken" (HSRC 2003). In practical terms, grassroots have always been used as the electorate, and in recent times, these are the people worst affected by the wrath of the state machinery as they face harassment due to participation in civic activities viewed as threats by the government.

The idea of democracy has been understood and applied in different ways, both temporally and culturally, with democracy

222

taking various forms in different societies. From a historical perspective, the direct democracy of ancient Athens has been transformed into the representative democracy that is common today (Norman 2005). However, all forms of democracy are based to some extent on the original Greek notion of demokratia, that is, "government by the people," from the words demos (people) and kratos (rule or power). This core concept still forms the crux of modern definitions of democracy, including the 1993 Vienna Declaration's statement that "democracy is based on the freely expressed will of the people to determine their own political, economic, social and cultural systems and their full participation in all aspects of their lives" (Vienna Declaration and Programme of Action n.d).

Shifting the discussion to human rights, it is interesting to note that international human rights language has swept across the landscape of contemporary world politics in a trend that began in the 1970s, picked up speed after the Cold War's end, and quickened yet again in the latter half of the 1990s (Thomas and Ron 2007). Yet, while this human rights 'talk' has fundamentally reshaped the way in which global policy elites, transnational activists, and some national leaders talk about politics and justice, actual impacts are more difficult to discern, requiring more nuance and disaggregation. Importantly, there may be substantial cross-regional variations, due to varying colonial and postcolonial histories and different trajectories in state–society relations (ibid). In Africa for instance, the missionaries and later the colonial regime propagated the myth that there was no conception of democracy and worse still that of human rights. They in fact, confused the African people's view of autonomy particularly African hostility toward individuality and autonomy. Yet a closer examination of the African people's way of life reveals a great passion for democracy and autonomous existence both at individual and group levels. At individual level, one had the right to express his/her opinion even during court hearings and elsewhere

(Mawere 2014). On the same token, autonomy of the group as a whole (including widows, widowers, orphans, and those physically challenged) was guaranteed through egalitarian systems both personal industriousness and collective work in the form of beer work parties (*nhimbe* in Shona or *ilima* in Ndebele) (ibid).

With the adoption of the Universal Declaration of Human Rights (UDHR) in 1948, the very term "human rights" came into a wider use both in academia and politics. Nowadays, speeches by political leaders, heads of enterprises, trade unions and non-governmental institutions rarely go without a reference to the commitments to the democratic principles and norms of the UDHR (ibid). By definition, human rights are a claim people are entitled to make simply by virtue of their status as human beings (Wiredu 1996: 157). The issue of human rights is worth discussing because it is currently topical and has been used by Europe and America to dismantle the African family institution and to cause a lot of civil unrest in some parts of Africa. As Donnelly summarises, "human rights are, literally, the rights that one has simply as a human being. As such, they are equal rights, because we are all equally human beings. They are also inalienable rights because no matter how inhumanely we act or are treated we cannot become other than human beings" (Said 2004).

Human rights are defined in several key documents, namely, the Universal Declaration of Human Rights (UDHR), adopted by the United Nations General Assembly in 1948; the International Covenant on Civil and Political Rights (ICCPR), adopted in 1966; and the International Covenant on Economic, Social, and Cultural Rights, also adopted in 1966 (Gutto 2002). The Vienna Declaration, adopted at the World Conference on Human Rights in 1993, further expanded the meaning of human rights. Originally, human rights were developed to outline a set of individual rights that states were required to respect or provide for their citizens. The framework not only included the prohibition of certain acts, but also the "imposition of the duty to perform certain obligations in order to promote and protect the enjoyment of certain rights" (ibid). In other words, abuse of human rights can take the form of both violations and denials. According to the UN, human rights are "rights inherent to all human beings, regardless of race, sex, nationality, ethnicity, language, religion, or any other status. These rights are deemed to include the right to life and liberty, freedom from slavery and torture, freedom of opinion and expression, the right to work etc.

Democracy and human rights talk as Africa's twin post-colonialproblems

It is indeed true that democracy and human rights are Africa's twin post-colonial problems. The shadow and ghost of colonialism is still haunting most African countries decades after the attainment of political independence. During the colonial era, administrative structures which perpetuated racial discrimination and segregation were set up. It is vital to note that colonialism did not cultivate a climate supportive of constitutionalism, but instead produced states that were "created to be totalitarian, oppressive, and exploitative" and to be supportive of the "colonial purposes of dominating African peoples and exploiting their resources" (Okoth-Ogendo n.d). To substantiate this point, Mimiko asserts that: 'the social fabric was completely devastated and a new culture of violence was implanted. Traditional African systems of conflict resolution were destroyed and, in their places, nothing was given. The democratic process, rudimentary though it was, but with great potential as accompanies every human institution, was brutally uprooted and replaced by the authoritarianism of colonialism. A new crop of elites was created, nurtured, and weaned on the altar of violence and colonialism armed with the structures of the modern state to continue to carry out the art and act of subjugation of the mass of the people in the service of colonialism (Mimiko 2010). Thus, colonialism not only set up a system of exclusion, but also established a pattern of state repression as a tool to deal with popular dissent. A pattern of previous state repression has been shown to be the single strongest predictor of a state's future human rights behaviour (Poe and Tate 1994).

Furthermore, Okoth-Ogendo (n.d) asserts that the independence constitutions of post-colonial Africa merely perpetuated the colonial institutions of control and coercion. It is widely believed thatupon attaining independence, most African governments simply inherited the governmental structures which were set up by the settlers. Surprisingly, the West shifted goal posts and started to criticise the very administrative structures that they had created on the basis that they are undemocratic and that they lack the rule of law. This was a stunning turn around which exposes the double standards of the West. Through Non-Governmental Organisations (NGO), and other lobby groups and civic organisations which were heavily funded and sponsored by the West, the issues of democracy and human rights took centre stage in most independent African states. We strongly suspect that this was a ploy to divert the attention of African governments from reflecting on past injustices as well as from addressing genuine developmental issues. Reports on both print and electronic media, highlighting the alleged violations of human rights in Africa were awash. To exacerbate matters, some of the Western governments in an effort to prove their claims to the world that there is no democracy and human rights in Africa, financed and funded opposition parties and civic groups to mobiles people to demonstrate against the ruling governments in the name of democracy and human rights. In some extreme cases that still remain the dark pages of history; the West sponsored civil wars in some African countries that ultimately costed several thousand lives. Most of these wars are perpetrated by the West and America, countries which see themselves as the architects of democracy and good governance. Consequently, the world was tricked into believing that unless African governments adopted the Western style of democracy, human rights will never be achieved in Africa. Because state creation in Africa differed so markedly from the European experience, the Western liberal conception of individual-state relationships does not easily apply to Africa. Western superpowers should not impose their particular forms of democracy on other societies and expect them to be accepted and sustainable. The Human Rights Watch (HRW) is a case in point. One would be surprised to note that: 'Human rights watch is founded on the idea that values of the United States are universal, and that the US must impose them on the rest of the world (Mawere 2014). Some perpetrating questions can be raised here: "By what virtue does the US have the right to impose its own values/ideologies on the rest of the world?" "Isn't it that the HRW is implying that the Americans are more human and rational than all others in the world?" (ibid: 59).

Narrowing down to the issue of human rights, the West from their long engagement with Africa knew that the African worldview placed the community ahead of the individual. Stereotypical thinking of Europe over Africa and the African people has never been neutral: it had emotional content and commonly associated with attitudes of hostility and hatred towards Africa (ibid, p 57). The argument being advanced here is that human rights reflect Western values, which give primacy to individualism, and thus run counter to traditional values that are strongly embedded in the context of the community (Ibhawoh 2000). In an effort to destabilise and break the African communitarian systems, the issue of human rights was introduced. As a result of this, the patriarchal system was severely challenged. The spirit of individualism and capitalism was inculcated in the minds of the African people. Women lobby groups in the guise of protecting human rights were established.

The extended family crumbled and moral values that glued the community were questioned and ridiculed. The number of divorce cases rocketed up and the problem of single mothers become the order of the day. Gradually the issue of human rights infiltrated into the education sector and sadly some African countries such as South Africa besides licensing children as young as twelve to indulge into sexual activities have openly allowed children to be pregnant while at school (see Mawere 2014). Worse still, they have legalised the issue of gay marriage, a thing that is unheard of in many African countries.

All this boils down to the fact that democracy and human rights talk are undoubtedly and undeniably Africa's two formidable challenges in the 21st century. This is mainly because most if not all the problems affecting Africa today can in one way or the other be traced back to these two Western derived ghosts haunting the African continent. A critical reflection of Africa's past and a purposeful self-examination of the current predicament of Africa will reveal that the discourse of democracy and human rights is empty rhetoric that is meant to destroy the African epistemological cosmos and render them identity less. Only when Africa is identity less, divided, confused and unfocussed can the West willy-nilly manipulate Africa to dance to its own whims. Africa must get out of this Western epistemic box and artificial cocoon to defend their values before they are diluted and thrown into the dustbin of oblivion.

Though human rights are a universal concern for all human societies, others have lost total faith in the whole Universal Human Rights Declaration (UHRD) as they see nothing but an empty document that is nothing more than deceit. Western and American governments have been criticised by critical scholars especially from the south for preaching the gospel they themselves don't follow (Mawere 2014: 65). Others see the 1948 UDHR as a mere marketing propaganda devised by the West to outwit populations from other countries (such as Africa) and create as well as convey to them a false message that the UDHR was indeed the basis for African liberation and of all the rights enjoyed today by all the individuals, communities, nations, continents, and indeed the world (ibid).

Democracy and human rights are clearly different notions; "they are distinct enough for them to be viewed as discreet and differentiated political concepts" (Langlois 2003). Whereas democracy aims to empower "the people" collectively, human rights aim to empower individuals. Democracy and human rights are distinct yet interrelated concepts, with democracy referring to government by the people, and human rights referring to universal rights that apply to all individuals in all societies. Human rights and democracy have historically been viewed as separate, albeit parallel, concepts. Thus, "democracies" exist that do not necessarily protect human rights, while some non-democratic states are able to ensure some, though not all, human rights.

It should be noted that democracy is a dynamic term which can take a variety of forms. This implies that there is no "one size fits all" democracy. As Beetham explains, "different societies and diverse circumstances require different arrangements if democratic principles are to be effectively realised" (Beetham 2002). In conformity with this understanding, Said noted that "the form of democracy is always cast in the mould of the culture of a people;" thus, he recognises its potential for variation and dynamism (Said 2004). For instance, the western liberals are criticised for projecting a one sided and Euro centric notion of democracy and human rights based on what is termed the Athens-to-Washington narrative of democracy and human rights. The Athens-to-Washington thinking is that democracy and human rights are products of the wisdom of people with "white skins", and as such are only organic to Western cultures (Zezela 1997). This approach is an idealistic and simplistic abstraction divorced from the complex universal human struggles against oppression and exploitation in non-Western part of the world.

It is important to set the record straight that democracy is not a western product as the principles and institutions that inform it are based on tenets that transcend national and political ideologies; thus, democracy is not exclusive to the West (ibid). The idea that democracy is not exclusive to the West can serve to caution superpowers to avoid imposing their models of democracy on other societies, and encourage them to instead assume a supportive role in developing democracy in local contexts. Likewise, superpowers should be cautious of pursuing national interests under the guise of democracy to prevent the association of democracy with Western imperialism.

Conclusion

Democracy and human rights have been practiced in various forms in all human societies since time immemorial. The emergency of modern states and the Universal Declaration of human rights brought in a new dispensation in the conceptualisation of democracy and human rights but with a bias towards America and the West. In all this, Europe and America assumed a self-imposed duty of being the adjudicators of democracy and human rights. Any understanding of democracy and human rights that does not satisfy the parameters set by Europe and America was unfortunately disregarded. Today most of the African states have remained paupers despite the fact that they remain loyal to economic liberalisation and all other dictates of globalisation which uses liberal democracy as a jump-starting condition. A whole century of evidence corroborates that liberal democracy has not been incompatible with social and economic inequality, with anti-democratic rule, with physical oppression, with partisan distribution of resources and systemic corruption (Sankatsing 2004). The chapter has shown that there is no universal understanding of democracy and human rights. Africa has developed a tendency of using Europe and America as templates and standard measures in issues to do with democracy and human rights. This is mainly because these terms though they existed in each and every human society in various ways, were repackaged and designed in the way that suit the Euro-American ideology.

References

Aborishade, F. 2002. Effects of globalisation on social and labour practices in privatised enterprises in Nigeria, *A Research Report Submitted to The Centre for Advanced Social Sciences*, Port Harcourt: Nigeria.

Abugre, C. 'In Defence,' 11– 13 (Cited in Biney, A. 2011. *The political and social thought of Kwame Nkrumah*, Palgrave Macmillan: USA).

African Gender Institute. 2014. *Feminist Africa: Pan-Africanism and Feminism*, Issue 19: September

African Renaissance Institute, 2000. *The amended version of the vision, mission and objectives*, African Renaissance Institute, Sandton, South Africa.

African Union Commission. 2014. *Walking the Talk: Gender Equality in the African Union, Women's Voices on* pan-Africanism *and African Renaissance.*
http://wgd.au.int/en/sites/default/files/Newsletter%20W alking%20the%20talk%20-%20English.pdf.
Accessed 8 August 2014.

Agbaye, A. 1991. *African Political Thought*, Ibadan: Department of Adult Education U.I., UP.

Agyeman, O. 1998. *Pan-Africanism and its detractors: A response to Harvard's race effacing universalists*, Harvard University Press: Harvard.

Ake, C. 2001. *Democracy and Development in Africa*, Brookings Institution Press: Washington Dc.

Ake, Claude. 2003. *The feasibility of democracy in Africa*, CODESRIA: Dakar, Senegal.

Akinpelu, J. A. 1981. *Introduction to Philosophy of Education*, London, Macmillan.

Akintoye, S. A. 1976. Emergent African States, Longman: Harlow.

Albrow, M. and Kind, E. 1990. (Eds.) *Globalisation, knowledge and society*, Sage Books: London.

Alli, W. O. 2005. "Pan-Africanism and National Question in Nigeria", in Warisu O. Alli (ed.) *Political Reform Conference, Federalism and National Question in Nigeria*, Enugu: NPSA.

Alofun, G.O.O. 2014. African Socialism: A critique. *IOSR Journal of Humanities and Social Science,* Volume 19 (8): 69-71.

Al-Rodhan, R. F. *et al.* 2006. *Definitions of globalisation: A comprehensive overview and a proposed definition*, Sage Books: London.

Aluko, M. A. O., Akinola, G. O. and Sola, F. 2004. Globalisation and the manufacturing sector: A study of selected Textile Firms in Nigeria, Journal of Social Sciences 9 (2).

American Philosophical Association. 1981. *Philosophy: A Brief Guide for Undergraduate*, Washington DC, USA.

Ameyaw, D. 2014. 'Renowned author: Ngugi wa Thiongo in Ghana for International Conference on African Studies', Accra: Ghana.

Anyidoho, K. 1989. The Pan-African Ideal in Literatures of the Black World, Ghana University Press: Accra.

Appiah, K. A. 1998. 'African philosophy,' *Routledge Encyclopaedia of Philosophy*. (Accessed August 31, 2015); Available at: https://www.rep.routledge.com/articles/african-philosophy/v-1/.

Armah, A. K. 1973. *Two Thousand Seasons*, Oxford: Heinemann.

Asante, M. K. 2000. *The Egyptian philosophers: Ancient African voices from Imhotep to Akhenaten*, Chicago: African American Images.

Asante, M.K. 1990. *Kemet, Afrocentricity and knowledge*, Africa World Press: Trenton, NJ.

Asfaw, B. 2003. Ethiopia: World's "oldest human remains" unearthed, *IRIN News*, 12 June 2003.

Asukwo, O. 2009. 'The Problem of Language in African Philosophy,' In: Uduigwomen, A. F. (Ed.). *Footmarks to*

Landmarks on African philosophy, p. 30-35, Obaroh & Ogbinaka Publishers: Lagos.

AU ECHO. 2013. Pan- Africanism and African Renaissance, Special Edition for the 20th AU Summit, Issue 05, 27 January.

Austin, J. L. 1961. *"Other Minds in Austin's Philosophical Papers,"*Urmson, S.O. and Warnock, C.J. (eds), Oxford University Press: Oxford.

Awuah- Nyamkye, S. 2012. Religion and Development: African Traditional Religion's Perspective, *Journal of Religious Studies and Theology*, Vol.31 (1): 75-90.

Awuah-Nyamekye, S. 2015. Indigenous Knowledge: A Key Factor in Africa's Sustainable Development in Mawere, M and Awuah Nyamekye (Eds,) 2015. *Harnessing Cultural Capital for Sustainability: A Pan-Africanist Perspective*, Langaa Research and Publishing CIG, Mankon, Bamenda.

Ayer, A.J. 1955.*The Problem of Knowledge,*Martins Press Inc: New York.

Ayittey, G. B. 2014. *The End of African Socialism*, The Heritage Foundation. Retrieved from www.heritage,org on 9th May, 2014.

Azenabor, G. 2009. *Odera Oruka's Philosophic Sagacity: Problems and Challenges of Conversation Method in African philosophy, Thought and Practice: A Journal of the Philosophical Association of Kenya (PAK)* Premier Issue, New Series, Vol.1 (1): 69-86.

Badejo, D. L. 2008. *Global Organisations: The African Union*, Series Editor: Peggy Kahn, University of Michigan-Flint, Infobase Publishing.

Bah, T. (Ed,). 2005. *Intellectuels, Nationalisme et Idéal Panafricain: Perspective Historique*, Dakar: CODESRIA.

Bamisaiye, O. A. A. 1989. *A Practical Approach to Philosophy of Education*, Ibadan AMD Publishers: Nigeria.

Barnett, D. 2008. *Philosophy: The Power of Ideas*, Seventh Edition, McGraw-Hill, Inc.

Beetham, D. 2002. "Democracy and Human Rights: Contrast and Convergence," *Seminar on the Interdependence between Democracy and Human Rights*, United Nations, Office of the High Commissioner for Human Rights: Geneva: 25-26 November 2002.

Bell, R. 2002. *Understanding African Philosophy*, Routledge: London.Bello, S. and Adesemoye, 2012. Western films and teenagers in Nigerian societies: The question of cultural promotion, *Continental Journal of Arts and Humanities*, 4 (2).

Benjamin, C. 2010. *An African Identity*, Available at: *http://www.chicagodefender.com/article-8928-anafrican-identity.html*. (Accessed 27/07/2015).

Bhengu, M.J. 1996. *Ubuntu: The Essence of Democracy*, Novalis Press: Cape Town.

Biko, S. 1978. *I Write what I like*, Heinemann: London.

Biko, S. Steve Biko, *I Write What I Like* (Chicago: Chicago University Press, 2002).

Biney, A. 2011. *The political and social thought of Kwame Nkrumah*, Palgrave Macmillan: USA.

Binsbergen and Wim van 2001. 'Ubuntu and the Globalisation of Southern African Thought and Society,' *Quest: An African Journal of Philosophy* 15 (1-2): 53-89.

Blankenberg, N. 1999. In search of a real freedom: *Ubuntu* and the media, *Critical Arts,* 13(2): 42–65.

Bloom, P. 2010. 'How do Morals Change?' In *Nature* ,Volume 464.

Bodunrin, P. 1984. 'The question of African philosophy,' In: Wright, R. (Ed). *African philosophy: An introduction*, Third edition, Lanham MD: University of America Press, p.1-24.

Brandom, R. (n.d). "Study Guide," In Sellars, *Empiricism and the Philosophy of Mind*.

Bridges, G. 2002. Grounding globalisation: The prospects and perils of linking economic processes of globalisation to environmental outcomes, *Economic Geography* 78 (3): 361-386.

Broad, C. D. 1923. *Scientific Thought*, Harcourt, Brace: New York.

Broodryk, J. 2002. *Ubuntu: Life lessons from Africa,* Ubuntu School of Philosophy, Pretoria: South Africa.

Browne, V. 2007. 'The coup that disrupted Africa's forward march,' Available at: http://politico.ie/articles/by/vincent/6/03/2007/. (Retrieved: 6 July 2015).

Bryson, A.A. 2009. *The view from the armchair: a defence of traditional Philosophy*, PhD Thesis submitted to the Graduate College of The University of Iowa.

Bukarambe, B. 2003. "Historical Overview of Africa's Development Efforts" In J. Ogwu (Ed) *NEPAD in the Nigerian Dock*. Lagos: NIIA Press.

Bunting, I. 1999. "The Heart of Africa. Interview with Julius Nyerere on Anti-Colonialism." *New Internationalist Magazine* 309 (January–February). http: //www.hartford hwp.com/archives/30/049.html.

Cabral, A. 1979. *Unity and Struggle: Speeches and Writings of Amilcar Cabral*. New York: Monthly Review Press.

Campbell, H. 1994. 'Pan Africanism and African Liberation', In Lemelle, Sydney J. and Kelley, Robin G. eds. *Imagining Home: Class, Culture and Nationalism in the African Diaspora*. London and New York: Verso.

Campbell, H. G. 2005. Walter Rodney and Pan-Africanism Today, Presentation at the Africana Studies Research Center Cornell University, Ithaca, New York.

Cervenka, Z. 1977. *The Unfinished Quest for Unity: Africa and the OAU*. London: Friedman Publication Ltd.

Cesaire, A. 1939. *Notebook of a return to the native land*, (trans. Clayton Eshleman & Annette Smith), Available at: kboo.fm/sites/default/files/AIME.

Cesaire, A. 1969. *A tempest*, (trans. 1985), Ubu Repertory Theater Publications: Paris.

Cesaire, A. *The Original 1939 Notebook of a Return to the Native Land: Bilingual Edition,* trans. A. James Arnold & Clayton

Eshelman, (Middletown CT: Wesleyan University Press: 2013), 95.

Chandra T. M. 1984. "Under Western Eyes: Feminist Scholarship and Colonial Discourses," In: Chandra, T. M. *et al.*, Eds: *Third World Women and the Politics of Feminism,* Bloomington: Indiana University Press: Bloomington.

Chimakonam, J. 2011. Why can't there be an African Logic? *Integrative Humanism Journal,* 1(2): 141-152.

Chimakonam, J. O. 2012. *Introducing African Science Systematic and Philosophical Approach,* Author House: Calabar.

Chime, C. 1977. *Integration and Politics among African States: Limitations and Horizons of Mid-Term Theorising,* Uppsala: The Scandinavian Institute of African Studies.

Chisholm, R. 1963. The Logic of Knowing, *The journal of philosophy,* Vol 6.

Chisinga, B. 2010. "Resurrecting the Developmental State in Malawi," In: R. Tambulasi (ed) *Reforming the Malawian Public Sector,* Dakar: CODESRIA.

Ciaffa, J. 2008. Tradition and Modernity in Postcolonial African Philosophy, *Humanitas,* Volume XXI, Nos. (1 and 2): 121-145.

Clapham, C. 1970. *"The Context of African Political Thought"* The Journal of Modern African Studies, 8, 1: 1-13.

Cole, M. 1961. The Story of Fabian Socialism, Heinemann Educational Books: London.

Cooper, F. 2002. *Africa since 1940: The past of the present,* Cambridge University Press: Cambridge.

Copleston, F. C. 1976. *History of Philosophy,* Doubleday: New York.

Copleston, F. 1993. *A History of Philosophy,* Volume 1: Greece and Rome, From the Pre Socratic to Plotinus, Image Books, Doubleday, New York.

Craig, E. 2002. *Philosophy: A Very Short Introduction,* Oxford University Press: Oxford.

Critchley, S. 1998. 'Introduction: what is continental philosophy?, In: Critchley, S & Schroder, W, *A Companion to Continental Philosophy,* Blackwell Companions to Philosophy, MA: Blackwell Publishing Ltd, Malden.

Da Costa, P. 2007. *Civil Society Organisations and the African Union: Towards a Continental Advocacy Strategy for World Vision*, Nairobi and Milton Keynes, World Vision.

Dagfinn. F. 1996. 'Analytic Philosophy: What it is and Why Should One Engage in It?', *Ratio*, n.s., vol. IX.

Danto, A. 1980. 'Analytic Philosophy', *Social Research*, 2 (57): 612–34.

Deleuze, G. and Guattari, F. 1994. *What is Philosophy?* Colombia University Press: New York.

Dieng, A. A. 2005. "Nationalisme et Panafricanisme", in Bah, Thierno, ed. 2005. *Intellectuels, Nationalisme et Idéal Panafricain: Perspective Historique.* Dakar: CODESRIA.

Donald, D. 1967.'Causal Relations', *Journal of Philosophy* 64.

Doresse, J. 1967. *Ethiopia*, (trans Coult, E.), Elek Books: London.

Duggan, W. R and Civille, J. R. 1976. *Tanzania and Nyerere: A Study of Ujamaa and Nationhood*, Maryknoll, NY: Orbis.

Ejanam, S. 2007. "Relevance of Pantaleon Iroegbu's Communalism in our times," In Ike Odimegwu (ed), *Perspectives on African Communalism,* Trafford publishing: Canada.

Ekwuru, G. 1999. *The pangs of an African culture in travail,* Totan Publishers Limited: Owerri.

Elaigwu, I. J. 1997. "From Might to money: The challenging dimensions of global transition to the 21st century", (*1995 NIPSS Distinguished Annual Lecture*), Kuru: National Institute.

Eliot, C. 1971. *The development debate*, London: SCM.

Encyclopædia Britannica, 2011. *Africa*, Encyclopædia Britannica: E-book: Chicago.

Enoh, O. A. 2001. *Patterns of Philosophy*, Jos: Saniez Publications.

Esedebe, P. O. 1982 *Pan-Africanism: The Idea and Movement, 1776–1963*. Washington, D. C: Howard University Press.

Evans-Pritchard, E. E. 1965. *Theories of Primitive Religion*, Oxford University Press: London.

Ewing, A. C.1951. *The Fundamental Questions of Philosophy*, Routledge and Kegan Paul: London.

Ezeani, E. 2005. *Philosophy as intelligent and pragmatic questioning*, Veritas Lumen Publishers: London.

Falola, T. 2003. *The Power of African Cultures*, University of Rochester Press: USA.

Falola, T. and Kwame, E. 2013. *Pan-Africanism, and the politics of African citizenship and identity*, Routledge: London.

Fanon, F. 1967. *The wretched of the earth*, Penguin Books: London.

Figueira, D. 2007. *Tubal Uriah Butler of Trinidad and Tobago Kwame Nkrumah of Ghana: The road to independence*, iUniverse.

Fortes, M and Evans-Pritchard, E. E 1940. *African Political Systems*, International African Institute/Oxford University Press, London, New York and Toronto.

Francis, D. 2006. *Uniting Africa: Building Regional Peace and Security System*, Aldershot: Ashgate.

Franken, 1969. 'African socialism is an attitude of the mind,' In: *The Arusha Declaration and Christian Socialism, 1967*, University College, Dar es Salaam: Tanzania.

Friedland, W. H., and C. G. Rosberg, (Eds.). 1964. *African Socialism*, Stanford, CA: Stanford University Press.

Friedman, T. 2005. *The world is flat broke*, Vanity Fair: USA.

Gade, C. B. N 2011. The Historical Development of the Written Discourses on Ubuntu, *South African Journal of Philosophy* 30 (3): 303-329.

Gaventa, J. 2006. Triumph, Deficit or Contestation? Deepening the 'Deepening Democracy' Debate, *IDS Working Paper 264*, Institute of Development Studies.

Germana, N. 2014. Steve Biko: The Intellectual Roots of South African Black Consciousness, *Proceedings of the National*

ConferenceOn Undergraduate Research (NCUR) 2014,University of Kentucky, Lexington, April 3 -5.

Giddens, A. 1991. *The consequences of modernity*, Polity Press: Cambridge.

Graness, A. 2012. 'From Socrates to Odera Oruka: Wisdom and ethical commitment,' *Thought and Practice: A Journal of the Philosophical Association of Kenya (PAK)*, New Series, Vol.4 No.2, p.1-22.

Gunder, F. 1998. *Global economy in the Asian Age,* University of California Press: Berkeley.

Gutto, S. 2002. "Current Concepts, Core Principles, Dimensions, Processes and Institutions of Democracy and the Inter-Relationship between Democracy and Modern Human Rights," *Seminar on the Interdependence between Democracy and Human Rights. United Nations,* Office of the High Commissioner for Human Rights. Geneva: 25-26 November 2002.

Gyekye, K. 1997. *Tradition and Modernity*, Oxford University Press: New York.

Haas, E. 1971. *Beyond the Nation-States: Functionalism and International Organization.* Stanford, California: Stanford University Press.

Hadjor, K. 1986. *Realist, dreamer or visionary?* The African Concord.

Hailey, J. 2008. *Ubuntu: A Literature Review Document,* Tutu Foundation: London.

Hakim, A and Sherwood, M. 2003. Pan-African history: political figures from Africa and the diaspora since 1787. London: Routledge.

Hallen, B. 2009. *A Short History of African Philosophy*, second ed., Bloomington: Indiana University Press.

Hamilton, A. G. 1980. *Logic for Mathematicians,* Cambridge University Press: Cambridge.

Hans-Johann, G. 2008. What is Analytic Philosophy? Cambridge University Press: Cambridge.

Harris, J. E. (Ed,). 1993. *Global Dimensions of the African Diaspora* [2nd edition], Washington, DC, Howard University Press.

Hattingh, J. 2002. 'On the imperative of sustainable development: A philosophical and ethical appraisal,' In Janse van Rensburg *et. al.* 2002. *Environmental Education, Ethics and Action,* Pretoria: South Africa.

Hegel, G. 1956. *The philosophy of history (adopted from Hegel's Lectures of 1830-1831),* Dover: New York.

Hegel, G. 1977. *Phenomenology of Spirit,* trans. A. V. Miller, Clarendon Press: Oxford.

Heidegger, M. 1956. *What is Philosophy?,* Trans. William Kluback and Jean T. Wilde (Albany: NCUP).

Hersh, Seymour, H. (09-05-1978), 'CIA said to have aided plotters who overthrew Nkrumah in Ghana,' New York Times: USA.

Higgs, P. and Smith, J. 2000. *Rethinking Our World,* Juta: Kenwyn.

Honderich, T. (Ed,). 1995. *The Oxford companion to philosophy,* Oxford University Press: New York.

Hopwood, B. *et al.* 2005. Sustainable Development: Mapping Different Approaches, *Sustainable Development,* 13 (1): 38-52.

Hountondji, P. 1983. *African Philosophy: Myth and Reality,* Henry Evans Trans. Bloomington: Indiana University Press.

Hountondji, P. 2002. *The struggle for meaning: Reflections on philosophy, culture and democracy in Africa,* Ohio University Centre of International Studies: Athens.

HSRC. 2003. *Democracy in African Societies and Ubuntu,* Centre for Constitutional Analysis: Pretoria. http://wssbd.com/wx/201503/a_Does_Africa_really_exist_.html. http://www.myjoyonline.com/opinion/2014/march-25th/nkrumah-the-untold-story.php. (Retrieved: 5 July 2015).

Hume, H. 1978. *A treatise of human nature,* edited by L.A. Selby-Bigge, (2nd Ed). revised by P.H. Nidditch (Oxford: Clarendon), I (3 iii): 146-147.

Ibhawo, B and Dibua, J. I. 2003. Deconstructing Ujamaa: The Legacy of Julius Nyerere in the Quest for Social and Economic Development in Africa, *African Journal of Political Science*, Vol. 8. (1): 60-83.

Ibhawoh, B. 2000. *Between Culture and Constitution: Evaluating the Cultural Legitimacy of Human Rights in the African State.*

Idoniboye-Obu, S and Whetho, A. 2013. Ubuntu: You are because I am' or 'I am because you are'? *Alter*nation, 20 (1): 229–247.

Ihuah, A. S. 2006. Scientific technology and globalisation, *Lasu Journal of Humanities,* 4 (1): 36-52.

Immerwahr, J. 1992. Hume's Revised Racism, *Journal of the History of Ideas,* 53 (3, 1992): 481-482.

International Monetary Fund (IMF). 2000. "Globalisation: Threat or opportunity", 12 April 2000, IMF Publications: USA.

Jagdish, B. 2004. *In defence of globalisation*, Oxford University Press: Oxford.

James, P. and Steger, M. B. 2014. A genealogy of globalisation: The career of a concept, *Globalisations 11* (4): 424.

Janz, B. 2009. *Philosophy in African places*, Letington Books: United Kingdom.

Johnson, U. 2011. "Hidden colours: The Untold History of People of Aboriginal, Moor, and African Descent" (documentary).

Journal for Activists, 4, November.

July, R.W. 1992. *A History of the African people*, Illinois: Waveland press, Inc.

Kam Kar, H. 2012. 'Africa Must Unite: ' Vindicating Kwame Nkrumah and Uniting Africa Against Global Destruction, *The Journal of Pan African Studies,* vol.4, no.10, January 2012.

Kant, I. 'On the different daces of humankind,' [1775 version]. Found In: *This is race: An anthology selected from the International Literature on the races of Man,* Comp. Earl W. Count. 1950. New York: Shuman.

Kanu, I. A.2013. Nkrumah and the Quest for African Unity, *American International Journal of Contemporary Research,* 3 (6): 111-114.

Keller, P.2006. What is Philosophy? Symposium de la SociétéSuisse de philosophie, Neuchâtel, May 19, 2006.

Khoza, R. 2005. *Let Africa Lead: African Transformational Leadership for 21st century Business.* Sunninghill: VezuBuntu.

Kingah, S. (n.d). *Africa's Integration Paradox,*United Nations University Institute for Comparative Regional Integration Studies, Bruges, Belgium.

Kiros, T. 2004. 'Zera Yacob and traditional Ethiopian philosophy,' In: Wiredu, K. and Abrahams, (Eds). *A companion to African philosophy,*

Kneller, G. F. 1964. *Introduction to the Philosophy of Education*: Second Edition. John Wiley and Sons, Inc, New York.

Koka, K. D. 1996. 'The African renaissance,' *Paper presented to the Ubuntu School of Philosophy,* Pretoria: South Africa.

Komba, D. 1995. "Contribution to Rural Development: *Ujamaa* and Villagisation." Mwalimu: The Influence of Nyerere. Ed. Colin Legum and Geoffrey Mmari. Trenton, NJ: Africa World Press.

Kornai, J. 2000. What the Change of System from Socialism to Capitalism Does and Does not Mean, *Journal of Economic Perspectives,* 14 (1): 27-42.

Kuper, S. 2013. 'Africa? Why there is no such place', *The Financial Times Magazine*: UK, Available at: http://www.ft.com/cms/s/2/c7e5e492-40ec-11e3-ae19-00144feabdc0.html (Accessed: 7 July 2015).

Langlois, A. J. 2003. "Human Rights without Democracy? A Critique of the Separationist Thesis," Human Rights Quarterly, 25 (4): 990-1019.

Larsson, T. 2001. *The race to the top: The real story of globalisation,* Cato Institute: Washington DC.

Leftwich, A. 1993. Governance, Democracy and Development in the Third World, *Third World*

Legum, C. 1962. *Pan-Africanism: A Short Political Guide*. New York: Frederick A. Praeger.

Legum, C., and Mmari, G. (Eds,). 1995. Mwalimu: The influence of Nyerere. Trenton, N J: African World Press.

Lehulere, O. 2003. "NEPAD: The Program of South African Capital," in *Khanya: A South African*

Lemelle, S. 1992. *Pan Africanism for Beginners,* London: Writers and Readers.

Lesole, I. 2002. 'Moral regeneration,' *Paper delivered at Youth Workshop*, Gauteng Department of Social Services, Johannesburg: South Africa.

Levy-Bruhl, L. 1922. *La mentalité primitive*, translated as *Primitive Mentality* (1923).

Levy-Bruhl, L. 1926. *Les fonctions mentales dans les sociétés inférieures* (1910), translated as *How Natives Think*.

Listowel, J. 1968. The Making of Tanganyika, London: Chatto and Windus.

Locke, J. 1999. (3rd Ed). *An essay concerning human understanding,* Pennsylvania University Press: Pennsylvania.

Louw, D. J. 2001. 'Ubuntu and the Challenges of Multiculturalism in Post-apartheid South Africa', *Quest: An African Journal of Philosophy*, 15 (1): 2.

Maduagwu O. M. 1999. 'Globalisation and its challenges to National Cultures and Values: A Perspective from sub-Saharan Africa', *A Paper presented at the International Roundtable on the challenges of Globalisation*, University of Munish, 18-19 March.

Makgoba, M. W. (Ed.), 1999. *African Renaissance: The New Struggle*. Cape Town: Mafube Tafelberg.

Makinde, A. 2000. "Philosophy in Africa", In: Momoh, C. S. (Ed). *The substance of African philosophy*, African Philosophy Projects' Publications: Auchi.

Makumba, M. M. 2007. *Introduction to African philosophy: Past and present*, Paulines Publications Africa: Nairobi.

Martin, G. 2011. Revisiting Fanon, From Theory to Practice: Democracy and Development in Africa. *Journal of pan-African Studies* 4: 7.

Masolo, D. A. 1994. *African Philosophy in Search of Identity.* Bloomington: Indiana University Press.

Mawere, M. 2012. 'Buried and Forgotten but not Dead': Reflections on 'Ubuntu' in Environmental Conservation in Southeastern Zimbabwe, *Global Journal of Human Social Science and Geography and Environmental GeoSciences*, 12 (10): 1-10.

Mawere, M. 2013. *Lyrics of reasoning and experience*, Langaa Publishers: Bamenda.

Mawere, M. 2014. *Divining the Future of Africa: Healing the Wounds, Restoring Dignity and Fostering Development*, Langaa Research and Publishing CIG, Mankon, Bamenda.

Mawere, M. 2014. *Environmental conservation through Ubuntu and other emerging perspectives*, Langaa Publishers: Bamenda.

Mawere, M. 2015a. 'Colonial heritage, memory, and sustainability in dialogue: An introduction,' In: Mawere, M. and Mubaya, T. 2015. *Colonial heritage, memory and sustainability in Africa: Challenges, opportunities and prospects*, Langaa Publishers: Bamenda, p1-10.

Mawere, M. 2015b. *Humans, other beings and the environment: Harurwa (edible stinkbugs) and environmental conservation in Southeastern Zimbabwe*, Cambridge Scholars Publishers: Cambridge.

Mazrui, A. 2004. *Nkrumah's legacy and Africa's triple heritage between globalisation and counter terrorism*, Accra: Ghana.

Mazrui, A. A. 1977. *Africa's International Relation: The Diplomacy of Dependency and Change.* Boulder Colorado: West View Press.

Mazrui, A. A. 1996. *The African Renaissance: A triple legacy of skills, values and gender.* Keynote Address at the 5th General Conference of The African Academy of Sciences, held in Hammamet, Tunisia, April 22 – 27, 1996.

Mazrui, A. A., and Mhando, L. L. 2013. Julius K. Nyerere, *Africa's Titan on a Global Stage: Perspective from Arusha to Obama,* Durham, NC: Carolina Academic Press.

Mbeki, T. 1998. *Statement at the African Renaissance Conference,* Johannesburg, South Africa, 28 September 1998.

Mbeki, T. 1999. 'Prologue', In M. W. Makgoba (Ed.), *African Renaissance,* Mafube, Sandton, South Africa, p. xiii-xxi.

Mbigi, L. and J. Maree 1995 *Ubuntu: The Spirit of African Transformation Management,* Knowledge Resources, Johannesburg.

Mboya, T. 1956. *The Kenya question: An African answer.* Fabian Tract No. 302. London.

McAllister, P. 2009. Ubuntu - Beyond Belief in Southern Africa, *Sites: A Journal of Social Anthropology and Cultural Studies* 6 (1): 1-10.

Mesembe, E. 2013. "Metaphysics, contemporary African philosophy and ethnocentric commitment", [Interactions in the History of Philosophy. *PHILHIST'13 Conference Proceedings,* EFE Duyan, AYSE Güngör Ed.], No 778, 2013. Mimar Sinan Fine Arts University: Turkey.

Mimiko, N. O. 2010.Tradition, Governance, Challenges and the Prospects of Change in Africa,In Niyi Afolabi, ed. *Toyin Falola: The Man, The Mask, The Muse,* North Carolina: Carolina Academic Press.

Mkandawire, T., (Ed). 2005. *African Intellectuals: Rethinking Politics, Language, Gender and Development,* Dakar, CODESRIA/Zed.

Momoh, C. S. (Ed). 1989. *The Substance of African Philosophy,* Auchi: African Philosophy Projects Publications.

Momoh, C. S. 1988. Modern Theories in African Philosophy, *Nigerian Journal of Philosophy,* Vol.1 No.2.

Momoh, C.S. 1985. African Philosophy: Does it Exist? *Diogenes: International Council of Philosophy and Humanities studies,* No.130.

More, M. 2004. 'Biko: Africana Existentialist Philosopher,' *Alternation 11* no. 1(2004): 86.

247

Morris, T. 1999. *Philosophy for dummies*, Foster City, CA: IDG Books Worldwide, Inc.

Moyo, D. 2009. *Dead Aid: Why Aid is not working and how there is a better way for Africa*, Farrar, Straus and Giroux, New York.

Moyo. B. and Ramsamy. 2014. African philanthropy, pan-Africanism, and Africa's development, Development in Practice, 24 (5–6): 656–671.

Mugumbate, J and Nyanguru, A. 2013. Exploring African Philosophy: The value of Ubuntu in Social Work,*African Journal of Social Work*, 3 (1): 82-100.

Mulenga, D. 2001a. Mwalimu: Julius Nyerere's Contributions to Education, *Convergence* 34: 17-41.

Murithi, T. 2007a. A Local Response to the Global Human Rights Standard: The Ubuntu Perspective on Human Dignity. *Globalisation, Societies and Education* 5 (3): 277-286.

Murithi, T. 2007b. *Institutionalising Pan-Africanism Transforming African Union values and principles into policy and practice*, Institute for Security State.

Museveni Y.K. 1997. *Sowing the Mustard Seed: The Struggle for Freedom and Democracy in Uganda,* London: Macmillan.

Nafukho F.M 2006. Ubuntu worldview: A traditional African view of adult learning in the workplace. *Advances in Developing Human Resources*, 8 (3): 408-415.

Nani-Kofi, E. 2013. 'Kwame-nkrumah-24th-february-1966-coup-and-the-international-progressive-movement', *The rising continent*, Available at: https://therisingcontinent.wordpress.com/2013/02/26/. (Retrieved: 6 July 2015).

Ndaba, W. J. 1999. The challenge of African philosophy: A reply to Mabogo More, *Alternation* 6 (1): 174-192.

Nelson, R. and Wright, P. 1995. *Making Democracy Work*, Princeton University Press: Princeton.

NEPAD. 2001. The New Partnership for Africa's Development. Paragraph 27.

New Internationalist Magazine, 2000. *A history of Pan-Africanism*, New Internationalist, Issue 326, August 2000.

Nicolaides, A. 2012. Globalisation and Americanisation: The hijacking of indigenous African culture, *Global Advanced Journal of History, Political Science and International Relations,* 1 (6): 118-131.

Nicolaides, A. 2014. Utilising Ubuntu to Inform Chief Executive Officer (CEO) Thinking on Corporate Social Responsibility (CSR) and Codes of Ethics in Business, Journal of SocialSciences, 41(1): 17-25.

Njoku, F. O. C. 2002. *Essays in African philosophy, thought and theology,* Owerri: Claretian Institute of Philosophy.

Nkrumah, K. (reprint 1973). *The autobiography of Kwame Nkrumah,* Macmillan: London.

Nkrumah, K. (reprint, 1962). *Towards Colonial Freedom,* Panaf: London.

Nkrumah, K. 1963. *Africa must unite,* Macmillan: London.

Nkrumah, K. 1965. *Neo- colonialism: The last stage of imperialism,* Macmillan: London.

Nkrumah, K. 1970. *Consciencism: Philosophy and Ideology for Decolonisation and Development with Particular Reference to the African Revolution.* London: Panaf Books.

Nkrumah, K.1973. African Socialism Revisited, In The Struggle Continues, Panaf Books, London.

Nozick, R. 1995. *The Nature of Rationality,* Princeton University Press.

Nussbaum, B. 2009. Ubuntu: Reflections of a South African on our common humanity. In: MF Murove (Ed.): *African Ethics: An Anthology of Comparativeand Applied Ethics.* Pietermaritzburg: KwaZulu-Natal Press.

Nussbaum, M. 2000. *Women and Human Development: The Capabilities Approach,* Cambridge University Press: Cambridge.

Nyamnjoh, F. B. 2015. Incompleteness: Frontier Africa and the Currency of Conviviality. *Journal of Asian and African Studies*, 1–18. DOI: 10.1177/0021909615580867.

Nyamnjoh, F. B., and Shoro, K. 2011. Language, Mobility, African Writers and Pan Africanism, in: *African Communication Research*, 4 (1): 35-62.

Nyarwath, O. 2010. Traditional Logic: An Introduction, 2nd edition, Consolata Institute of Philosophy: Nairobi.

Nyerere, J. 1967 (1973). *Freedom and Unity,* London and Nairobi: Oxford University Press.

Nyerere, J. 1968. *Freedom and Socialism,* Dar es Salaam and New York: Oxford University Press.

Nyerere, J. 1997. Opening speech on Ghana's 40th anniversary duped: 'Africa at 40. Vol. 1. No. 3. April 1997.

Nyerere, J. K. 1962. Ujamaa: The basis of African socialism. Dar es Salaam: Government Printer.

Nze, C. *1990. African Philosophy & Okolo's Interpretation: Okolo on African Philosophy and African Theology,* Cecta Nigeria Ltd: Enugu.

Nziramasanga, T. 1999. *Report of Presidential Commission of Inquiry into Education and Training,* Curriculum Development Unity: Harare.

O'Rourke, K. H. *et al.* 2000. When did globalisation begin? *NBER Working Paper,* No. 7632.

OAU, 1982. *Lagos Plan of Action for the Economic Development of Africa,* 1980-2000, Geneva: International Institute for Labour Studies.

Obenga, T. 2001. *Le Sens de la Lutte Contre l'Africanisme Eurocentriste,* Paris: Khepera and L'Harmattan.

Ochieng –Odhiambo, F. and Iteyo, C. 2012. Reason and Sagacity in Africa: Odera Oruka's Contribution to Philosophy, *Thought and Practice: A Journal of the Philosophical Association of Kenya (PAK) New Series,* Vol.4 No.2, December 2012, pp.169-184.

Odera Oruka, H. (Ed.) 1991. *Sage philosophy: Indigenous thinkers and modern debate on African philosophy*, Nairobi: African Centre for Technological Studies.

Odera Oruka, H. 1978. 'Four Trends in Current African Philosophy,' Alwin Diemer (Ed). *Philosophy in the Present Situation of Africa*, Wiesbaden: Franz Steiner Verlag GmbH.

Odera Oruka, H. 1983. Sagacity in African philosophy, *International Philosophical Quarterly*, Vol.XXIII No.4.

Odera Oruka, H. 1990. *Trends in contemporary African Philosophy*, Nairobi: Shirikon Publishers.

Oduor, R. M. J. (n.d). *African philosophy, and non-human animals: Interview talks to Antneh Roba and Rainer Ebert*, University of Nairobi: Kenya.

Ogunjini and Bayo, 2005. *Introduction to African oral literature and performance*, Africa World Press: New Jersey.

Okeke, O. I. 2011. Pan-Africanism and Pan-Arabism in Africa: The -anti thesis and Imperative for Synthesis, *Kuwait Chapter of Arabian Journal of Business and Management Review* Vol. 1 (1): 87-106.

Okoth-Ogendo, H.W.O. (n.d). *Constitutions without Constitutionalism: Reflections on an African Paradox, in* Constitutionalism and Democracy, *supra* note 2, at 69.

Okufolake, O. 2014. African Socialism: A critique, *IOSR Journal Of Humanities And Social Science,*

Olela, H. 1981. *From Ancient Egypt to Ancient Greece*, The Black Heritage 1 Corporation: Georgia.

Olinger, H. N, Johannes, J. Britz and Martin, O. 2007. Western Privacy and/ or Ubuntu? Some Critical Comments on the Influences in the Forthcoming Data Privacy Bill in South Africa. *International Information and Library Review*, 39 (1): 31-43.

Oliver, B. 2011. *Personal identity, numerical and qualitative,* Available at: http: //sammelpunkt.philo.at: 8080/1356/. (Accessed: 26/07/2015).

Olu-Adeyemi and Ayodele. 2007. The Challenges of Regional Integration for Development in Africa: Problems and Prospects, Journal of Social Sciences, 15 (3): 213-218.

Omi, M and Winant, H. 1986. *Racial Formations in the United States. From the 1060s to the 1980s*, New York: Routledge and Kegan Paul.

Omoregbe, J. 1991. *Knowing philosophy*, Lagos: Joja Educational Research and Publishing Company.

Omoregbe, J. 1993. *Ethics: A Systematic and Historical Study*, Jaja Educational Research Publishers Ltd: Lagos.

Omoregbe, J. I. 1999. *A Simplified History of Western Philosophy*, Volume One: Jaja Educational Research Publication: Lagos.

Omoregbe, J. I. 1999. *Metaphysics Without Tears: A Systematic and Historical Study*, Jaja Educational Research Publications: Lagos.

Oni, A. A. 2005. Globalisation and its implication on African culture and development: Challenges for education, *International Journal of African and American Studies* 4 (2) July 2005.

Onyewuenyi, I. 1982. A philosophical reappraisal in African belief in reincarnation, *International Philosophical Quarterly*, Vol.22 No.3.

Oppenheim, C.E. 2012.Nelson Mandela and the Power of Ubuntu, Religions, 3: 369–388.

Osabu-We, D. T. 2000. *Compatible Cultural Democracy: The Key to Development in Africa,* Ontario, Canada and New York

Otchere-Darko, G. A. 2014. Nkrumah: The untold story, Available at:

Outlaw, L. 1987. African philosophy: Deconstructive and reconstructive challenges, *Contemporary Philosophy: A New Survey*, Vol.5.

Owomoyela, O. 1991. 'Africa and the Imperative of Philosophy: A Skeptical Consideration,' In: Serequeberhan, T. (Ed.) *African Philosophy: The EssentialReadings*, Paragon House: New York.

Ozumba, G. and Chimakonam, J. 2014. *Njikoka Amaka: Further Discussions on the Philosophy of Integrative Humanism*, 2014 Series Vol 2. Third Logic Option: Calabar.

p'Bitek, Okot. 1979. *African religions in Western scholarship*, East African Literature Bureau: Nairobi.

Paramaribo: Democracy Unit – Anton de Kom University of Suriname.

Paul, M. 2005. *Civil Society*, Polity: Cambridge, England.

Pixley ka Isaka Seme, 1906. 'The Regeneration of Africa,' In *The African Abroad*, April 5, 1906.

Poe, S. C and Tate, C. N. 1994. *Repression of Human Rights and Personal Integrity in the1980s: A Global Analysis*.

Porter M. E. and Kramer M. R. 2006. Strategy and society: The link between competitive advantage and corporate social responsibility, *Harvard Business Review*, 84 (12): 78-92.

Praeg, L. 2008. An Answer to the Question: What is [ubuntu]? *South African Journal of Philosophy*, 27 (4): 367-385.

Priest, G. 2006. "What Is Philosophy?" *Philosophy*.

Pyke.S. 1996. *Philosophers*, Zelda Cheatle Press.

Quarterly, 14(3), 605-624.

Quatson, K. B. 2015. 'The man Nkrumah: Those who betrayed him', Available at: http://nkrumahinfobank.org/article.php?id=109&c=12. (Retrieved: 6 July 2015).

Radu, M. 2001. *Does Africa exist? Foreign Policy Research Institute* (FPRI), Philadelphia: USA.

Ramose, M. B 2002. African Philosophy Through Maim, Mond Books, Harare.

Ramose, M. B. 1999. African Philosophy through Ubuntu. Harare: Mond Books.

Ramose, M. B. 2003b. 'Globalisation and *ubuntu*' in Coetzee, P. H. and A. P. J. Roux (Eds,), *The African Philosophy Reader*, 2nd Edition (Ed,), Routledge, London.

Ramose, M. B. 2009. 'Ecology through Ubuntu,' In M. F. Murove (Ed.), *African Ethics: An Anthology of Comparative and*

Applied Ethics, Pietermaritzburg: University of Kwazulu-Natal Press, South Africa.

Robertson, R. 1992. *Globalisation: Social theory and global culture*, Sage: London.

Rodney, W. 1981. *How Europe Underdeveloped Africa*, Zimbabwe Publishing House, Harare, Zimbabwe.

Rorty, R. 1979. *Philosophy and the mirror of nature*, Princeton University Press: New Jersey.

Rorty, R. 1992. 'Philosophy as Science, Metaphor, Politics,' In *Essays on Heidegger and Others: Philosophical Papers*, Volume 2, Cambridge University Press: New York.

Rorty, R. 1994. 'After Philosophy, Democracy,' In *The American Philosopher*, ed. Giovanna Borradori, University of Chicago Press: Chicago.

Rosen, M. 1998. 'Continental philosophy from Hegel', In: *Philosophy: A Guide Through the Subject II*, p. 663-704.

Russell, B. 1967.*The Problems of Philosophy*, Oxford University Press: New York.

Said, A. A. 2004. "Let Us Be Democratic About Democracy." Al-Hayat 27 June 2004.

Samkange, S. and Samkange, T. 1980. *Hunhuism/Ubuntuism: A Zimbabwean Indigenous Political Philosophy*, College Press: Harare.

Sample, I. 2015. Jaw bone fossil discovered in Ethiopia is oldest known human lineage remains, *Guardian News*, 5 March 2015.

Sankatsing, G. 2004. Political Democracy, Social Democracy and the Market in the Caribbean.

Savage, T., and Sonkosi, Z. 2002. Ritual, Reparations and Reintegration: The Challenge of Reconciliation in Post-Conflict African Societies, *Institute of Justice and Reconciliation*, Cape Town, South Africa.

Schiele, J. H. 1994. Afrocentricity: Implications for higher education, *Journal of Black Studies, 25(2)*: 150–169.

Schneider, J. 2011. *Philosophy and problems of the definition of Extra-terrestrial Life*, Paper Presented at the Conference, "The History and Philosophy of Astrobiology" Tycho Brahe's Island Ven, Sverige (27-28 September 2011).

Seeman, E. R. 2010. Reassessing the Sankofa Symbol in New York's African Burial Ground, *William and Mary Quarterly* 67: 101-22.

Sellars, W. 1962. "Philosophy and the Scientific Image of Man," In *Frontiers of Science and Philosophy*, ed. Robert Colodny, Pittsburgh: University of Pittsburgh Press.

Senghor, J. C. 2009. Going Public: How Africa's integration can work for the poor, Africa Research Institute, London.

Senghor, L. S. 1975. What is negritude? In G. C. M. Mutiso and S. W. Rohio (Eds.). *Readings in African political thought* (pp. 78-90). London: Heinemann.

Senghor, L. S. 1977. *Liberté III: Négritude et Civilisation de L'Universel*. Paris: Le Seuil.

Serequeberhan, T. 1991. 'African philosophy: The point in question". In: Serequeberhan, T. (Ed.). *African philosophy: The Essential Readings*. New York: Paragon.

Sithole, N. 1968. *African Nationalism*. London, Nairobi, Ibadan, New York: Oxford University Press.

Sloth-Nielsen, J., and Gallinetti, J. 2011. "Just Say Sorry"? Ubuntu, Africanisation and the child justice system in the Child Justice Act 75 of 2008. *PotchefstroomElectronic Law Journal*, 14 (4): 62–90.

Snowden, M. F. 1976. 'Ethiopians and the Greco-Roman world,' In: Kilson, M. L. and Rotberg, R. I. (Eds). *The African Diaspora: Interpretive essays*, Harvard University Press: Harvard.

Sodipo, J. O. 1972. Philosophy and Culture, *Inaugural Lecture Series 6*, University of Ife Press: Nigeria.

Sogolo, G. 1993. *Foundations of African philosophy*, Ibadan University Press: Ibadan.

Sogolo, G. 2003. 'The Concept of Cause in African Thought,' Coetzee, P. H. and A.P.J. Roux (Eds), *The African philosophy reader*, second ed., London: Routledge.

Solomon, R. C. and Higgins, K. M. 2010. *The Big Questions: A Short Introduction to Philosophy*, 8th Edition, Wadsworth, U.S.A.

Spinzak, E. 1973. African Traditional Socialism: A Semantic Analysis of Political Ideology, *The Journal of Modern African Studies*, 11 (4): 629-627.

Stoger-Eising, V. 2000. *"Ujamaa* Revisited: Indigenous and European Influences in Nyerere's Social and Political Thought," *Africa,* Vol. 17, No. 1.

Sumner, C. 1976. *Ethiopian philosopher, vol. V: The Fisalgwos,* Commercial Printing Press: Ethiopia.

Sumner, C. 1985. *Classical Ethiopian philosopher*, Commercial Printing Press: Ethiopia.

Sumner, C. 2004. The light and the shadow: Zera Yacob and Walda Heywat: Two Ethiopian philosophers of the 17th century,' In: Wiredu, K. and Abrahams, (Eds). *A companion to African philosophy*, Blackwell: Oxford.

Suny Global Workforce Project. 2015. 'What is globalisation?' *The Levin Institute*: The State University of New York.

Tambulasi, R and Happy K. 2005. Can African Feet Divorce Western Shoes? The Case of „Ubuntu" and Democratic Good Governance in Malawi. *Nordic Journal of African Studies* 14 (2): 147-161.

Teffo, L.J. 1996. The other in African experience. *South African Journal of Philosophy,* 15(3): 101–104.

Tempels, P. 1945. *La Philosophie Bantoue,* (trans. 1959 by Colin King), *Bantu Philosophy*, Paris: Presence

Thomas, O. N. T. and Ron, J. 2007. 'Do Human Rights Violations Cause Internal Conflict?' In *Human Rights Quarterly,* 29 (3).

Tieku, I. 2004. Explaining the clash and accommodation of interests of major actors in the creation of the African Union, *African Affairs 103*: 249-267.

Traore. M. 2015. Pan-Africanism, Marxism and Sustainable Development in Jacques Roumain's novel Gouverneur de le rosee (Masters of the Dew), In: Mawere and Awuah-Nyamekye, (Eds), 2015. *Harnessing Cultural Capital for Sustainability: A Pan-African Perspective*, Langaa Research and Publishing CIG, Mankon, Bamenda.

Tutu, D. 2000. *No future without forgiveness: A Personal Overview of South Africa's Truth and Reconciliation Commission.* London: Rider Random House.

Udah, H. 2015. Africa: Diversity and Development, Agenda 2063: Africans in Australia and the Building of a New Africa, *African Studies Association of Australasia and the Pacific – AFSAAP 37th Annual Conference* – Dunedin – New Zealand.

Uduigwomen, A. F. (n.d). 'Philosophy and the Place of African Philosophy,' In: Uduigwomen, A. F. (Ed.). *Footmarks to Landmarks on African philosophy*, p. 30-35, Obaroh & Ogbinaka Publishers: Lagos.

United Nations Development Programme. 1994. *Human Development Report*, New York: Oxford University Press.

USAID Democracy and Governance. 2001. Center for Democracy and Governance Bureau for Global Programs, Field Support, and Research-Technical Series.

Vallega, A. A. 2011. Displacements – Beyond the coloniality of images, *Research in Phenomenology* 41 (2011): 206-227.

van Binsbergen, W. 2001. '*Ubuntu* and the Globalization of Southern African Thought and Society', *Quest: An African Journal of Philosophy*, 15 (1): 2.

Van Hook, J. M. 1993. African Philosophy: Its quest for identity, *Quest*, Vol.VII No.1.

Van Stam, G. 2014. Ubuntu, Peace, and Women: Without a Mother, there is no Home. In M. van Reisen (Ed.), *Women's Leadership in Peace-Building: Conflict, Community and Care.* Trenton, NJ: Africa World Press.

Venter, E. 2004. The notion of ubuntu and communalism in African educational discourse, *Studies in Philosophy and Education 23,* Netherlands: Kluwer Academic Publishers.

Vienna Declaration and Programme of Action, United Nations GAOR, World Conference on Human Rights, 48[th]Session, 22nd Plenary, Management, Part I, Paragraph 8.

Wa Thiong'o, N. 1998. *Penpoints, gunpoints, and dreams: Towards a critical theory of the arts and the state in Africa,* Clarendon: Oxford.

Wa Thiongo, N. 1986. *Decolonising the mind: The politics of language in African literature,* Heinemann Educational Publishers.

Wamba-dia-Wamba, E. 1991. 'Philosophy and African Intellectuals: Mimesis of Western Classicism, Ethno-philosophical Romanticism or African Self-Mastery?' *Quest,* Vol.V No.1.

Warburton, N. (Ed). 1999. *Philosophy: Basic Readings,* 2nd Edition, Routledge, London and New York.

Waters, M. 1995. *Globalisation,* Rutledge: London.

Waters, R. 1997.*Pan-Africanism in the African Diaspora: An analysis of modern Afrocentric political movements,* African American Life Series: Wayne State University Press.

Whitehead, A. N., & Bertrand, R. 1967. *Principia Mathematica,* Cambridge University Press: Cambridge.

Wichtner-Zoia, Y. 2012. Could the philosophy of ubuntu support community connections, development and economic prosperity in your community? Available from: http: //msue.anr.msu.edu/news ubuntu_is_powerful _thinking (Accessed 5 June 2013).

Wikipedia. 2008. Portal: Sustainable Development. http: //us.f905.mail.yahoo.com/ym/showletter?msgld.

Wiredu, K. 1980. *Philosophy and an African Culture,* Cambridge: Cambridge University Press.

Wiredu, K. 1995. "How Not to Compare African Thought with Western Thought," In: Mosely, A. (Ed.), *African Philosophy: Selected Readings,* Prentice Hall: New York.

Wiredu, K. 1996. Cultural Universals and Particulars: An African Perspective, Indiana University Press.

Wittgenstein, L. 1993. *Philosophical Occasions* 1912-1951, Indianapolis: Hackett.

Wojtyla, K and Aguas, J. J. S. 2013. Ethics and Moral Philosophy, *Kritike*, 7 (1): 115-137.

World Commission on Environment and Development: (WCED). 1987. Our *Common Future*, Oxford: Oxford University Press.

Yai, O. 1997. The theory and practice in African philosophy: The poverty of speculative philosophy, *Second Order: An African Journal of Philosophy*, Vol. 1 (2): 1997.

Young, C. 1982. *Ideology and Development in Africa*, New Haven, CT: Yale University Press.

Zonke, S. 2014. 'Where are we with Intra-African Trade?' *Sawubona*.

CPSIA information can be obtained
at www.ICGtesting.com
Printed in the USA
LVHW081526291019
635705LV00013B/1372/P

9 789956 763016